TWENTY
TEACHERS

Also by Ken Macrorie

Writing To Be Read
Uptaught
Telling Writing
A Vulnerable Teacher
Searching Writing

TWENTY TEACHERS

Ken Macrorie

OXFORD UNIVERSITY PRESS
New York   Oxford

Oxford University Press

Oxford New York Toronto
Delhi Bombay Calcutta Madras Karachi
Petaling Jaya Singapore Hong Kong Tokyo
Nairobi Dar es Salaam Cape Town
Melbourne Auckland

and associated companies in
Beirut Berlin Ibadan Nicosia

First published in 1984 by Oxford University Press, Inc.,
200 Madison Avenue, New York, New York 10016

First issued as an Oxford University Press paperback, 1987

Oxford is a registered trademark of Oxford University Press

Library of Congress Cataloging in Publication Data
Macrorie, Ken, 1918–
Twenty teachers.
  1. Teaching. 2. Learning and scholarship.
3. Teachers—United States—Interviews. I. Title.
II. Title: 20 teachers.
LB1025.2.M324 1984   371.1'02'0922   84-14839
ISBN 0-19-503464-3
ISBN 0-19-504982-9 (pbk.)

10 9 8 7 6 5 4 3 2

Printed in the United States of America

A learner with the simplest,
  a teacher of the thoughtfullest,
A novice beginning
  yet experient of myriads of seasons . . .

(from "Song of Myself" by Walt Whitman)

ACKNOWLEDGMENTS

Most of all, I thank the twenty extraordinary teachers and their students who consented to tell me the stories that comprise the heart of this book. They have made the last seven years stirring and delightful for me.

I thank the individuals who introduced me to those teachers I didn't discover on my own: Professor Yetta Goodman of the University of Arizona—Vera Milz; Professor Carl Berger of the College of Education at the University of Michigan—Don Campbell; Professor Bill Barker of Bowdoin College—Tom Smith. Professor James Gray, director of the National Writing Project at the University of California, Berkeley—Stanyan Vukovich; and my son, Michael Macrorie—Fred Bartman. I also thank Robert L. Erickson, chairperson, Department of Speech Pathology and Audiology, Western Michigan University, who supplied materials for my presentation of Charles Van Riper.

I thank the photographers who took the pictures of these teachers in action.

Two of the interviews require a word. I chose to ask Marcia Umland to tell something of her childhood experiences with reading because I wanted at least one of the teachers to be revealed as a person with a personal past as well as a present in the classroom. I didn't have space to include extensive biographical material for all of the twenty teachers, but wanted to make the point as I did in my contextbook *Searching Writing* (1980), that when we become acquainted with the personal history of powerful persons or "authorities"—with their frailties and experiences often so much like our own—we can entertain the notion that we also might become leaders in our fields.

I gave the last teacher in the book a pseudonym, John Sheffield, because I haven't been able to locate him since my army days, when I stored up the memories which comprise my portrait of him as a teacher. All the other teachers in the book had the opportunity to read what I wrote about them before it saw print.

I thank my editors: At Oxford University Press—Curtis Church, who in many ways helped me make this book what I wanted it to be, and

John Wright, who first believed in it and then made major suggestions for improving its form. And Anthony Prete, who printed in shorter form eight of these interviews in the magazine *Media & Methods.*

Finally, I thank Joyce Tiefenthal Macrorie for her usual helpful criticism of my writing.

CONTENTS

INTRODUCTION

The idea behind this book is so simple that it may sound at first like tomfoolery.

Seven years ago I set out to find teachers whose students did *good works*. By that term I mean what learners write, speak, or construct that counts for them, their fellow learners, their teachers, and persons outside the classroom.

I wasn't looking for teachers who were popular with students, had reputations for being hard taskmasters, or were approved by principals or deans. Nor was I looking for scholars who had published many articles or books, had won prizes for research, or were dazzling lecturers. I was looking for teachers whose students did good works.

I asked these people to show me the good works of their students and tell me what happened in their classrooms. I found they all believed in pretty much the same ideas and were using pretty much the same methods—although they were teaching, for example, woodworking to rich kids in Pennsylvania or history to poor kids in California, space engineering to university students in Michigan or mathematics to sixth graders in Massachusetts. They were not *teachers* in the usual sense—persons who pass on the accepted knowledge of the world and get it back from students on tests, but *enablers* who help others to do good works and extend their already considerable powers.

Of all teachers, professors think least about what they do in classrooms, and in general, teach worst. And yet they are the models for all instructors, the teachers of teachers. For this book I sought out more professors than teachers at other levels because I wanted to demonstrate that their position doesn't necessarily prevent them from being enablers, too.

To make clear how these twenty teachers enable their students to do good works, I've presented what goes on in their classrooms in more detail than is common in writings on education, which customarily discuss theory and illustrate it with short examples. A half dozen or so books of the late sixties told rich stories of youngsters struggling to come together and learn in school. But college and university classes have seldom been revealed in detail, probably because their activities have been traditionally abstract and impersonal. The professor arrives at the last moment, steps to the lectern, delivers a lecture, and asks for questions in the final seconds of the period. As the course continues, he (there are many more he's than she's) assigns papers, conducts quizzes and examinations, and seldom gets to know students as persons—as if learning were best done outside of human acquaintance, sharing, and engagement.

Here I present many of the good works done by students of these enablers and many of the exchanges, spoken and written, between teachers and students. Without such documentation, my assertion that the teachers and students in this book are genuine learners would be only a claim, not an established fact. To furnish case histories of traditional classrooms would be ridiculous, for in them students seldom ask questions or exercise their curiosity in ways that make evident the origin of their thoughts.

The twenty teachers who make up the cast of these dramatic pieces write and talk to their learners as human beings, in what James Britton, the author of *Language and Learning*, calls "expressive" language, the everyday lingo of human beings, which derives from their early childhood acquisition of their Mother Tongue. This is the language of people at work and play who see each other as equals in humanity, if not always in knowledge. We say that if two people are to live together with some degree of harmony they must communicate well. That's also true for teachers and learners. Their language must suit themselves and each other, or the trust and respect crucial for producing good works will not develop. They must enable each other to meet at their best.

It is good works, not minimum competency, that these enablers bring about in their classrooms. Most traditional education fails to produce works any more significant than rote test answers and knowledge (or more often, recollection) of disconnected bits and pieces of information. That fact is both cause and effect of those powerful instruments called "Minimum Competency" or "Scholastic" and "College Aptitude" tests. They are administered impersonally to thousands of students who are by the nature of the process destined to be seen as educational units—average, above average, or failing. These tests can't measure a person doing good works. They are designed not to teach, but to judge. Unwittingly, administrators and teachers, as well as the general populace, have elevated them to such a position of unquestioned authority that we now find many courses in schools and universities tailored to prepare students for these standard tests rather than to produce good works that help people become ongoing, creative learners. A sadder notion of education can hardly be imagined. The result is that traditional educational experience appears even more useless to learners than it actually is.

Few people think of school as a place where persons live together; but in fact most citizens live the major part of their childhood days in school, and those who go on to college and graduate study stay there well beyond the age at which we say they become adults. Too often, enduring classroom hours is more like doing time in prison than living in a place characterized by civility and intellectual and emotional growth. What we get from school in widening and extending our perception often comes only from the social moments we enjoy with our peers on the playground, in the corridors, in the cafeteria, or at parties on weekends. This social life is intense and valuable. It's especially so when enablers make it part of the classroom experience—the student becoming both more individual and more social while learning with others. In traditional school, social life lacks intellectual rigor, and classroom life lacks sociability. There is the fun outside the classroom and there is the unpleasant stuff inside it, as if learning can't be exciting and enjoyable. In traditional school, most studying is not learning. It is drudgery, and it is not exciting and not enjoyable.

Our picture of school in novels and movies is almost unrelievedly dismal—it's a coercive, drill-and-question, punitive place, except for conversations on the stairways or in the rest rooms, a term I use here not euphemistically. Some years ago when I learned that Benjamin Franklin had in 1749 published "Proposals Relating to the Education of Youth in Pensilvania," I turned to his collected papers with eagerness, because I knew he was one of the greatest "renaissance men" (the term should be *persons,* so as to include women) and yet a self-educated wonder, who was formally schooled for only two of his eighty-four years. I found that in his proposals for an academy the members of the corporation he projected would

> ... make it their Pleasure, and in some Degree their Business, to visit the Academy often, encourage and countenance the Youth, countenance and assist the Masters, and by all Means in their Power advance the Usefulness and Reputation of the Design ...

I looked up the word *countenance* in the *Oxford English Dictionary* and found that it once meant to "look upon with sanction or favour ... to encourage, 'back up,' or bear out."

And then Franklin went on to say that the members of the corporation should

> ... look on the students as in some Sort their Children, treat them with Familiarity and Affection ...

A reader who doesn't know Franklin might think that he was merely being saccharine in writing a proposal to attract financial support for the new school; but however suave and diplomatic he was, in matters of substance he wrote plainly what he meant. Nowhere in the document is there a hint of "Lay it on those stupid, lazy kids. They must be kept in line."

I cite Benjamin Franklin because he seems the godfather of the good teachers presented in this book, although I doubt most of them ever read his proposal for educating the youth of Pennsylvania. They support and encourage learners because they sense that coercion cripples learning and paralyzes thinking unless the habits have been fully developed previously. In every interview in this book the enablers are seen treating learners with familiarity and affection. In a number of ways these teachers, taken together, could be said to be working at Franklin's Academy. His emphasis on making knowledge useful speaks to their practice of eliciting *good works* from their students.

Before I present these enablers, I want to describe a pattern that repeats itself again and again in their classrooms. It's the fusing of polar opposites. These enablers don't expect learners to be objective or subjective, but both objective and subjective—not learning only from the experience and ideas of "authorities" or only from their own experience and ideas, but from setting up a conversation between the two and listening to it. I call this kind of learning *Moebian,* after the 19th-century topologist August Moebius, who invented the imaginary figure now known as the Moebius Loop. You can make one by cutting a half-inch strip off the side of a piece of typing paper, giving one end a twist, and taping it to the other end, like this:

The applications of the Moebian notion in learning are endless. If you think of the act of reading, for example, which as leading researchers in reading are now saying, is a *composing process*—making meaning out of the way the reader's experience and expectations encounter a text—you can see that the meaning of a piece of writing is a function of both text and reader. The text means something different for every reader and at every moment she or he encounters it. The meaning isn't all in the text or all in the reader. Another way of revealing this relationship is to ask, "Where does the text leave off and the reader begin?" Only such a figure as the Moebius Loop can suggest a precisely responsive answer to that question. Write *text* on one side of the Loop and *reader* right behind it on the other side. Then place your pencil point on *text* and pull the Strip along underneath it. Soon you'll find that you have reached the word *reader*. This two-sided figure is one-sided. In the descriptions of classrooms that follow, you'll see enablers and learners again and again doing things that bring together polar opposites—process and product, enabler and learners, individual and group, experience and theory, doing and thinking.

This book presents profiles, largely in their own words, of twenty enablers in action. Then a summary of the principles, methods, and attitudes that make up their classroom habits. And finally, an "Open Letter About Schools" discussing how schools have developed, often unwittingly, a tradition that runs counter to the way these enablers work.

TWENTY
TEACHERS

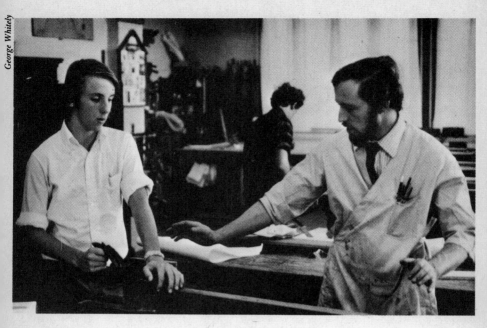

Sam Bush helps a learner get the feel of planing wood.

1

SAM BUSH
Woodworking, Prep School

At Hill School in Pottstown, Pennsylvania, Sam Bush, the woodworking master, and I entered a building and passed under a six-foot long board of red oak displaying delicately chiseled Gothic letters that read,

> *The invisible things of God may be clearly seen, being understood by the things which are made.*

We were in a high-windowed great English-Gothic room filled with work benches, woodworking tools, and saws.

My companion, a man of twenty-eight, medium build, and sharply angled beard and mustache, led me over to a chest of curved drawers, opened one of them, and showed me the dovetailing. All around the edges of the room stood pieces of furniture in various stages of completion. Sam Bush ran his fingers over the raised leaves and flowers on a bureau. "Isn't this beautiful work?" he asked.

I agreed, thinking it must be his or that of the master craftsman who had preceded him as teacher there.

"These are pieces not yet finished by the boys."

"I can't believe it," I said.

"The boys are fourteen to seventeen years old," he said.

Although Sam Bush's family was not well to do and lived in Oregon, he himself had gone to this private boarding school as a boy, on a scholarship. Among other subjects, he had taken woodworking under Karl Pacanovsky, a master who had come over from Slovakia in 1913. After graduating from Hill, Sam entered Reed College in Portland and majored in art history. He said to me:

After a while, I began to feel that *studying* great art and accomplishment isn't enough. Writing a thesis about art didn't seem to be as fulfilling as trying to make the art. I had the special background with Karl together with the exceptionally academic nature of Reed, and then I stumbled onto William Morris, and things began to coalesce. One day I went to Lloyd Reynolds, the great calligrapher and teacher

at Reed and showed him pictures of my wood work. I asked him what
he thought I should do. He said, "You have a teacher who helped you
make this? I think you ought to leave Reed immediately and go to
him."

I finished out the year, my sophomore year, but after that meeting I
was on my way. I wrote a zillion letters to European craft schools and
universities where I could study woodwork, not realizing at that time
that further work with Karl was a possibility, and eventually I was
accepted at two—Carl Malmsten's school in Stockholm and the Royal
Academy in Copenhagen. I was actually on my way there when I
stopped in Pottstown to see Karl and stayed ten years.

In the spring *Alumni Bulletin* of Hill School for 1972, I began an
article about Karl in this way—

> Born in a tiny self-sufficient village at the foot of the Tatra Mountains of
> Slovakia, Karl Pacanovsky . . . was apprenticed in woodworking at eleven
> and a half years and took his first job at fourteen; as a journeyman he
> traveled through much of central Europe. Perhaps most influential were
> the years he spent building the monumental carved Gothic altars which
> were the expression of religious faith in his region.

Pacanovsky came to the United States in 1944. In twenty-eight years
at the school he built a powerful foundation for the philosophy which
we embody today. When he retired I merely took up where he left off.
His influence still lives in this room. And he's alive, too. I see him every
week or two. We have lunch together. We think woodworking is wonderful, but it is a means to an end, which is understanding. Woodworking involves a part of man's nature which is only vaguely recognized
and not expressible in words. It has to do with the permanence of
tradition and the reality of day to day life.

A boy comes to me, and asks to build a chair. Right from the first I
put all the decisions on him. What kind of chair—narrow? low? modern? dark brown? At first that approach usually throws the boy, but he
recovers, and we start drawing.

I insist on lots of drawing, to the point of getting a reputation in the
school for it. Before you start cutting you must know what you are
doing. And I want them to attempt a project which as nearly as possible
parallels their dream or idea of that project.

When a boy begins working, I go over his drawing until I see what
he's after, and then ask questions to hear him support his choices, his
ideas. I do this so he will feel we are working from his impetus, that his
decisions are taken seriously, and because often his ideas are better
than mine. Then I make him draw the idea over, in scale, with T-
square, triangle, and so forth. I'm not concerned about a perfect draw-

ing, but want to see the construction problems laid out and the proportions solidified. At this time I make suggestions that I think will be improvements, without being overpowering. If I tell him outright that he *has* to do a certain thing, he will do it, but he will also hate me for stealing his project. At this time I have to make a quick character analysis of the student as to potential so I can encourage him as much as possible without getting him in over his head.

If a fellow is really obstinate about some point—I let him do it. The boys depend on me, but I try to meddle as little as possible. The atmosphere of the shop suggests that they can do things they never before dreamed of, and I take them seriously in their attempts. It's more important to me that they feel able than that they make the project. At the same time I really stick it to the kid who won't decide for himself. I tell him that I'm not making it. He is. "So get in gear and think." I ask him who he thinks is going to live the rest of his life for him. I want him to draw up a personal expression with conviction, stick to its construction with courage, and see in its completion a measure of his integrity. I don't allow students to use outside plans, except for boats.

The drawing phase is important in clearing cobwebs from the brain and getting the boys started in habits of constructive thinking. There is nothing mysterious or from on high about woodworking, no right answers in the back of the teacher's copy of the book that the kid has to match. The unknown solutions are available through concentration, effort, and study. More important, drawing is essential because no wood can be cut until all the facts are in and decided upon. No pay as you go plan, and, of course, the drawing period is the hiatus in which I decide how much good wood I'm going to invest in this guy.

Then we start building. I take each plan as if I were building it and advise the boys step by step. I explain each tool as it is required and with the expectation they will think about its function and use it by themselves without relying on me telling them anything more. I tell them all the required capacities to do the work exist within them, waiting to be released by their struggling. And I tell them as often as possible that the release and development of these capacities—perseverance, imagination, courage, and decisiveness—are the value of the work and the point of the course. They are to develop qualities of lasting value applicable not only to this proof or that translation but to the constant vagaries and vicissitudes of life. They usually don't understand me, but there is reason to believe that they will remember, and reflect, later on.

Most of the boys come from wealthy Eastern families. I have two kinds of pupils—those in a regularly scheduled class and those who come in on their own time because they want to do something with their hands as a relief from other school work. They ask me how to go about working in this shop. Tradition in this place does much of the teaching for me, so it's a bit hard to define exactly what I do. The pieces of furniture you see standing around waiting to be finished by last semester's boys say more to the boys than I can say. When they walk into this great room, they see that they are expected to do work of a very high quality. You see evidences of Karl Pacanovsky here—this beautiful carved tool chest he left, and the mottoes about work habits that appear around the room, like that one: "How well, not how much."

In my regular class I open the year discussing design, proportion in particular, also line. I show slides, solicit the boys' opinions. For the second class they must produce a short paper discussing their expectations for the year's experience, why they signed for the course, and what values it may have for them beyond the obvious ones of learning to use tools, producing a nice table, and so forth. Then, during that class, after I've collected their thoughts, I tell them my theories and feelings—and we're off.

Throughout the year I expect my class boys to keep hopping. I don't like them sitting down or with their brains on idle. They came to work—so work. Woodworking is a means of building strong character. Few people today care about strong character. In the studio, the boys' drawings become the idea. I don't allow any weak moment changes. Just before they take out the boards, when they're standing there with a plan, which, even for beginners, is usually far beyond their highest hopes—partly because when they were drawing I encouraged them to do more and partly because construction is complicated—while they're standing there with a plan beyond their highest hopes, I take a moment to tell them that if they have the courage and fortitude necessary to meet all the problems of their design they will get good results. Their own selves are all that stand between them and whatever they wish to accomplish.

I never assign projects. I never want them to think they have to do something because I told them to. They tell themselves, or at least I try to keep it that way. First I ask them what they want to make. I never say, "Oh no, you can't do that—too difficult for a beginner." In fact, I never say they can't make what they want to make, except for boats. I had to draw the line there because boats were taking up so much studio space that we couldn't work rationally.

Some visitors at first think that the boys are taking on tasks too demanding of them—for example, this bureau with curved drawer fronts. But there are ways to approach the work. If a boy wants to make a little table for his mother's bedroom, I tell him there are three possible kinds of legs for it. One, straight legs, the easiest to make. Two, tapered. They require more work. Three, curved, as in this period piece. The curved ones will require learning the use of special tools and take a lot more time to make. It's important that the boys feel they can make the project. Confidence and quality go together. Most of the work done here is of high quality, although occasionally—well, take this little desk, the dovetailing in the drawer here. Look at those spaces where there should be a snug fit. That's such slipshod work. I let it go because the boy was so inept that this represented good work from him. But I don't often do that. The standards must be high.

There are lots of ways of maintaining standards. As I've said, here are all these models around the shop. At most furniture stores you can't buy pieces made as well as these. No nails. Few screws. Mostly mortise and tenon joints and most of those done better than most professionals do them. When a *New York Times* reporter interviewed me for a story [February 26, 1976], she mistakenly said that I don't let students use any electric tools. That's not true. We use power tools sometimes, for example, a router bit, but more often the boys are carving by hand. Always in this studio we deal with something beyond the machine. The boys create a design and then they bring that design into being in wood.

Do you see this mirror? Isn't that turning done beautifully? And the way that design is laid on there. That piece means something special to me because it was done by a boy who was falling apart in life and couldn't get it together here in the shop either. One day I noticed him turning legs for a table and having a bad time. Later I went up to him and said, "How you comin', Ned?"

"Oh, fine," he said, "no trouble at all."

A few minutes after that I was walking by a trash bin and noticed a badly mangled leg that I recognized as belonging to Ned's table. He had already shown me the four he had finished, accompanied by self-congratulation. I took the leg out of the bin and walked over to him. "No trouble at all, eh?" I said, holding it up to him. I couldn't let him lie like that about the craft that was our concern. The process of his project was much the same as the process of any big undertaking he would face in life. I let Ned and other students know that school is the training ground for developing the personal qualities requisite to those larger undertakings. After that, he turned around and began to do first-rate work.

I try to confine my help to advice, but actually I get involved with every facet of every project, and so I know when a boy is having difficulties and failing. When he starts, we take one step at a time, day after day, until the job is done. Some boys work faster and more ably than others, but the method is the same for everyone. I have to size up every one and subtly scale him up or down in complexity, based on my estimate of his character. A boy's first project may be very involved if he wishes. Then it just takes longer. Such a teaching formula consumes vast amounts of my time. As yet I haven't been able to conceive any other way of getting results. It's hard to find time to do my own work, but I find it. I feel it's important for me to be creating my own objects in the shop, so that the boys' efforts are not so much in a school shop as in an active, creative studio.

The problem of presenting woodworking as education rather than simply manual labor is difficult in this country. It's first necessary to dignify the work. Materials are lying about the studio which picture the rich diversity of human expression, contemporary and antique. An opportunity is before the boys to make something excellent. It's a rare student who doesn't sense that immediately.

I'm trying to draw out what is in the boy rather than pile it up on him. It's a process of introducing him to his own makeup, insisting that he deal with his discoveries maturely. Every time a problem comes up I speak to each student or the group so as to keep before them the idea that their participation and effort here is not separate from other things that they do, or from their core as persons. Interestingly, the kids are much hipper to these notions than parents, teachers, and other adults, who somewhere, deep inside, remain convinced that woodworking exists in school so that later on you'll be able to change light bulbs by yourself.

Because I work in a boys' school you may think I believe that woodworking belongs to boys. I've worked in other settings with girls and women, and they are fine learners. Boys or girls, I find that the kids are more idealistic and eager than adults. I want them to dive into that idealism with high expectations and then measure up to the challenge. All the work we do is hard. The problems they have bitten off in their designs demand their full attention and effort. If they do a sloppy job, I usually ask them to do it over. In this studio they must grow up to do a good job.

I think we've met with so much success in product and theory because the boys are energetic and the school leaves us alone. What could these young men do if they had more than a few hours a week to devote to woodworking? The possibilities are endless. These kids are a warehouse full of raw material and we are showing them how to use it.

I use the word *we* when I'm talking about teaching because I know I'm working in a tradition. Karl Pacanovsky's influence still lives in this room. So there it is. I'm more interested in what the wood does to the boy than what the boy does to the wood. I want my students to learn that they can never lie to their work.

That was in 1976. Eventually Sam wanted to take on new challenges, and he had become tired of trying to reconcile his philosophy of teaching with the rules and regulations of conventional school. He resigned from his position and returned to his home region in Oregon, where he began teaching at the Oregon School of Arts and Crafts in Portland. He wrote me of his new beginning.

Things have changed, shifted and moved in my life. It's exciting, challenging, as usual. Teaching has been my core activity since last August, building up a spirit of opportunity at the Oregon School of Arts and Crafts, but I've just recently decided not to follow up on these efforts—not there at least, as various institutional frustrations this spring have left me feeling a little out of step with the school. It's not a good place for me to make my stand.

So for the first time in eleven years I won't be doing students—no, actually that's not true. I will have a few classes. How could I get away? But the major focus will be on *my making*. I have rented an equipped wood studio and am looking forward to putting out the goods. I have lots of ideas to build and try. One recurring feeling I've had all along—I remember it at the Hill as a student, and at Reed College when I was there—is a need to actually do the wood work. I get kind of weird when I go too long without making, and Arts and Crafts has not been a good place for me to work—questions, interruptions, noise, and so forth.

A little aside here: I watch the contemporary wood scene grow in huge leaps and I see the usual effect of people *talking* the subject a lot. It's valuable to communicate but what if all that word energy were work? I've always felt the wood was the best teacher. It's amazing how many people want to be told the *rules*. They want to understand intellectually and memorize the processes. They'll have to be more flexible than that with me. I want them to sense the material, get their other perceptions involved. The techniques are only guidelines, starting points, systems that work. These people may very well invent something tomorrow that revolutionizes the way *I* do wood—so it wouldn't do to let them copy or memorize. Besides, since every piece of wood is different, a fixed rule doesn't apply. They have to be on their feet, thinking, touching, analyzing, dreaming at all times, to do good stuff and be themselves. That's part of why I think woodworking is so good for people.

Naturally the rapid expansion of interest in wood has sponsored some blind adulation of older makers by younger makers. The admiration for a man is so strong that it twists up what the new guys have to offer. They imitate. Some of the big wood schools have the same effect on people. I'm interested in individuals. You never know which one of them might be the next Michelangelo. It wouldn't do to say "I am the great Sam Bush and this is how it's done." Or wipe out their contributions. I've learned more from students than they have ever learned from me.

Anyway, I've met some good people out here—dedicated, try-hard types who really respond, and I'm gratified and assume that my teaching is productive outside of the Hill shop as well.

I've done away with rulers because people were so number conscious. One fellow had a tongue and groove that didn't fit. He was semi-mad at me, saying "I used a 3/8-inch bit and set the saw for 3/8, so what's wrong?" My response was "Who cares about 3/8 of an inch? Why not concentrate on making one part relate to the other?" So folks have been making cardboard mockups, cutting and bending and using masking tape until they get the shape right—putting the mockup next to their chair at home to see what height or size is *really like,* how it relates, rather than picking a number. Then we take the cardboard to the wood and take off our lengths from there—no ruler. I want them to see where accuracy, which they're addicted to, is important and where it isn't. The proportions of a little box are considerably more important than the lengths falling on even inch measurements. What is important is that the two ends be exactly the same length *as each other,* not as the ruler. When students have to have the middle or center line, I cut a piece of paper the length of the side, and fold it in half, presto—centerline! People are dazzled by this, and really go for it. It's so simple. In a world of high tech and experts, individuals are lost, self-conscious, lacking confidence. But as usual, that's where all the strength for our national fabric lies. It doesn't do for our world to neglect individuals so—in school, in television, in government.

Incidentally, I went to the area high school wood projects show and was appalled. Utter garbage from top to bottom. Bad everything. I didn't know it was possible to do so little with the natural enthusiasm and energy of young people. That reminds me to tell you how much I miss the high-school students, and young learners in general. One thing I feel strongly—students in their adolescence are at just the right moment for beginning and participating in woodworking. Not only are they old enough to handle the rigors of the craft, but they are young enough to absorb the intangible lessons, the non-intellectual aspect of the work, in a non-intellectual way. They can feel what is happening to them and respond with deep enthusiasm.

But most of my current learners are adults. The seemingly natural direction for me to go now is to open an advanced craftsman's school—in-depth apprenticeships, fine woodworking. In fact I have worked out the particulars and this is quite do-able. But a certain other part of me wants to have a school for children, a regular grade-school total learning environment, except in this one making is at the core and studying is seemingly on the periphery. The aim is to get kids to make their education rather than receive it. To start right away nurturing rather than destroying the self, the spirit. I have all kinds of ideas for how this could work, what kinds of other teachers I'd want. It's clearly a few years down the road yet, but it sure feels right.

2

RICHARD LEBOVITZ
Writing, High School

The Outer Banks, that angled shank of sand off North Carolina surrounded by ocean, are captivated by water, one part of the United States not accessible by airliners. I'll let Richard Lebovitz's letters from Buxton, and samples of writing from his high-school students at Cape Hatteras School, speak for what he does in the classroom.

Buxton, North Carolina

Dear Ken,

There are gale warnings up on the coast tonight. The wind's blowing fifty to sixty miles per hour and the tide's about as high as I've ever seen it, washing over the bulkhead across the street, crossing the road in low areas, and flooding the Soundside marshes. People have moved their cars to high ground to protect them from the rising water. I had to wade through water a foot and a half deep this evening to check on the *Sea Chest* sailskiff. We had hauled it ashore for the winter, and it was sitting high and dry on the knoll where we hauled it up. The Sound was churned up, the waves big and white-faced like the ocean. I shined my light to the water's edge and saw a long white pole that turned out to be the spritpole we lost early in the winter. It must have been buried under some eelgrass and was dug out by the waves. Things are easily lost and not very easily recovered around the water. The sea has a way of taking and not giving back. Two young fishermen disappeared on the ocean this fall. No trace of them, their boat, debris, nothing, in spite of the largest and longest search and rescue the Coast Guard has ever undertaken in this area. Just the other day another fishing boat went down. Two waves came over the stern and the boat sank just as the captain was radioing his coordinates. A friend of mine, three miles away, heard them and came to the rescue. He was there in fifteen minutes. The two fishermen, clinging to a net buoy and Igloo coolers, were so exhausted from fighting the current and the cold

Richard Lebovitz acts as editor, on the side of the writer.

water that they couldn't help themselves into his boat. They, luckier than the other two, survived . . .

Richard

On the Outer Banks people live in water. It surrounds them, laps at them, suspends them day and night. Most of Richard Lebovitz's students know that sea better than he does because they have lived longer with it. Many come from parents and grandparents and great grandparents who worked in the coastal rescue service in decades past. Now these young people are part also of the mainland culture, knowing drugs, drunken driving, and all of the other escapes from the humdrum and frustration of life that we look to. But the sea is too enveloping for them to forget. In Richard's class they write of it:

While riding down the beach one day, my friend and I ran across some trails which led back into the dunes. That same night we went down the trails in a truck. Back in the dunes near the surf was a hill about 35 or 40 feet high. We drove up the trail and parked the truck. While getting out we noticed that the roar of the ocean was very loud and very clear. We went back to the truck and got a flashlight and started walking back towards the sound of the surf. My friend was carrying the flashlight and was about 10 or 12 feet to my left. As the light shone over the top of the hill, the other side seemed to disappear as if it were cut straight off. But before the thought crossed my mind, I fell—about 25 feet straight off the side of a dune! After making my landing I looked, and there, about a foot in front of me, lay the great Atlantic.—Richard Quidley

Another testament to the water came in the form of a story by Terri Midgett. Its matter-of-fact voice reveals his closeness to the practice of rescuing, which has dominated the history of his family for generations.

It was in the winter of '76. The Sound had had a layer of ice on it for at least a week. Now it was slowly beginning to melt. I went to the edge of the creek. As I walked on the ice my boots seemed to want to slip out from under me. I slowed down just enough to where I thought I wouldn't fall, and about that time, BAM! I'd slipped, falling hard on the ice, its wetness cold to my face.

I stood up, my face numbed from the cold. Looking ahead, I saw three figures waving at me. It looked as though they needed help. I ran toward them, falling several times before reaching them. One of the boys had fallen through the ice. He was wet and cold and wanted to lie down, but I knew if he did, it would only be a matter of minutes before he'd die. I pulled off my waders and some of my extra clothing. I made him take off his wet ones and get into mine. They were a little too big, but would keep him dry and warm. I finally got the other two boys to run on home to get my father. The boy couldn't walk, so I put him in my arms and took the shortcut over the frozen creeks. When I arrived at my house, I yelled for Dad, but it was too late. The boy had frozen to death.—Terri Midgett

Richard wrote me that Terri's story was fictional, a Jack London-like tale of death in the cold. He said that he encourages his student writers to let their topics choose them. Here's another story, this time nonfiction.

It happened about ten years ago. The night was cold as I drifted off to sleep. Not a sound was heard except the trees outside my window. The house seemed unusually quiet. I had fallen asleep for a while, I guess, until noises woke me. Our house made all kinds of weird noises but these were different. As I lay back with my eyes and ears opened wide, I heard them again. I knew it wasn't Mom or Dad, or even my brother. An eerie feeling came over me; someone was in the house. I was stiff in my bed, wanting to scream, but nothing would come out. As I lay in the voiceless silence I felt the presence of another energy nearing my room. All of a sudden it was with me—in my room! I could see the figure: black like the shadows. Unable to scream or move, I watched the intruder creep about my room. Finally it walked out. At this time something told me to jump out of bed and run to my brother's room. I jumped right on top of him like you would a horse. He waked up and I told him what had happened. At that time we heard the front door slam. I lay trembling in the dark with my arms around him.

Finally we went to the bottom of the stairs and called for Dad. He came down, and we told him about it. I don't think he believed us. That night I slept with the hall light on.—Susan Lynch

In the past three or four years, Richard has been writing articles for teachers' journals, attending conferences, and getting to know the work of leaders breaking new ground in his field.

Buxton, North Carolina

Dear Ken,

I've been sharing Donald Graves's research reports [of his two-year research project done at the Writing Process Laboratory at the University of New Hampshire] with some of my friends in the elementary school here, and they're trying out his ideas. My younger daughter, in one of my friends' first-grade class, brought home a twelve-page diary the other day. I was tickled. I got a fascinating letter from Vera Milz, whose workshop I attended in Cincinnati. She is a Michigan school teacher who uses what she calls a "whole language approach" in her first-grade classroom. She has her kids writing the first day of class. Ordinarily, first-grade kids do nothing more than practice writing letters and words. Some of her students have even written to her before they arrive. I've never realized how much restraint the schools put on children's learning. At every level the kids are capable of much more than we let them do.

Richard

In his classes, Richard began to challenge his students rather than restrain them. Here's a piece of writing done by one of his students:

One day when I was testing my Camaro out, I decided to go to Avon. I was going the speed limit through Buxton. When I left Buxton, I started winding her out at about 60 m.p.h. She was running really well that day. When I got to the smooth part of the road I threw it on her— 65–70–75–80–90–100. I felt really good. When I got to a 100, my blood started to circulate, and I kept pouring it on. Finally I slowed down enough to pull in at the parking lot at Ramp 20. She was running just right, without one miss in her. I pulled out on the highway again, squealing, and slammed the gas pedal to the floor. I got up to 120, and still faster. Then something went "bang, bang, bang, bang."

"Oh no!" I said. "I just blew an engine!"

It scared me so I was shaking all over. I slowed down and looked, and when I did, I saw the seatbelt hitting the back window. I stopped, put it inside, shut the window, and drove home slowly.—Nick Stemple

Richard often asks his students to write down their experiences a month or a year later, when they have cooled enough to be recorded more objectively. For example:

December 29, 1979, was a beautiful day for that time of the year. I was the only person at home; everyone else was fixing flowers and organizing things. I was so scared and nervous I couldn't get my make-up on right and my hair wouldn't curl. I wanted to cry. I was almost ready to give up when my mother came to the rescue. She got my hair fixed and make-up on. I was finally ready. Everyone was getting dressed, so I decided to go ahead by myself. I needed to think about what I was doing.

I walked down to the clubhouse and it was magnificent. Flowers, candles, and cake. I loved it. I went to the bathroom and dressed. I had never been so scared of anything as I was of this. Then people began to come in. My friends came to where I was and they hugged me and cried. Then the music started.

Daddy was beside me. I was crying. He kept saying, "Sandy, you don't have to go through with it." That made me cry worse. I walked without knowing it. I saw the preacher and then Jimmy. He was also crying, but he winked and whispered, "I love you!" and that was all I needed. The preacher pronounced us man and wife.—Sandra New

Richard believes that if some day Sandra's daughter says to her mother, "I'm so scared about getting married. What did you feel like? Sandra can say to her, "I've got a paper I wrote long ago in Mr. Lebovitz's class on those very feelings."

Buxton, North Carolina

Dear Ken,

I'm enclosing more of my students' writings. Some aren't as memorable as others I've sent you, but they're strong in their way, and I'm still pleased with the results I'm getting. My seniors have just finished writing case histories, and I want to send some of these when I get around to typing them. The first drafts excelled anything this particular class has written before. I think they're getting the idea that writing can be a natural and satisfying form of expression. In one of them, Kim Fagley looks at herself:

> I was standing at the lighthouse talking to Bobby when I turned around and saw these people gathering around someone. I saw Ame lying on the ground rolling back and forth, and crying. I ran over to her to try and find out what was the matter. I bent down beside her.
> "Ame, what happened?"
> "Nothing, just go away and leave me alone."
> "Ame, tell me what happened!"
> "Get away from me!"
> About that time I saw Joni standing to the side crying. I walked over to see if she knew what happened, but she was too upset to talk. I walked back over and bent down beside Ame.
> "What happened to you?"
> "My leg, I think it's broken."
> "Ame, are you sure? Where does it hurt?"
> "I hurt all over."
> "What do you want me to do, take you to a doctor or your mother?"
> "Just get the hell away and leave me alone!"
> I walked over and talked to Joni. We decided to take her to the doctor. They put her in my car, but I was too upset to drive. My sister was at the lighthouse and she told me that she would drive. After we got Ame in the

car and were almost ready to leave, it suddenly hit me that we were going to the hospital and I just couldn't go because I'm really afraid of them. I don't know why, but I am.

I was standing talking to Bobby. I think he was trying to calm me down, but it wasn't helping, knowing my friend was hurt and they were taking her to the hospital and I was too scared to go with them. Then all of a sudden, I don't know what happened, but I just put it in my mind that Ame was going to the hospital and she might need me, and I was just going to have to get over my fear of them. But when I turned around to get in the car, it was gone, and so was everyone else that was going to the hospital.—Kim Fagley

I think Kim showed some insight into herself in that paper, a turning point in her life.

Richard

Buxton, North Carolina

Dear Ken,

Some of the writings from my senior *Basic English* class are so personal I wasn't sure how to react. None of these students is college bound. Many are going into the service. Some will go to work. One or two may be going to a two-year college.

Since I attended a workshop in Cincinnati, I've been incorporating individual writing conferences into my instruction. My students are responding very positively to these conferences. They like my reaction to their writings, and they like to be asked what is important to them.

I'm trying to formulate a series of questions that throws the decisions back into their laps. Questions like:

"What would you like to ask me about your writing?"

"Which part of your writing needs fixing? What are going to do about it?"

"Have you said everything you want to say?"

"How do you feel about your beginning? Ending?"

"How does the writing compare to other writings you've done?"

"What have you learned to look for in your writing that needs improving?"

I've been impressed by the intelligence of students' responses to these questions. They've developed a greater sense of the writer's craft than I expected. The conferences appear to elevate the writing process to a higher level of significance. Maybe a conference gets across the message "This matters. We're going to work hard to make this right. And when it's done we won't throw it in the wastebasket."

Richard

A couple of years ago Richard sent me a copy of the magazine Sea Chest, *which students at Cape Hatteras School write and publish following the lead of Eliot Wigginton's* Foxfire *books. Richard has served as the faculty sponsor for seven years. On the back cover of Volume 5, Number 1, which contains many photographs and drawings, appears this statement:*

> *Sea Chest* is a project involving the young people of Cape Hatteras School in the research and collection, using tape recorders and cameras, of materials on the culture and history of Hatteras Island and North Carolina's coastal area. The materials are published in a bi-annual magazine, *Sea Chest.*
>
> By conducting extensive interviews with the older members of the community, the students are able to document the wisdom and capture the essence of their cultural heritage as well as obtain a wide range of skills, such as photography, darkroom, tape transcription, writing, editing, design, layout, office management, circulation, and marketing.
>
> *Sea Chest* also demonstrates the applicability of their scholastic work to their everyday lives and increases for all those involved their understanding and appreciation of the unique heritage of the Outer Banks.

Below that statement is a photograph of a state historical marker which reads:

"MIRLO" RESCUE

> A German submarine
> sank the British tanker
> "Mirlo" off coast nearby,
> Aug. 16, 1918. Coast Guard,
> led by J. A. Midgett,
> saved most of the crew.

And inside that issue of Sea Chest *is a reproduction of a letter written in flowing script, which reads in part:*

> Mount Pleasant July 12, 1859
> > > Mr. J. A. Midgett
> > > > Dear Sun this is to lit you no that I am not well but I hope these lines will find you and your family well.
> > Also I understand from B. W. O'Neal that all the land belonging to my fathers estate conveyid to my farther by Hambleton Doe on a count of the Seaflower also a track of land on the North bank Crone by Willis Tillet. Now if these rights can't be found in my farthers papers they can be found in the registers office in Currituck . . .

Here's an excerpt from one of the varied and fascinating articles in the more than dozen issues of Sea Chest. *Appearing in Volume 4, Number 2, 1977, it's entitled "Three Lifesavers: The children of Urias Gaskin Isaac Jennette, and Edward Midgett tell about the lives of their parents."*

Urias O'Neal Gaskins was born in the village of Hatteras, October 9, 1878. He died February 24, 1919, while he was still in the service. Mrs. Leona Jennette, his daughter, said, "My dad was one of 23 children by the same mother. . . . He married a girl from Buxton, my mother Catty Midgett, and made his home at Buxton instead of the village of Hatteras. They had five kids and I'm the oldest of the group. . . . He weighed 208 pounds, wore a mustache, and could sing like a nightingale. Everyone in the church would turn and look at him when he sang.

What education he had, he got in the Hatteras school, but of course at the time it was quite limited. With his energetic way of wanting to do things and get places, he studied and applied himself until, at the time of his death, he was the officer in charge of the Cape Hatteras Coast Guard Station and had papers from the commander of the Seventh District, Edgar Chadwick, for having the best work in the Seventh District. Mrs. Leona remembers, "It was quite wonderful to us as children having a dad with such limited education that was able to reach this place in the service where he was commended for his ability to take care of the Coast Guard Station in time of war. . . ."

Some writings by Richard's students have been so truthful that they have startled and unsettled him.

Buxton, North Carolina

Dear Ken,

I especially wanted you to see this paper by John Russell (a pseudonym I'm employing for the writer's protection). I think he did a very good job of rewriting, but I'm not sure whether my comments to him or those of the two students in his editorial group encouraged him in his efforts. You know, I don't remember what I said to him about his writing.

We were sitting in my brother's den getting wound up. Billy was going crazy on the guitar. Edward was lighting another joint. (Again, pseudonyms for protection.)

We had been drinking Scotch and smoking pot all morning. Before I go on, let me get this straight. This happened over eight months ago. I don't smoke or drink any more, nor do I take speed or coke any more.

I was just sitting there listening to Billy and watching Edward. Out of the blue I said, "Lets hit the woods boys. We've got some new equipment to try out."

That got instant results.

"You boys ready?"

"You want to go down to Trent?" said Edward.

"Lets get going," said Billy.

So, ten minutes later we were on the way to Trent. We stopped at Buxton to get some beer. We all carried about ten hits of speed apiece. Billy had a bag of pot and some hash. Edward carried a gram of coke.

After buying the beer, we decided to go in the Buxton woods. Trent was too far to go. We were in a hurry to get going. It was about 1:00 and we wanted to stay in the woods as long as possible.

We parked the car down by the Coast Guard housing. We dressed out in the woods and hid the bags (with our clothes in them) near the car. We used the woods until we got to Open Ponds Road then followed it to a cross road. Then took a trail that would take us to the camp ground on the point.

It was hot and humid. I soaked my uniform with sweat. My brain was starting to clear when we reached Open Ponds. It started to drizzle. We got behind a huge tree to get out of the rain. Billy opened up a bottle of Scotch. I popped a couple of black beauties in my mouth and used the Scotch to drown them. I don't really know where we went after it stopped drizzling. We had finished the whole bottle of Scotch and smoked about three joints and a lot of hash.

I was just following their foot steps. Several times I would look up and not see anybody. I would get on the radio and ask where they were, then run to catch up.

We were walking down Open Ponds Road, heading toward the hills, when a man stepped out of the woods right in front of us. I popped out of my trance and dove to the side of the road. At the same time bringing my M-16 off my shoulder.

Billy and Edward both reacted in the same way at the same time. All three guns were trained on the man. He took a step backwards, his face turning white. We moved slowly around. His eyes followed us all the way around. He started walking one way, us the other.

If he only knew how close he came to getting shot. Our nerves were shot so bad we decided to head on home.—John Russell

That's just the way John turned in his second draft, a few slips in grammar and punctuation, but it's good writing, far better than any paper he had ever done before. I doubt that there is anything else he could have done to seize on the terror of that moment, when half crazed with drugs and booze, he and his buddies point their weapons at the man in the woods.

That the writing frightens me shows how well it communicates. I knew about John's war games. His comrades and he dress up and play war in the woods surrounding the village. He summed up a book report with a statement that said, more or less, "This is a great book for anybody who loves war." And he was serious! I don't believe I've ever encountered anybody who actually "loved" war, have you? I didn't know about the drugs he and his friends used, and that too is scary, though he states in the writing that he doesn't have anything to do with them any more. He was recently saved at a church revival.

As you can see, I'm reacting to his writing on several different accounts, which I suppose is what good writing makes a reader do. At the same time I'm wondering if I should know everything he's telling me. I think I would feel more secure in my ignorance.

I'm also wondering about the energy released through the method of free writing. I think of a teacher I heard of who requires his students to write 20-page research papers on drugs, among other topics. There can be no creative energy in those papers. They're safe, harmless, like a chemical safely bottled. I had a wonderful teacher at the University of North Carolina, Chapel Hill, several summers ago—Gerald Unks, who told us that there are some teachers who become myths. They are bad but as the years go on their faults are not only accepted but extolled.

Richard

Over the last few years Richard wrote me that he was brooding a lot about his teaching. In 1983 the North Carolina English Teachers' Association named him North Carolina's Outstanding English Teacher.

Randy Werner makes sure a boy will kick the ball.

3

RANDY WERNER
Physical Education, Elementary School

The Sunday, December 21, 1975, issue of the Kalamazoo (Michigan) Gazette *carried a story about an elementary school gym teacher who set up games for kids not considered athletically adept. The five photographs on the fullpage spread showed kids playing in the gym, their faces and bodies registering absorption and joy. The reporter quoted a piece written by the teacher, Randy Werner, twenty-three, who used it to recruit children for his after-school workouts in the gym. It began: "Strike three, strike three, strike three, you're out. You're too slow, you're too slow, you're too slow! You're out. You're out of bounds, you're out of bounds, you're out . . ." Randy wanted kids to reply to that by saying, "I might hear, 'Strike three, you're out,' or 'You ran too slow,' but no matter what happens, I'll learn and have fun."*

A secretary at Randy's school said he had left teaching and was working as a salesman for the Shakespeare Company, a Kalamazoo manufacturer of fishing equipment and golf club shafts. I called Randy and he agreed to meet me when he returned to Kalamazoo on one of his check-in trips to headquarters. We could talk at the airport over coffee.

I was a few minutes late. "Don't worry about that," said Randy. "I've been fine, waiting here. I just called a couple of children I worked with, and feel great. It was so good to talk to them." He laughed and smiled. He was charged up.

I asked him how he got into teaching. Well, he said, his eyes searching the pictures of old planes on the wall of the airport restaurant, I was always in athletics. I looked up to P.E. teachers and coaches, and they helped me tremendously. One of those was Coach Frank DeFelice of the high school in Swampscott, Massachusetts. In junior high I was an active kid—a discipline problem, I guess you'd have called me. Coach DeFelice was very disciplinary, but warm. I trusted him. I still do, just phoned him last week. I keep in touch with him regularly. He's straight with people, no bullshit. He had a way of approaching things that was simple, basic. I didn't get along well with women teachers, and DeFelice, while talking about me with an administrator, just said, "Well, if that's true, just give him men teachers."

When I was in fourth and fifth grade, I was uncoordinated. Then in junior high and high school I became a jock. Eight or nine out of a hundred kids would get selected—jocks who got special privileges. In college I began to think about that, and remembered Fred, who was a wonderful guy but didn't play sports. We jocks stuck together and never mingled with other people, so I never got to know him as well as I should have. And I thought, what if I have children? Will one of my kids be like Fred—outcast because he or she's not good in competitive athletics? In high school you can expect that the competitive system will begin operating, but should kids seven and eight years olds have coaches yellin' at 'em?

Where I went to school for three months and taught for three months, in Brookline, I was teaching kids K through Five and I found that I loved those kids. I love children. I've got a three-month-old boy now, and I expect to have a lot of children in and out of our front door in the next few years.

I guess I began teaching in the conventional way. The kids were so enthusiastic—about everything, even the way I talked, the way I walked. I knew that in the older grades kids weren't always enthused about P.E. Most phys. ed. teachers were coaches, and at 2:15 or 3:00 they went out the door—to coach. Being a phys. ed. teacher was simply a step on the way to becoming a coach. Yet all the kids couldn't play on school teams. What about the other kids? They were the majority. I had always wanted to be a coach, but one day I said to myself, "You like kids, you enjoy being with them in the gym. Why don't you make something out of their lives there, so they both have fun and learn?"

I evolved another way of teaching. In the gym I told them I had three rules, just three. "One. Always wear rubber-soled shoes. They don't have to be tennis shoes. Maybe you can't afford *them*, but *rubber* soles. If you run around in just socks, you might slip and get hurt. Two. Don't run to the door." In that first gym there were glass windowpanes in the door. "You crash them and you get cut. Three. See this whistle? If I absolutely need attention for anything, I'll blow it and then you stop whatever you're doing immediately. It's an emergency."

I was responsible for the kids' safety so I had these rules. I think I blew that whistle only twice all year. You don't have to worry about discipline if the kids are having fun and doing things. But otherwise, beyond those rules, anything went. They could yell, scream, whatever. I told the kids that the most important thing in this class was to have fun. I said I didn't care who won the race. If you improve your time, that's O.K. Our one goal was that we all would do well in something. A lot of conventional teachers make statements like that but don't back them up with action. Many teachers sit around and talk about modern concepts. "Let's let 'em learn," they say, and the next minute they're shoutin', "Get the hell back in your seats!"

I taught kindergarten kids how to tell time. I bought forty hula hoops and asked each kid to sit in a hoop. "The little hand, that's your feet. The big hand, that's your hands." Then I drew a clock on the board. "If your feet are pointing straight forward, that's twelve. And if you bend forward and stretch with your hands toward your feet, that's the minute hand on twelve. Twelve o'clock. Now move your hands over to this position. What time is that?" So the kids learned how to tell time—and they loved it—while they were exercising their muscles. In the after-hours class I had them play games without any idea of winning or losing. I changed the rules in basketball so that two points were scored if a kid simply hit the rim or the backboard with the ball.

Most P.E. classes are a drag. I hated them in school: "Line up, take roll, everybody do this exercise." I never take roll like that. I do it while the kids are loosening up. It's no big deal. I began asking them who wasn't there, and eventually in one class they would come in and say, "You don't have to ask, Mr. Werner. Sally and Jack are absent, everyone else is here." It's not hard for me to communicate with these kids because I enjoy being there so much myself.

Randy had often moved into present tense as he talked of the job he no longer held. Now he recovered himself.

I was like one of the kids. I participated in all the activities. If it was jump rope, I was jumping rope. If they were lying on the floor, I was lying on the floor. If there were teams, I was on a team. Sometimes I would go wild in gym, just for the fun of it. I'd start throwin' balls around, chasin' kids—it was crazy. And I told them I had my dog in the closet of the gym. At recess I'd hide in the closet and while they were comin' in, I'd bark like a dog. They loved it.

I found that children of elementary-school age are extremely ego-centered, but it was no problem. One day I noticed the gym was blah looking, so I said, "I want everyone to bring a picture of themselves, and I'll put it up here on the wall." It quickly became the thing to have your picture in the gym. Eventually we had the picture of every kid in school on that wall. And I had a great big drawing of a cake on the wall, and when your birthday came, your name went up there on the cake.

Once a boy got a record from his parents for Christmas. "Would you like to hear it, Mr. Werner?" I said, "Sure." The next day we did exercises in gym by that record. Leslie was in heaven. I used to have kids come in the door and say, "Gimme five, Mr. Werner!" and slap my hands. The principal didn't like that. She thought you should maintain a certain distance between yourself and the children. That's part of discipline. I was often told I had to make children know they were Students and I was Teacher. I hated that system.

I remember one of the few discipline problems I had. It was after-hours intramural program, and I saw an icy snowball flying while we were getting started. "Who threw that?" I said. "I did, Mr. Werner," said John, a kid who was pretty wild in school and had a lot of trouble with other teachers and the principal. "John," I said, "what if that had hit someone?" John said, "I know I was wrong." In front of the class I told him to wait outside until I decided what to do with him. And when he came back, I said he couldn't come to the next after-school session. I was wrong. If I had that to do over, I would never send a kid out of class. Children can't learn anything outside class standing in the hall-way with their nose against the wall. There's really nothing on the wall they can learn from.

I should have sat down with that kid, as I usually did with the others. If a child hit someone in class, I'd say, "Why did you do that?" Maybe the kid would answer, "I had to." And I'd say, "Maybe you had to. If that's true, then it's o.k. But if it's not, it's a bad thing to do." I never had any problems with discipline. If the kids were all talking when I was trying to set up the activities for the hour, I'd say, "If you don't want to listen, go over there and form your own group. I'll talk only to those who want to listen." Soon the listeners were back. They didn't want to be left out.

But it wasn't always easy. The evening of the day I told John not to come to the Thursday after-hours session, his mother called me and said, "John idolizes you. And he says he's not coming to school tomor-row." I told her to tell him I wanted to see him. So the next day when he came in, I said, "John, I need some help. You know I don't hold grudges. Forget it. What'd you have for lunch yesterday?" He said he didn't remember. "See," I said, "yesterday's lunch is gone and so are other things of yesterday. I'd like you to help me set up gym equip-ment every morning." Everyone else in school had made him feel bad. I had to make him feel good about something. Just then the principal came in and said, "Why is John here?" I told her John was going to be my special helper. "After yesterday's performance," she said, "he de-serves no special privileges," and sent him from the gym. "You go back to your class." I saw he was near crying. I couldn't forgive her for that. John's one of the kids I just called up on the phone. We had a great talk.

For movement education, I say to kids, "Now let's walk across the gym as quiet as you can be." Naturally they walk on their tiptoes. I ask them how they walked. Then I ask them to walk across the gym as noisy as they can be, as low, as square, as round, as flat, as spread out. And like it's raining out, and like it's the nicest day. And in each case we analyze how they did it. When one kid does a specially good job, I say, "Let's give Leslie a hand for doing it so well. Show us, Leslie, just how you did it." *I noted that Randy was back in present tense.*

That idea I got from a course in elementary education at Northeastern University. And I taught these little kids square dancing—something they ordinarily wouldn't think of being seen doing. Professor Hal Ray—he's head of phys. ed. at Western Michigan University—he helped me. In his class we did things that really prepared us to be teachers. He wasn't the type of teacher I am, but he helped me a great deal.

My objectives are for the kids to be able to perform the acts they're supposed to learn before they enter the next grade. First of all, as I said, I want them to have fun—to enjoy—while they're gaining motor skills, endurance, eye-hand coordination, and body awareness. So one day a month I have them do eight stations. I call it "The Obstacle Course." They don't even know it's a test. Kids love it. They say, "Can we do the Obstacle Course today?"

At these stations they have to do different things, and if they do them well, I praise them. I never tell a kid he has done bad. I teach them to skip, hop, jump, gallop, stand on the right foot for five seconds. Sometimes I do that with the game I call "Shipwreck." I mark off the gym figuratively—the bow is the front, starboard is over there, and so forth. Then I say a storm is upsetting us. Run to the bow! Now two in a boat, find partners for life-boats, pull in sails—reach up and pull while jogging in place. All hands on deck—put hands on the floor. A shark is coming—they have to go to the black lines fast for safety. I would get down and make shark noises. I found out that you learn by doing—they learn, and you, too, if you get down and do it with them.

Some of the kids are badly coordinated, can't catch or throw a ball. So I throw them a bean bag instead of a ball. It doesn't bounce off their hands. It flattens and sticks. I guess I'm moving them from success to success. Too many phys. ed. teachers see the kids come into the gym, throw a ball out on the floor, and go back into their office to drink coffee for the rest of the hour. I honestly believe that phys. ed. is as important as any other class, and it makes me mad that teachers in other subjects never come in the gym and sit through an hour and watch what we do there. They ought to visit and find out how the kid acts who they've been having trouble with in their classrooms.

I'm going to make every kid do something with their body that's good, but it's gotta be good, no phony praise. And they'll enjoy it. Of all the guys I knew in high school football, eighteen went on to play college football, three went on to professional. Let's not put all our time on those guys. Let's not eliminate everybody so early. Let's let 'em have fun till they're thirteen or fourteen at least. You know, kids' hockey or Rocket Football is tough. They have majors and minors in hockey for kids. In my gym my kids are all in the majors.

When I was in elementary school gym, they gave us a ball, we played the ball games, and we didn't learn anything. Just played ball. After I got into regular teaching I said to myself, "I'm not going to teach like that." Jess Walker, a professor of education at Western Michigan University, introduced me to letting kids be themselves while they were learning something. And I'd be myself. Why be on a pedestal? When I first changed my teaching, we didn't learn anything. We didn't have any set goals. Now I know it's o.k. to do just anything occasionally, but I found I wanted to go beyond just being myself and having the kids be themselves. I wanted to build some foundations in physical education.

I loved teaching, but eventually I felt I had to leave it. I wanted to earn more money so my wife and kids could live decently, but partly it was the system. Other teachers were jealous of me, but I wasn't trying to win any popularity contests. The system is hard. Too often it's against the kids. Once while I was teaching I met an athletic director at a high school who had known me before. He said, "How ya doin'?"

"Havin' a lot of fun," I said.

"God!" he answered. "I don't hire people who say they're just havin' a lot of fun."

"Don't worry," I said. "You're not hiring me, anyway."

I know of teachers who kept kids out of my P.E. hour in order to punish them. Geez! Because the kid didn't do what they wanted him to do in English, he has to miss the fun in my class! I really question education. At three o'clock, if you don't get out of the doorway fast, you'll get run over—by teachers going home. Once I had left my class to go to the office—I trust my kids and they trust me—and as I was coming back, I noticed there was absolute quiet in the gym. I poked my head in the door and yelled as loud as I could, "What's wrong here—all this quiet?" The kids were standing in line at attention. I didn't want anyone in my gym standing at attention. As I glanced at the side door I saw a teacher looking in. Later she left a note for me in the office, which read:

> The policy here, as you know, is that students always walk through the halls quietly.

What was she talking about? The kids weren't in the halls. They were in the gym, and my policy wasn't that they should be quiet there. I went to that teacher's room and crumpled the note into a ball and threw it at her right before her kids, and said, "Don't you ever put this kind of junk in my mailbox again!" I shouldn't have done that, but I was mad. On second thought, maybe I should have done that.

I had my problems with the system. The kid that had thrown snowballs in the gym—remember? I really like him. He was a little hyper, but a good boy. He was put on Ritalin to control his behavior. I was told a doctor prescribed that. His father said, "He's wild." And I said, "So am I." I didn't want him on that pill. The kids would refer to it, saying, "In a half hour he'll have to take his pill," or he would say, "Oh, I didn't take my pill!" The teachers couldn't control him, they said. I had no discipline problems with him except in that one instance with the snowballs. I wasn't trying to control him. I was trying to help him learn to control his own body.

The greatest things happen in this kind of work. I remember one girl—I'll call her Joan—disliked phys. ed. Her parents came to me at Parent Teachers Association night and said, "Joan's got a poor self concept, but she really likes you. Could you do something for her?" So Joan joined the after-school group. I chose her for the special team that would be performing the Centennial exercise at the university. We practiced every morning before school, twenty-four children using this big parachute. They would spread it out on the gym floor, and each kid would pick it up where a cord was attached and walk around in a circle. It was heavy. Then they would skip or hop. They would raise it as high as they could—good for the cardiovascular muscles, you know. One day I said, "Now look straight up in the air and then drop the cord." While they were looking up, I ran under the bubble and the parachute came down and I was gone, disappeared. Then I poked my head out the hole in the center and everyone was surprised. I had a lot of fun in that class. That's why I taught. It was so much fun. I like to act like a kid sometimes, and I could do it there. Some people think that's not good, but I do. You know you could develop large muscles in kids by having them skip from one end of the gym to the other and back again, but that isn't much fun. I had these kids holding this heavy parachute skipping around in a circle and they loved it.

Competition is good. I believe in it. I myself became very competitive in athletics. But I'm talking about a coach versus a P.E. teacher. Till eighth or ninth grade I'm against competition for kids. Up until then the effort should be to improve skills. Let's enjoy. Let's build a foundation of body control. Reminds me, a teacher at a nearby school once called me and said, "Will you choose eight boys to compete with my fifth-grade boys in various sports this year?"

I said, "I don't know." I was thinking of Bill, a boy with limited ability, who would have loved to have come. "If I come," I said, "I'll bring about forty kids."

"What do you mean?" he said. "I want four schools to compete and we're planning on the best competition possible."

"It wouldn't be fair to the other thirty-two kids," I said.

"Oh God!" he said, "I know some day you're going to change but right now you're ruining our whole thing."

I had no regrets. If Bill had asked me, as he surely would have, "Why can't I come?" I would have had to say, "Because you're not good enough." I'll never tell any kid that.

Doreen MacFarlane-Housel and learners talk about their writing.

4

DOREEN MACFARLANE-HOUSEL
Literature, High School

Several years ago I visited Bunnell High School in Stratford, Connecticut, and talked with students and teachers. A year and a half later a woman there sent me ten long papers that told students' experiences in reading the works of a poet they liked. Opening the package and reading the cover letter from Doreen MacFarlane-Housel, I thought, "I'll put these aside and force myself to read some of them later so as not to hurt Doreen's feelings." No teacher or student reads for pleasure a high-school paper about a poet.

But before returning the papers to the envelope, I looked at one and was caught, just as Doreen had been when she brought them home one weekend.

I remember coming home from a party at 11:00 one night. It was spring. That's when we do poetry. [*She laughs.*] I glanced at one of the papers I had brought from school that afternoon and couldn't stop reading until 3:00 in the morning. I was reading with delight!

> "Mousemeal" is a story of a man's thoughts as he watches a cartoon with his son. The man sees "the unbridled violence and hostility of the imagined world" and of course, like any good father would be, he is shocked by the fact that his son is amused by something he finds to be a drag, and that the real drag is that the imagined world is modeled after the world that we live in. Mr. Nemerov is criticizing society for its tolerance of amusing violence for children and adults, and I am with him in his criticism for basically the same reasons. When I had finished "Mousemeal," I found myself remembering a day when I was in a department store and I overheard a child asking his mother for a S.W.A.T. rifle and bullhorn so he could shoot Tommy tomorrow. The child could not have been older than 8, but he had seen enough to want to be like one of his heroes . . . (The above is from a me who once thought that he could never care for kids. I guess it's in me to be a guardian if I could.)

I got papers like that in an honors class in a school located in a town with a large population of both professionals and factory workers. Eleventh grade. Twenty students. Only two people in that class wrote poor papers—two boys who felt that before reading a line they had to go to the critics and copy down what they said. The other papers that I didn't send you would be considered outstanding in most classes, but these ten were simply incredible. The writers had broken loose from the authority of books and articles about poetry and begun to respond to the works themselves. For example, when Ray Fernandes went to something he had overheard in a department store, he was extending Nemerov. And that's what poetry is—extending. It conjures up all those images, the intellectual as well as the emotional.

I think these papers were so good because they were honest. The students were honest about their responses to poetry and so was I. We had a good time. We had just been having a good time all year.

At the beginning of the work on poetry I asked each student to choose two poems from the anthologies they had, and for two weeks we discussed those poems. Obviously there was no way that I *Knew*—you know, with a capital K—all those poems in two anthologies. So they felt free to make their own judgments.

The only requirement was to choose two poems from these two books, except that if you have a poem from somewhere else you really care about, then bring it and we'll xerox it, so we have it in front of us. I can't read a poem once to people and then have them respond to it satisfactorily. You can choose a poem for any reason—because you like it, or for whatever reason you want the class to deal with it. It might be because you initially started to read it and said, "What the hell is he talking about?"

They brought in the poems. I would read one out loud and then we'd all read it kinda to ourselves. "Give me your reaction," I'd say. "Whatever it is. It can be 'I like the way he put those two words together,' or it might be 'It's the most wonderful thing I've ever heard and I haven't got the foggiest notion why.'

I knew that many of these people had been turned off from poetry by teachers asking pointed questions like "Now we're going to look for a point of view. What is the point of view in the first stanza?" I tell them if it's really a great, great poem and they understand it right off, then they're either very brilliant or it's not great. Because poetry's not meant to be—it's an experience, that's what it is, more than any other kind of reading. And it seems to me that you observe as you wander through it. And you've got to keep touching it because it's such a combination of emotion and intellect. So don't be afraid if you don't immediately understand it. It's better if you don't understand it.

I remember once as we discussed a poem in class I began to realize that my interpretation had been absolutely wrong. When I finished giving it, I thought, "How am I going to backtrack on what I said?" And then I heard an inner voice saying, "You had just better tell them that you were wrong. You don't have to be right all the time." And I told them why I believed one thing before and why I now believed differently. I think a lot of them saw that it was O.K. for me to be wrong.

Here in his paper a student says: "The poems that I remembered best I felt more certain about and generally liked more. These are the poems I chose to examine in this paper." Of course! But those are the poems that most teachers never give them to deal with. We say, "You don't have to like them or relate to them or enjoy them—any part of them. You just have to deal with them." And somehow or other, of course, all the way through the experience they are supposed to recognize that this is incredibly fine poetry!

When these people arrived in my class, many of them had already learned to trust themselves. They were fortunate. Several were especially strong people in themselves and some had done things in theater with Len Mozzi and in English with Jean Smith that gave them confidence. They had been with teacher adults who literally mean what they say. Other teachers of course, had said, "I really want you to write from your heart," but if the students didn't produce a nice bibliography, they were punished. So my students wrote excitingly. For instance Nancy Sasso, after talking about the stanza form, rhyme, punctuation, and sentence structure that her poet employs, says, "So much for the mechanical aspect. Now we get to the stuff that really matters: what his poems do to me." And she goes on:

> His poems stimulate my mind, spark my imagination. I'm pretty sure that the emotion that I felt was excitement. After reading each poem I was forced to go back and read it again, and then I couldn't help but say "Yeah!" He was so right. He had put into words things that I had contemplated once, as well as really great ideas of his own.

In setting up this project, Doreen had issued a Guide Sheet to her students. Here are excerpts from it:

> Glance through some anthologies—read some poetry and find your poet. Get in touch with why you chose the person. Remember why. Then, read several of the poet's works. Choose some to explicate. Get in touch with why you chose the particular poems and remember why. Listen in class and talk and share the discovery of the poems we discuss and use what you can to enhance your individual discovery of your own poet. Let yourself react, and trust your reactions. Let first impressions imprint themselves, but stay open to change. As time passes and you learn to know your poet, things will come clearer, just as learning about any new persons becomes clearer as you see them behave and hear them speak. Approach your poet as a new acquaintance. Get to know him or her. Somewhere

along the way you'll know whether you want to be friends; you may not, and that's o.k., too. Try to refrain from judgment too soon, though.

In the second part of the Guide Sheet, Doreen issued a challenge to her students to exercise their own judgment, encouraging them to ask questions which when followed through would result in what we call "thinking."

... begin to explore the puzzle that is poetry—the "how did he or she get me to react like this?" Play with the poetry, arrange the puzzle pieces, fool around with the rhyme, the non-rhyme, the phrases, the images, the spaces, the juxtapositions that make clear the soul's concern with life and death, beauty and ugliness, pain and joy. Find the how that produces a precise reaction, the very reaction the poet felt when he or she initially experienced the poem in real life ... Do not try to move too quickly. Experience the poem first, really experience it—over and over, and then look for why it happened.

When you write your paper, try to recreate your search, your reactions, how you got your hands on the poetry, what steps you took, the mistakes you made that were not really mistakes because we learn from what is by what isn't, the conclusions you came to, the joys, anger, shock, frustration, boredom, *whatever*. Don't be afraid of your conclusions—keep checking them out against the WHOLE poem, against what you feel and what you intellectually perceive the author to be saying. Trust yourself and use your inner self to best advantage.

The paper itself should reflect, in as clear and organized a fashion as possible, the search you have made. You may consult other people's work in the subject, but do not replace *your* search with others' searches—it is you I am primarily interested in, not some critic that I can read about myself. This is not totally a research paper; it is an I-Search paper as well. It is probably the most self-disciplined paper you will be asked to write because your search will generally be based on primary sources—you and the poems in question.

Type the paper, please. Or have it typed. Use footnotes and bibliography if your paper calls for them. Check MLA [The Modern Language Association Style Sheet] for current usage. I'll be around to help and other teachers can help. Jean Smith is a super resource person. . . .

Sorry about the typing. It's late and I'm about wiped out. Try to do a better job of typing your papers than I do of mine.

What I wrote in that Guide Sheet was not altogether a surprise to these students, because they had been prepared by the preceding semester with me and by experiences with other teachers who respected truthtelling. That's how I talk to them, so it wasn't like "Now we're going to be doing some big thing that's different from anything we've done before." I'm talking about consistency—not about "hobgoblins of the mind" but a certain kind of consistency that reassures students that you're always coming from the same place. And you have to remember that this was April, and they had been with me since September. I don't think anyone could go into a class in September and in November get papers like that.

At Bunnell we've been changing over and offering full-year courses. It's necessary at all levels and it's certainly necessary at the lower levels of ability, for students to learn to trust the person they're with, to feel that they can make mistakes, that it's o.k. in the classroom—even in a paper like this—to be wrong. You can see in the way that Ray Fernandes starts his paper that he trusts his audience. He's willing to let his thoughts go:

> The poem "A Primer of the Daily Round" is a collection of individuals, each involved in an action that is in no way directly related to the actions of the other individuals. After I read this poem I thought about all of the persons that I came to know in my life, how through each of these persons I came to know at least one other person, and how I am thus related in some way to a person that I would otherwise have never met. This idea led me to think about how a friend of a friend at one end of my friendship spectrum was related, no matter how indirectly, to a friend of a friend of a friend at the opposite end of my friendship spectrum. Then again, I could be at either end, or anywhere in between, of anyone else's spectrum of friends.

And then soon after that, he writes this passage, which I like so much:

> So once again I have come up with a part-whole type idea. That seems to be what I get out of everything and I don't know if it is because I see what I want or because I see what is there.

And yet these are the young people so many teachers call unperceptive. In these papers they come up with perceptions about themselves, about the world, about their brother, friends, about how people relate. It's just wild. These people are writing freely, as professional writers do. That's why they're so exciting. Nancy Sasso lets herself say,

> The poet's name is Joseph Francis Murphy (I love three-word names; they sound so neat. Olivia Newton John, Francis Scott Key, Robert Francis Weatherbee . . .)

In the Guide Sheet Doreen had said, "Try to recreate your search . . . the joys, anger, shock, frustration, boredom, whatever." In her paper Sue Colicci wrote:

> One night Sandi came home more-than-usually excited. She said they had discussed and written poems and she showed me a poem that I assumed Jean Smith had typed and dittoed as an example. It was called "The Fish" and was by Elizabeth Bishop. I really liked the poem and I

should have immediately looked up Bishop when we were assigned this I-Search project, but I had decided to start at the worst place to begin, the top. That meant reading and explicating poems by William Shakespeare. Well, I should have realized sooner that Shakespeare was just too big for me, I had to settle for somebody smaller.

Then one day after school Mrs. Smith and I started discussing poets. She told me the romantic story of Elizabeth Barrett Browning and gave me a book on contemporary poets. I skimmed through the poems but none of them reached out and slapped me across the face, so I scratched them.

The next morning when Gail and I went to the library, the first person I looked up was Elizabeth Barrett Browning. Somehow I had confused her with Elizabeth Bishop and thought they were the same. But when I looked, the library had no real good books on her, so I gave up. I didn't give Elizabeth Barrett Browning/Bishop a second thought. Then I looked up Helen Lowrie Marshall, whose books had been taken out by some other person, and Nikki Giovanni, whose name I couldn't even find in the card catalog. And then Gail suggested a few such as Dorothy Parker, Langston Hughes, and Edna St. Vincent Millay. She pulled one of Millay's books off of the shelf and read to me a poem about a candle burning at both ends. I liked it. Later I realized it was the only poem of hers I would like. I did give her a fair chance though, I brought home five of her books and sat through hours of her poetry and I didn't like her. Stuck again . . .

Then Sandi said something about Elizabeth Bishop and "The Fish." Then it hit me! I mean the poem. I couldn't imagine how I could have gotten Elizabeth Barrett Browning and Elizabeth Bishop confused. So the third time I went to the library, I looked her up and there it was. Bishop. Elizabeth. The Complete Poems. 811 B622C. And that was who I settled on.

That was the introduction to an I-Search paper. After it, Doreen wrote, "I think I love this already!" Writing about Elizabeth's Bishop's poem "The Colder the Air," Sue went on to say:

This poem took me a while to figure out, which is why I liked it, because at least it had something to see in it, not like her other poems. At first I thought it was just a lady hunting because of the word *game*. But after reading it again, some things didn't seem to fit. It even dawned on me that she was some type of cupid, but that didn't fit either. Her perfect aim, I knew, was because no matter where she shot "her shot was right." But what gave it away was when it said "air's gallery marks identically the narrow gallery of her glance." I figured it could mean that the boundary of her glance is as extensive as air, which is great, but it said "identically," which started me comparing where she shot in air and maybe *she was* "air's gallery" or "winter air." So, with this in mind, everything fit. She knows there's a time for her winter air and she knows it well and can't forget it because the "ticking loud" in her pocket would keep reminding her. It's hidden though, and she doesn't care because she won't consult time,

"she'll consult not time nor circumstance" but instead she'll call on atmosphere—*air* atmosphere, for her result, the cold.

What struck me about Sue's paper, and most of the others was that
they carry that authoritative statement—"I feel it's this because of so
and so." Or, "I recognize that I may be coming from—" It's all there.
It's part of the I-Search concept. Because the person is there in the
paper,˙you know some of the biases and prejudices and the state of
mind at the time the paper was written. Instead of the last word in the
automatic response system.

On their own these students picked up the poetic devices in the
poems they were reading. Pat Stavola talks about E. E. Cummings:

> The odd spacing in the above poems is not merely there to be different, as
> is charged, but rather to serve a specific and designated purpose. Cum-
> mings uses this spacing to control the tempo of the poem; his strange
> punctuation acts as additional controls. Often Cummings will completely
> isolate one word such as "him," the last word in the poem. This is for extra
> emphasis upon the word. Parentheses are also used frequently by Cum-
> mings, as is illustrated in the above poem. Such parentheses are used to
> interrupt a thought, to register an aside. Sometimes Cummings will only
> put down the opening or closing marks of the parentheses. This creates an
> impression that the phrase is a fragment and something is left unsaid.

The students were not doing exhaustive treatments of a poet, but they
were learning how to read poems and they learned terms as well. While
they were doing the papers, a lot of students would come to me and
say, "I know we talked about this. I don't remember the name, but I
know what it does." And I would say, "Well, who cares about the name
if you know what it does? But for the purposes of the paper—to make
it clear to other people—maybe you need to know the term."

One student reported she had had a teacher who gave the class a
page full of definitions of poetic devices, which they then were supposed to memorize. And she would bring in two lines from a poem and
they would have to find the poetic devices in them. That was the past
experience with poetry of about a half dozen of my students.

I think you must realize that these students had had a chance to
develop as writers about literature before they wrote these papers. In
the semester previous they wrote about what they read, but we took
things pretty slowly. In studying *Hamlet* we wrote the speech "To be or
not to be" in a humorous way. We took something that was classic and
said, "We're going to fool around with it." And we also did academic
papers on *Hamlet* as well, but people chose their own topics. I said to
them, "You choose something that means something to you. Do you
have a problem of ambivalence as Hamlet did?" [*She laughs.*] Or what-

ever. Something that makes sense to you. Not "Let's do the Oedipal Complex, all of us together."

When I talk about writing essays, or poetry papers, I say that much of our evidence comes from ourselves. I'm not saying, "Because you feel this way, therefore it's true," but "If you've had this experience or seen someone else in the family, or wherever, have it, that's as valid as some other expert coming along and saying, 'Well, I've witnessed this, too.' "

People ask me if I love my students. "Oh, of course," I say. How could you not love them when they write like Joan Krystiniak? In her paper she told how she went through poetry books till she found a poet "whose works made complete and total sense" to her. She quoted a poem by Helen Lowrie Marshall that contained these lines:

> I think my heart would burst in two
> Without a God to give thanks to.

And then Joan wrote: "The poem made absolute sense to me. I liked what it was saying, but I realized that Helen Marshall was in a Hallmark way."

5

LAVERNE GONZALEZ
"Remedial" English, University

Beginning in the fall of 1970, a developmental program in English Composition was founded at Purdue University as a "growth center for students with low scores on the Scholastic Aptitude verbal test." The language of that description is an attempt to get away from the term "remedial." Frequently about half the students were either black or of Spanish descent and some of them had not customarily spoken or written Standard English.

The results of a test given in 1971 showed that on an average, as a result of taking English 100, a student improved from a D+ to a B— in writing. Some of the engineering students who took the program received their English credits and were dismissed from further English courses. Several were assigned to special creative writing courses. One received the first-place prize at the all-university Purdue Literary Awards Banquet for the Informal Essay as well as the President Hovde Award that was given for the best of all entries. I learned of the program in English 100 from its director, Professor LaVerne Gonzalez, who described her work in this way.

Of course, statistics are meaningless except as they are translated into specific individual achievement. Whether or not the program really succeeds depends wholly on whether or not the participating students' lives were significantly changed by this experience. That evaluation can be given only after much time has elapsed.

I was in charge of training "teacher assistants" for English 100. They taught the hundreds of students enrolled each semester in the program. I have several file folders full of notes and letters I've received from these young teachers, many of them written after the teachers had finished working in English 100. Here's one of those letters:

> I walked by your English 100 class today, as your students were writing their Pre-tests. It was out of curiosity that I lingered briefly and surveyed your class, and soon my eyes fell upon you, at the "head" of the class (so unlike you, I think) writing your heart and head away—into infinity. And

LaVerne Gonzalez writes with her students as an equal.

upon your face I saw a smile, your lips were loosely curved. I think your smile was a contented one, full of good thoughts for this semester with your students. I thought: I must have looked similarly today when I wrote as my students wrote, and I casually looked at their faces and frustrations. I must have smiled too when I thought of the unknown areas I would travel and explore with these, my students, these, as yet total strangers. I felt happy inside when I saw you sitting there writing. We were/are doing serious work in this confused world, and living life.

I was writing on the first day of class with those undergraduates, just as I expect the T.A.s to do. Students should see teachers writing.
  Another T.A. wrote me:

> I have been using "free writing" with some kids at the Community School in West Lafayette. . . . Here is poem I shared with my English 100 class. It was written in my class by an eight-year-old girl:
>
>> if this poem was perfect,
>> it wouldn't be good at all.
>> Because perfect is nothing wrong and
>> all tidy and neat and no feeling at all—
>> so don't blame me if this poem
>> isn't perfect 'cause perfect's
>> not really good at all.

Here's another letter from my file:

> I should begin the letter with a series of thank-you's—for opportunity to learn from you this summer, for your sending my journal and writings to me, and for your remembering me with copies of English 100 minutes and publications.
>   The school year has been moving so rapidly for me. Besides teaching, I am taking the Real Estate Salesman's Course at Purdue. I never seem to arrive on campus early enough to see you, so am hoping my letter will serve as the messenger of my thoughts . . .

And another letter:

> We went to Yosemite National Park this past weekend: camping and gathering information concerning at least two backpacking expeditions that we're going to take before December-January. It was beyond belief! ("Bob, you've got to have better descriptions than that"—I can hear you.)
>   My English 100 is coming in handy in writing "Man-hours" reports. It will especially help when I start writing pre-operational procedures, test procedures, etc. I found myself correcting grammar in an engineer's memo that I was typing. It's all your fault! Proud?

At the end of each semester, I require all teaching assistants to write comprehensive evaluations of their teaching experience. Here's an excerpt from one of them:

> I remember you saying, "Your students will think they are in the most informal class, but they will constantly be learning discipline." I didn't believe you, and assumed from the start that the students would readily accept the responsibility of learning what was to be offered—that they would learn what they wanted, and that they wanted to learn composition. I therefore gave nearly no structure at all to my class, and the students saw little need to accomplish what was not *demanded* of them—and I demanded too little.
>
> By the time I realized my mistake, I felt damned. It was nearly mid-semester, and I thought that changing my style then would completely ruin my class. Students abhor inconsistency in a teacher—I know I do—and I felt that to make a major change in my approach would cause an even greater loss of interest, a notion of "what-the-hell-has-gotten-into-him?" and a final rebellion against cooperation. Instead, I elected to let the students do as they wished, pointing out that I was aware that they were taking advantage of our lack of form.
>
> I wanted them to see that it was imperative for them as adult human beings to undertake responsibility for themselves. I am not a good nurse-maid, and I could never see that as my job. Consequently, the most mature of my students improved their writing the most. Others sloughed through the course as it appears they slough through most of their present life. This is terribly depressing to me, its reality vivid and shocking. I honestly wish I could have changed their attitude, and I see the need to be firm on this point from the first day of the semester. A developmental teacher has the monumental task of helping students to grow up!

Many of the undergraduate students in English 100 thought of themselves as failures in writing the American-English language, and school had branded them as such. For the uncertain teaching assistants, meeting a college class for the first time in their lives, these students were threatening. I gave them some advice out of my own experience teaching the course. For example, here are some excerpts from a handout I distributed to the T.A.s:

> At least three-fourths of my students have been minority group members. During these six years I have learned my value system operates only for me—even then sometimes it has proven inadequate. I valued a tenet of mine: students who come to the university must sever home ties. "Do not go home until Thanksgiving," I announced authoritatively. "Why do you think the army has a six weeks basic training period? The first semester at the university must be devoted to inuring yourselves to the academic environment." . . . I remember one young woman in particular—intelligent, eager, well motivated. But she went home every week-end. "Look," I said

maternally, "you will never make it through Purdue like that." She answered, "If I don't touch home base every week-end, I cannot bat—I must constantly be renewing my spirit." Her religion meant family and God; she spoke in religious terms often; she graduated from Purdue with a 5.2 out of a 6.0 index; she now teaches elementary school in South Bend.

. . . One summer I was working with a group of Upward Bound students . . . I spoke in enthusiastic terms of the tremendous potential lying dormant in each of them—a potential I had observed as I read the first set of papers they had written. One young man turned sullen and said cynically, "Don't talk about potential. I'm sick of hearing about my potential. What about me right *now?*" Yes, what about him right now? I know what he was saying to me. "If you cannot accept me as I am, forget it."

. . . In order to learn from you, an Anglo teacher, the student must *like* and *trust* you. [Educators say:] "We must consider the background and not make too many demands." Such reasoning is faulty. A part of the respect for student and teacher comes from the demand by the teacher for excellence—excellence of teaching, excellence of performance . . .

I would hasten to add that the professor who feels he has a mission to save the black or Chicano has written his own death certificate.

In the black community the ability to rap is a virtue; in the Latino community a professor is *"una persona de respeto."* The Latino student would feel his proper response would be to listen. If the student comes from a very conservative Latino family, he will even avoid that all important eye-to-eye contact, believing that contact disrespectful.

One T.A. told me, "One of my students said he wouldn't be in class because his mother had been in a serious accident and he was needed at home immediately. Later I saw him in the Sweet Shop laughing with his friends. What a fool he must take me for. I'll never trust him again. They're all alike." One of the hard lessons we have learned is to treat lies objectively. Usually a teacher may gauge his value to the student in terms of how elaborate the lie is. If the student does not "feel" like coming to class, he will give you a lie. His reasons for not "feeling like" attending class vary: he is a night person; he finds the material boring; he has some work due for another class; it's raining—or one of a dozen other reasons. Whatever the cause, he will not embarrass or insult you with the truth. He will fabricate: the better his imagination, the better your image, the better the lie. He honors you with his lie. You accept the honor; but you also let him know that you know it is a lie, albeit a beautiful one. And you insist that the missed work be made up. Regardless of how puritanical your background or how "straight" your moral code, he does not subscribe to the same value system. He doesn't *have* to; all he needs to do is master the material.

I try to be frank with the T.A.s and treat them as peers. And often they reply with equal candor. One, a fundamentalist Christian, wrote me this after leaving Purdue:

I never wrote to you thanking you for the pamphlet of English 100 writings, not because I didn't read them, but because I didn't know what to say. I still don't know what to say so I'll let the Lord do the talking.

I remember that you taught me to always write truths. That, I remember, because I couldn't always write truths. I would have to make things up as I went along. This is wrong. I learned this from the Bible . . .

Another T.A. wrote me:

You cannot know what incalculable benefit you have had on my thinking. I always knew how to dream, but now I know how to believe in dreams, and run after them.

I treat the students in my own undergraduate courses the same as I do the T.A.s. Here's one of them writing me:

I have a problem. I have to drop English 105 and it's kicking my ass. At first I thought it was alright, I had it all figured out. I was going to start a journal on my own and write everyday. After reading the valuations and criticisms you gave to me my mind began to change. I dropped English 105 yesterday and won't be attending Stan's class today. Oh how I remember the good times in English 100. God knows I don't want to stop now. Mrs. Gonzalez, I am confused, I can't think. I feel empty. I feel as if I cut off my arm by dropping English. I must write and have my stories, articles, or whatever read, but what can I do? My schedule won't allow it. What can I do? I love to write, I must have that class. You know I just realized that I'm talking myself out of dropping English. Well, so what, shit! I want it. I'll just drop something else, but I must have English . . .

The way we take an interest in the students' lives is a calculated risk. It's dangerous. T.A.s may get too close to their students and lose objectivity. They have to be aware. All their students are high-risk, borderline people who have more than the normal number of life and academic problems. But college is training for life, and good writing grows out of life situations. The president of the university called the entire Purdue staff together and made a plea for faculty to entertain students in homes. So we arranged that some of our T.A. staff meetings would be held in their apartments.

From the first day of class to the last day of class you always had new ideas. Regardless of how you felt, it seemed that you were always in a good mood. At first I had a hard time writing in my journal, but you saw that and helped get me on a good start. When I would turn in my journal, I couldn't wait to get it back. I wanted to see what good things you said about my sloppy writings, and start writing in it again. Dr. Gonzalez, you are like a high school teacher; you are always concerned about how your students are adjusting to college life and if you can help them. So far, I have been unable to find professors as willing as you are to go out of their way to help a student.

Thank you for everything that you have done for me and if you ever need any medical help in eight years, when I am a doctor, feel free to look me up and give me a call.

Our work in English 100 is difficult—often successful and often unsuccessful. Many students and T.A.s are still struggling with the fundamentals of the craft. But they need to believe in their own abilities. And the teachers must be willing to take first efforts and say, "You did something good here." Now you can go on from there. Grammar has to come after writing gets under way. It must come out of what's going on.

Writing is what we're teaching. In our staff meetings everyone does some free writing. Last fall a bunch of T.A.s decided to get together on their own and write and respond to short stories, poems, journals. I remember seeing a journal entry from one of those sessions about a student who had moved one of these young teachers.

But not everything is positive. Bob Miller was the professor who originally proposed this program and gave me the job of launching it. When he died, we set up an annual award in his name for the outstanding student writer in the whole program—not for just one paper, but for continuing good performance by one student. The prize was to be voted by the T.A.s, who were supposed to bring good student writing to a meeting. Some simply didn't bring any papers, and didn't participate in the discussion except to say they didn't believe the writing being judged was good enough. And once, the award went to a writer who half the teachers didn't agree was the best. And then people complained about the person chosen as winner. I was disgusted.

I got a Christmas card from eighteen students in one of my T.A.s' classes. It said:

> We thank you for all of the miracles, big and little, which you have worked on our behalf, despite the Engfish Establishment ["Engfish" is a student-coined name for the dead academic language most school papers are written in.]

You may wonder how students in someone else's class came to make this gesture toward me. I visit the T.A.s' classes to help them improve their teaching, so the students get to know me. I'm looking for teachers' rapport with students. I watch for every lead that students give the teacher that isn't followed up. When I hire these people, I interview them all. I don't turn down many, but those who have a negative or condescending attitude toward students, who say, "These poor benighted people"—they don't get hired. So once teachers have been hired, they know I trust them. My job is to challenge them with this exciting and important task they're about to undertake. I tell them that any time you have what could be a problem in teaching, one that puts you on the defensive, you must turn it around so it's an advantage. You must act aggressively.

It's not surprising that after they left, these T.A.s kept in touch, because at the weekly staff meetings they talked about their experience—what was going on in their classes, what needed to be done. I told them that we would assume responsibility for students. We would expect them to come back to us after they left the course, because we would discover where they were, what their needs were, and go on from there.

The students who take English 100 have known failure in writing throughout their school careers. In most schools, such a course would be dubbed "remedial," but here the student has at once freedom to find his own voice and discipline, and to discover more professional craft to supplement his already considerable language skills. Total respect for student expression distinguishes the course. A person learns to write by writing, and a person who writes is by definition a writer. Therefore students in this program approach writing as professionals. Each student keeps his own grammar charts which allow him to concentrate on any recurring problem. From that activity, a slide set on punctuation evolves. Grammar books appear, composed of dittoed material driving home a point.

In such a hard challenge for student and T.A., enthusiasm is necessary, and we see it. Randy Brooke, one of my T.A.s, sent this poem to me:

AWESPIRING TEACHER OF WRITING

LaVerne will yell, shout
eagle eye you
shake her finger in your face
speak so sincere and serious
that you feel like part
of an historical event
and it is too
this is the revolution
we must change the system
the old ways just don't work
and all of these new teachers
are listening
heart-throbbed staring
feeling like they've been transported
back to the days of protest

they haven't heard anybody
talk like this for years
faculty meetings are supposed to be tedious
and boring
no one says anything new
but here
IT IS THE REVOLUTION

WE WILL CARE ABOUT THE STUDENT
WE WILL NOT LET HIM GO
UNABLE TO WRITE

Raise your right hand
and repeat after me
I SWEAR
TO UPHOLD AND PROTECT
THE CONSTITUTION OF ENGLISH 100
THAT ALL WRITERS ARE CREATED EQUAL
AND SHALL KNOW HOW TO SURVIVE
AND PURSUE THE HAPPINESS AND BLISS
OF TELLING TRUTHS
THAT WILL GRIP
THEIR PEERS BY THE BACK
OF THEIR CRANIUMS
THAT ALL WILL ACT WITH CONVICTION
AND WRITE WITH CONVICTION
NOT TO PERSUADE FALSELY
NOT TO WRITE EFFECTIVELY FOR THE SAKE
OF EGO OR POWER EXHIBITIONS
NOT TO DECEIVE
BUT SPEAK FROM THE GUT
THE TRUTH
NOTHING BUT THE TRUTH
SO HELP ME GOD.

In the center, Twila Papay smiles at the good conversation.

6

TWILA YATES PAPAY
English as a Second Language, College

In 1972 I met Twila Yates Papay in West Lafayette, Indiana, when she was a graduate teaching assistant at Purdue University. In 1978, after taking a job teaching at Caldwell College in New Jersey, she sent me a copy of a mimeographed newspaper called International Thoughts, *containing writing in English by her foreign students. It was printed on bright-colored sheets of legal-sized paper and contained pieces such as this one, titled "The Wise Men from Beginning to End" by a woman from Ecuador. Here are excerpts from it:*

It was January fifth of 1967, and I remember as now that I went back of my house. I cuted up some of the grass and brought it into my house. I put it under my bed. Then I went and I asked my father many question as a child of seven years old do when they are not sure about. He usually sat with us on the front porch, and told us things about the old times of his youth. As this time he explained to my brothers and I from where the tradition of the three wise king came from . . .

This day was very special for me because I was the day I descovered the real truth about this famous holiday in Puerto Rico. Also, when all my dreams of childhood broke out. I remember as now that I gave my father the list of toys for the three wise king. I always had ask my father to tell the wise to bring my a set of kitchen to play with my dolls and friend. But I didn't know that day my father was going to go and never come back home. That day I went to bed and I didn't found anything just the old grass I had cuted out and the glass of water.

I ran crying into the kitchen where my mother was cooking breakfast. I remember that I asked her why they did not brought gift to us. She said that there were many thing difficult to explain to a child like my. I was so sad that my mother called me and explain that the existence of the three wise was only a tradition and that such thing about three men coming at night and put gift under the bed were only a lie. I asked my mother who were the person who put the gift under the bed all this year. She said that she went to town bought the present and when we were slept my father and her will put it under the bed and take with them all the grass and water put it away where we couldn't see it. I was so sorprise with all this thing I started to cry not only for the descoverement but for my father absent and knowing that he will never come back.

Year later I had grew up and I was twelve years old then I could realize that the tradition of the three wise king was not only for fun but for have a nice remembering of it. I also learned that we have to acept the truth of life and learn to live by finding the best way for us, live it. Now I have a good experience for myself and for the children I will have in the future.

Twila Papay published International Thoughts *monthly, and sent me issues of it for two years. One was twenty-six pages long but I couldn't resist reading through it.*

In October 1982, on Long Island, when I met Twila for the second time, I asked her to tell me something of her last ten years as an enabler.

As a graduate student at Purdue, my first year of teaching, I didn't know what I was doing. But I discovered I liked the students. I liked talking to them. In my office they enjoyed talking to me, but when they wrote, their words were so empty. They weren't writing about the things they were talking about, so I started asking them to do so. I was experimenting.

The following year we started the Developmental English Course, English 100, where I worked with LaVerne Gonzalez [*see Chapter 5*]. I think she and I influenced each other. She had more energy. She's a powerhouse. She sees teaching in different political terms than I do because she believes in the American dream—people pulling themselves up by their bootstraps. I come at it from a different political view. I'm a sixties liberal. We end up doing the same things in the classroom, believing students can do anything and persuading them of that. And insisting they do it. When LaVerne got her Ph.D., she became the coordinator of English 100 and I continued for two years in that program dedicated to helping underprepared students. Some of them had parents who were first-generation Americans, so I was unwittingly readying myself for teaching positions I later held at St. Peters College and Caldwell College in New Jersey.

When English 100 was created, and I was asked to teach it, I said I couldn't because I didn't know anything about it. And they said, "Well, we don't have anyone else." So I said I'd do it, and they handed me a writing textbook which presented the work of ordinary students doing "free writing"—that is, writing fast about whatever mattered to them, without worrying about correctness. I asked my students to do this and discovered they had ideas and that I could believe in those ideas and their right to them. Most of us don't start teaching this way because we think students don't have anything in their heads. I began to develop the confidence to try all kinds of things and to go beyond that book.

I could try new things because I realized that it didn't matter if they didn't all work. I could ask students to do odd things. I could tell them I was bored with what was happening and I wasn't going to read any more boring papers. I could hand back papers and say, "You don't care about this, so I don't care. Write something else." And that was freedom.

When I went to Caldwell to teach students for whom English was a second language, I decided to try all the techniques I'd developed for poorly prepared students. After going through the Caldwell writing program once, I saw that if students did something which didn't work, it didn't mean they couldn't do things. It simply meant that *that* thing didn't work. If an assignment doesn't work and students come in with some dreadful piece of drivel they've written, you can talk about what went wrong and you can get at why what they did didn't work. Sometimes I get them to write about such an experience in a journal.

Another thing I learned from that textbook is that any one piece of writing can be thrown away. So doing a lot of writing is essential and no one piece of writing matters all that much. That's the way professionals work when they have the chance.

At Caldwell I found that foreign students are helped by free writing. They can just put down words in English without worrying about correctness, so they begin to think about meaning and develop a flow of language. My students discovered they knew more English than they or I thought they did. I told them, "I don't care what you say in your journals. These writings aren't going to be graded. I just want to know what you're thinking about a few things. Write about your past, write about growing up in your country. Don't write all that trivia you find in travelogues." I forbade them to do that. I said, "Only write about your own country as it relates to you."

They were intrigued. They enjoyed telling me and each other these things. We started reading the journals aloud to give them practice speaking English, and I discovered that exactly the same techniques worked for them that had worked for what are wrongly called "remedial" students. With some differences, of course. My Caldwell students were generally better motivated. Remedial students have had an experience of failure. My foreign students were terrified because they were locked out of communication, but desperately wanted to learn. They came in to my office and talked to me about their writing. They would say how terrible a paper was and I would pick it up and say, "I know what this says," and they would be amazed. Although it wasn't written well by our standards, I understood it, and that motivated them. They came to believe in themselves. I was giving them the confidence they needed to use the English language.

At Caldwell about twenty to thirty students come each year for the program in English as a Second Language. Originally nearly all of them were Latin Americans, but then as the program became known we began to get other people—students from mainland China, doctors and nurses from the Middle East, a lawyer from Cyprus. Also we had people from the New Jersey area whose wives and husbands had been brought into the United States to work for a year, and the spouses wanted to learn more English. One year well over half my class was from Latin America, the next, only a fourth. I soon found if my students were not just doing exercises in the English language but using it to say something they wanted to say, they learned English quickly. To learn a foreign language one must be confident. One of our students from Korea demonstrated this painfully. Lily had been in and out of Caldwell several times. Before I met her, she had known three other Korean students at the College who made fun of her because she had forgotten how to speak Korean. She hadn't learned English, so she was without language. One of the nuns—Caldwell is a Dominican women's college—said Lily used to go off to a closet and close the door and when they'd open the door to get something, there would be Lily sitting in there crying. They couldn't get a Korean counselor for her, and apparently that wouldn't have done any good because her Korean was lost.

By the time I had Lily in class she had picked up a little English. She had a lot of emotional problems, had had them for many years. So what I did for a long time was to tell her just to sit in the class and do whatever writing assignments she wanted to do. When she presented some writing to a small group, they didn't want to admit they didn't understand, so they would pretend, and respond with something. I would make her repeat things. Finally when she realized the others in the class were there to try to understand her, she began to spend hours over pages, and she'd come into my office with them.

Then I published something of hers in our newspaper, *International Thoughts*. I cleaned up her writing a little bit. It hardly made any sense. But I thought the idea I could see running through it might be picked up by other people. On that little campus everyone read the newspaper. I put her piece on the front page. Everyone knew her because she had been in and out so often. So people were stopping Lily and saying, "How nice. You wrote something and it was in the newspaper!" And this helped her, but more importantly, some people understood it. She was saying she wished she were a stone "because stones can't cry and they don't have feelings." A couple of weeks later she came into my office. She started talking but didn't make sense, and I said, "I don't understand you," and she began to cry. She cried a lot, and it took her two hours to explain to me she had a lot of problems but she couldn't think about them because she didn't have words to think about them in. And she hadn't realized that, because she hadn't been thinking in words, and now she was. She wanted to learn more words.

I got a tutor for her, a student who just walked around with her, talked, pointed out things, and gave her the nouns for them. Lily became enthralled with this. She never did graduate from Caldwell, but she completed two out of four courses with me. At the end she was writing so I could understand her. Here's an excerpt from a piece of hers published in the magazine:

> Winter doesn't need decoration for his body. It is a very honest season. that keeps silence in the outside world. If there is cold, it is only a present at low and lower temperature for us. But they could feel this. Which showed to us that it is very honest . . . humble and beautiful is winter. When the wind is so strong and passing through beside the trees and they make so noisy a sound. It is so scared in winter.

One day when we were doing personal experience papers—it was toward the end of the class—Lily read hers. None of us could follow it at all. I said, "We're too tired to do this right now. We'll do it again next time and I'll read it to you." So the next day we came into class and Lily was nervous. I started to read from her paper and someone said, "No, let her try it again. We'll listen harder this time." I made her read slower, and she said to the class, "O.K., when you don't understand a whole sentence, raise your hand," and they did. And she tried over and over until we understood enough of the paper to critique it. We never did understand the whole paper, but the fact the students wanted so much to help her was part of our success.

Eventually Lily got a job in a store where she was able to communicate with customers. A great achievement for her. She also quit crying and made some friends.

I think I'm good at working with people who have difficulty writing because I have difficulty too. Lately I've been talking to a colleague about how empty my writing seems to me. I can skim the surface of things really well, but I'm not writing about things that matter to me in the way I want to. This same colleague observed me teaching. The students were reading their personal experience papers to each other and giving suggestions, and then they were going to revise them. This teacher thought the class was fine but then wanted to know what such work had to do with expository writing, which the students were supposed to be doing. And it struck me—unfortunately not until I had left him, but I'll have to tell him some day—the trouble with my writing is I was never given the opportunity these students have. That's what it is. I've never written regularly about my experiences and gotten responses to the writing, and so I've never learned to start that way with a paper. That's what's making the writing of these students exciting and remarkable for me. When they do it, they find their voices. They use metaphor and sensuous words. The incidents in their papers come up strongly, with finely delineated, precise details. These things aren't hard to do if we don't get self-conscious about them. But I'm too aware of audience. When I make a presentation at a teachers' conference, I *say* it well, but when I go to write it out I'm afraid I can't do what my students do. I'm afraid I won't say what I know is true—or maybe afraid the truth is something I'm not ready to look at or admit. Learning to write is hard because I've always been told I do it so well, but I know differently. I skim the surface. I have a sense of urgency about wanting to write things that really matter to me in teaching.

The skills you learn in narration are helpful in exposition. Narrative writing is essential. It ultimately does more for us as human beings and is more interesting to read than what we're expected to teach—exposition and argumentation and all those things about structure. When students are writing exposition I encourage them to use personal experience examples. I forbid them to write about anything they don't care about. You know, you have to forbid them. You have to say absolutely, "You may not write about this if you're not interested in it." I talk to them about how to take assignments in other classes and turn them into things they care about. I know it's subversive. Students don't ordinarily write things that count for them in college. But they do in my classes. And when they learn to write this way, they're free to make choices. They can write anything in any mode they choose.

At Caldwell, Graciane Birotte from Haiti, whose first, or at least formal, language is French, wrote this story:

SUBWAY RIDE

I had a very bad experience when I came in the United States. A few days after arriving here, my husband and I wanted to go to New York. We took the bus from Newark to Port Authority, then the subway. We were fascinated through the whole trip. We went out of the subway, shopped a little, and by nine o'clock we decided to go back to Newark.

We got back to the subway station. Hundreds and hundreds of people were waiting for the subway. Some were all dressed up. Some girls had beautiful gowns and sophisticated hairdos. Their escort wore elegant tuxedos. Some others wore shorts or blue jeans, and some had sloppy, dirty, smelly clothes. It was a saturday night. What a contrast!

As the subway approached, we could hear a big, loud noise. It got louder and louder and the whole platform was shaken just like a tornado was coming. The subway stopped, the doors opened and everyone rushed without any courtesy, pushing and shoving each other.

I entered the subway without even knowing it. I looked around and saw my husband not too far from me, standing by the door. We stood up because we could not find a seat. The door closed, and the subway started to move. I had to hold the steel bar to keep my balance. God! what a noise. The man sitting in front of me was sleeping. The lady on my right was reading her newspaper peacefully. How did they manage in such madness?

When we got to our stop, I did not even know it since it was my first trip to New York. My husband told me, "Get ready! This is our stop." I nodded. As soon as the doors opened again, everyone rushed out. I was afraid that I was going to fall down, so I waited patiently for my turn to go out. My husband was already outside waiting for me. "Hurry up Honey!" he said as I was moving slowly.

What's the matter with him? I thought. *Is he becoming an American so soon?* I was about to tell him that when . . . Surprise! The subway door closed in front of me. I could not believe what had happened to me. How had the door closed? I looked at my husband. His eyes were wide open. Just like me, he was shocked. I stood up in front of the door for a few minutes motionless. I looked around. I could only see strange faces without expression. I got scared because we had always heard of so many bad things happening in the subway. I glanced at the man next to me. He was wearing a black suit, black shirt and a white tie. Could he be a gangster? He looked very unfriendly anyway. I held my pocketbook tightly. The train kept moving faster and faster. I counted every minute, every second. Was the train ever going to stop? I thought. It seemed it was going slower now, Good! The train stopped.

Quickly, like everyone this time, I ran out of the door as soon as it was opened. Without thinking I followed the crowd and went upstairs. My hands were cold and wet. I did not want anyone to know that I was new in the United States. I kept walking and walking without knowing where I was going.

Finally, I spotted a policeman. What a relief! I ran toward him and told him, "me want to go to Newark."

"Where?" said the policeman. "New York?"

"No," I said. "Ne-wark." I remembered I had a pen and a piece of paper in my bag. I took them out and wrote NEWARK.

"Ah," said the policeman "Come, little girl, and follow me," I don't think I will ever forget these words. I walked by him and followed him everywhere. When we got another stairs, he said, "There you are." The bus was right in front of us. I thanked the policeman. He smiled at me and left.

I paid my bus fare and got in the bus. I sat in the front row and watched carefully. When we got to Newark, I took a taxi and went home.

My husband had waited for me, thinking I was coming back to his station. After about one hour, he thought I had managed to go back to Newark. He called to make sure that I was home before he could return himself. I was already home. We were both scared.

When he arrived one hour later, he hugged me very tightly. Then he got mad at me and asked, "Why did you do that? You were walking just like a turtle." I did not answer. I smiled at him and he said, "Anyway, I am glad you are safe."

Now whenever I am in the subway which happens very seldom, I always manage to stay close to the person who is with me, and like everyone else, I try to go out as soon as the door opens.

In Haiti, Graciane had been an elementary-school teacher. She had been in this country a good while when she came to my class. I suggested she become a Boy Scout leader, and she did, working with her small sons' American friends a good bit, and there corrected her idiomatic problems with English. But she made a great improvement in the class, conquering her habit of omitting the word *the,* solving her problems with prepositions, and learning to develop detail. But the point is she learned fast because she was using English to say things that meant something to her.

At present I'm the director of the composition program at Hofstra University on Long Island, 1100 students every year, several different courses—Freshman English 1 and 2, Business Communication, which has another 500 students, English 4, which is an extra practice course. I've found that the same basic truths about learning to write have applied to all those I've taught—the so-called "remedial" students in English 100 at Purdue, the people learning English as a second language at Caldwell College, and the American college students, many of whom are majoring in business, here at Hofstra.

Last year in this new job I got to teach an elective course called "Writing from Experience." It was one of the high points of my career because there were only twelve students and I got to do all the things I've wanted to do but didn't have time for in the past because I was worrying about other kinds of writing.

For the big paper, I asked students to take some important, growing thing that ran through much of their lives. One woman wrote about the loss of her mother at fifteen—she was now forty and had just gotten over it, she thought. And one man wrote about fathering. He had had two fathers and three children. These papers ran twenty to thirty typed pages. We talked about them several times in class, and I had little sessions open to the public and faculty where the writers had to present their projects and read a portion of them. The students complained. "Ms. Papay, you got to read the whole papers, but we heard only little pieces of them." And so they traded each other's papers. One student wrote about why she was such a romantic. Another tried to trace why she was so retiring and what she could do about it. One wrote a marvelous piece about coming to terms with his family. We teachers learn so much from students when we let them write like that.

One of my colleagues said he wouldn't assign personal experience writing because "They would all write about the death of their grandmothers and there's no way you could evaluate such papers." A lot of teachers don't want to come close to their students. They believe there's no way you could talk about writing that is this personal. I don't see any point about talking a lot about any other kind of writing. That's my problem. What do we read by choice? We read fiction. We read stories, because they're so involving. My students have the opportunity to write them themselves.

Next semester I'm teaching a new course I call "Autobiographical Writing." I see it as a step beyond Writing from Experience. I'm going to get students to fictionalize some of their experience. Some of them worry a lot about whether they're being honest when they make things up. We'll talk about different kinds of truth and honesty. I'll have them read *Sons and Lovers, Look Homeward, Angel,* and others. It's a reading and writing course. For me, I think it's going to bridge the gap between experience and fiction. I've taught creative writing, and I've taught writing from experience, but I've never taught moving between the two.

Sometimes I've wondered where my faith in the powers of students came from. Earlier in my life, I never believed I was capable of much of anything. All through high school and college I got A's, but I always felt I was bluffing. Some day they would find out I wasn't very bright. I was a long time believing that. I think I was in graduate school before I became convinced of my own intelligence.

I've always taught students by thinking of how I felt when I was a student. If I were doing the assignment I was giving my students, what strategies would I have to use to approach it? I grew up so badly wanting to succeed in school. I think it was my own insecurity. I was succeeding and getting attention from teachers but never believed them when they said I was good. Later, when I became a teacher, I constantly worried. "Am I doing that same thing to my students?" I very much wanted them to feel secure.

I suppose one of the things which developed my belief in the powers of students was seeing what they wrote in their journals. In the first two years of teaching I didn't assign journals—for the same reason every teacher I ever talked to didn't—I didn't know what to do with them. I was afraid of them. Could I ever read them all? What kinds of marks could I put on them? But I just decided to do it. I told students I wasn't going to grade them. I was only going to write positive things, because I didn't know what else to do. The students who were so frustrated in their first year on the campus were delighted to have someone listen to them. They opened up! Told me all sorts of things about themselves, and I became fascinated with their problems and hopes.

I found myself starting in the journals to respond to their problems, which I'd always been told as a teacher you never do. I saw that the more I responded, the more they came in to see me, and the more we ended up talking about writing. The more I responded, the more they wrote, and the more they wrote, the better they wrote, because they had a real audience. I think what happened to me—I couldn't have voiced it then—was that I began to realize you can't separate the writing from the person, as most writing teachers are doing. That's why they want to teach expository writing and nothing else, because in expository writing you never have to touch the human being.

Of course people accuse me of being a therapist rather than a writing teacher. And there's something to it, because writing is therapy in a way. You're your own therapist when you write, in the writing that comes out and the responding you do to it. Finally I said, "All right, I'll be a bad teacher." Once I acknowledged this and discovered the students were so much better writers for it, I developed a confidence in that as a method—and said, "If I'm going to be teaching human beings, I'm a human being responding to human beings." Now I realize I talk to them as much about their thoughts, their ideas, their dreams, and their problems as I do about how they are structuring their sentences and paragraphs—more, in fact.

At Hofstra I found my students needed the same kind of response as students at Caldwell. After all, language is a human activity. At Hofstra I had better students than I had ever had before, in a way. At first I thought, "They don't need me." But I said, "Well, I'll do the same thing I've done before and see if they think it's too low level." They didn't. I've received some phenomenal writing and I've had some students changing their majors because of my course. I've gotten students who were here for four years learning how to become middle-management somethings or other, and students who have never thought about their education or themselves and things they ought to know—who are really growing as human beings. They see Composition is not a service course, although it's that, too. It's a liberal arts course. I say this with confidence, but I don't see much hope of convincing most teachers of writing in this country that that's so. To make writing a meaningful experience can't be done by teachers who don't want to touch students.

I have a group of five teachers using one Sunday's *New York Times* for students' reading material. We have a *Times* writer coming in to talk to the students, George Vecsey. He was called upon to write an article about Jimmy Connors, the tennis player, in forty-five minutes, because the paper needed a filler. He's going to tell our students everything that's wrong with doing this but he's also going to tell them how you have to learn to write under pressure like that. That's so real it makes essay writing look ridiculous. Vecsey is a graduate of Hofstra.

I do some of my best work when I go to another school as a consultant. When you go somewhere else and talk about writing, you can say with conviction what you believe, and have no concern about the repercussions. The small schools I go to often bring their whole faculty together for one meeting. I find a lot of teachers outside of English would like to do something with writing and have no idea what to do. I tell them they don't have to mark every line. They think teaching writing is marking grammar. It's such a relief to them to be told it isn't, that they are willing to do other things.

My experiences in teaching writing have begun to affect the way I teach literature courses. I want to mention one exam question I gave in a literature course in English Romantic Poets. It was, "If you could go out to dinner with two of the Romantic poets we have studied, which two would it be and what would they talk about all evening?" I learned more from the answers to that question than from anything else I did with them all that summer. Only the more adventurous students took that question—I gave everyone a choice. I've never had so much fun grading a final exam. You know I realize now I could have given them the question before the exam. That's an idea hard to convince teachers of—you can measure things even if students know ahead of time what you will be measuring. We give a proficiency test in writing at Hofstra and I think we could measure the writing better and the students would write better, if they knew the topic ahead of time. "Come in with some notes, some free writing, and then compose your answer."

Last summer I had a literature course with all business majors. I had learned at Caldwell how much a group of peers can help a student, so I had them working on projects in small groups. The literature course was required, so they were in there. I had been talking about how terrible some Long Island students are—never use New York City, which is so near. Never go to museums. Never go to anything in the city. I had three students come to me who had been working as a group discussing poetry and writing responses to it and talking about it. They told me they had decided to go to a museum in the city. And now every weekend they are going to the city to a museum. They're thinking together now, they're talking together. I'm not sure most people understand that this is what education is supposed be about in this country. Those three students are taking initiative.

Notepaper in hand, Bill Barker listens to a student at the chalkboard.

7

BILL BARKER
Mathematics, College

We had exchanged letters. We walked into a lounge in the student union and I took a seat behind a semi-circle of easy chairs in which students were sitting. At one of the three portable chalkboards in the room he wrote:

> *A metric space M, d is complete if all Cauchy sequences are convergent.*
> *Suppose M, d is complete, and A M. Then is A, d complete? or are additional conditions necessary on A?*

He turned, faced the fifteen students, briefly reviewed what the class had last taken up, and suggested that the questions he was now asking grew out of their last meeting.

"O.K.," he said, "let's go!" and the fifteen split immediately into three groups, one leader—chalk in hand—at the board before each group. Instantly the leader began drawing a diagram of a Cauchy sequence of points and started into a proof.

Group Two's leader paused and looked at the four others with him. One cued him what to write next. Then he found a stimulus in his own mind. Chatter and studying of notebooks, laughter and sudden spurts of words spoken aloud by the chalk wielder to himself and the others. Ideas were picked up and thrown around the group, many eventually appearing as marks in chalk on the board.

This was Math 32, Introduction to Analysis and Topology, Bowdoin College, Brunswick, Maine—teacher, Bill Barker, age thirty-two.

When a group seemed stalled, Professor Barker walked up and asked a leading question. All five students looked hard at him. One young woman put her hands on the side of her head and said, "Ooooooh" in rising tone, and then spoke the next step they were looking for.

John Leeming, a teaching assistant who had earlier taken the course with Bill Barker, said to me, "Did you notice that one group is writing the proof in words and one in numbers and symbols? We don't care how they get the answer as long as it's logical. I'm pleased to see that one group is composing one way and a second group another."

As I sat there, I realized that John and Bill aren't directing the groups, rather teaching from behind the lines. Bill is on tiptoes in mind and body, watching, waiting for moves that advance toward the answer. He tightens his lips, nods his head, his whole body saying, "That's it! That's it!" And then, his lips form, "Oh, no!"

He whispers to me, "The hardest thing is to hold back and let them struggle. When they're learning, there are many physical reactions in the room. When they're not, the room can be lifeless. This method allows me to see students working out a problem. I can watch people thinking mathematically."

Bill joins a group. "Great!" he says to the students, elation lighting up his face, "you couldn't have done it better. Beautiful!"

In the third group, Mike Cain stands at the board, right now joking about his predilections in working problems. His colleagues laugh with him. One points his finger at Mike and says, "That's why this is so." The finger jabs the air again. Mike places the chalk in the pointing hand and says, "Will you put that up here so I can write it all down?" and he is now seated in the group before a new leader.

After class, Bill and I spoke.

In my own undergraduate experience I took so many courses as a student where I sat in class writing as fast as I could to get the material down—I wasn't talking at all—I wrote it down in order to take it back to my room and work on it. That doesn't seem like a human way to utilize a classroom. I didn't get as much out of undergraduate studies as I should have. I was getting A's in my math courses and hence assumed I was learning all that was necessary at the time. I memorized too much for exams and remembered too little afterwards.

That's why I can't forget Bill Transue at Ohio State. Students called him "Smiling Bill." A gentle man, he taught a two-term class in "Topology and Functional Analysis." He didn't use the standard lecture mode, but made us students learn from each other. Every day he would assign a section of the text along with the corresponding problems. The next day he would ask us, "Which ones did you get?" He took your word for that, and then he'd ask a person to go to the board and present one of those problems he thought he had solved. Transue sat in the back, smoking his ever-present pipe, and didn't say much. Maybe someone in class would find errors or misdirections. When Transue found something wrong, he never announced it in a way that put a student down. He was a good teacher, who got us to do our best work, and a good mathematician himself.

But I must also mention Allan Ziebur, with whom I had five courses. He was a man of incredible energy and great warmth. He had, and still has, a broad grin that could disarm Attila the Hun. He used to love standing in front of his 8 A.M. class (he always taught at 8 A.M.), his eyes twinkling, and exclaim that it was a wonderful day and he would give anyone of us an A if we would blow up the smokestack down the road that was polluting the air and ruining the view. I never saw him treat a student with anything but understanding and respect. I learned from him although he always lectured. I wish he had had the desire to use a discovery method format in the classroom. Another teacher, Dick Wick Hall, ran his class like the Kaiser. He would call on you if he thought you weren't paying attention and in his booming voice demand answers to questions. But he was an incredibly good lecturer. He loved mathematics with such a passion and boomed it out at you with such enthusiasm that only a complete dullard was not swept away by the obvious importance and awesome beauty of the subject. You began to realize he was tough on students because he cared that you saw the power and majesty of mathematics. I would never, never teach the way he did, but I might still take another course from him if I had the chance.

Now in this course in Analysis and Topology I'm finding the group method is so much slower than the traditional one that I've had to add an extra meeting per week in the evening, and often we stay fifteen or twenty minutes beyond the hour. But the students don't complain. Sometimes they don't realize what time it is. Sometimes they do, though. If people hang back, things go badly.

I give this mimeographed handout to students. It's titled "Traditional material in an innovative format, or mathematics as if people mattered." I decided to do something different. Under the heading "Course Structure," I wrote, "Does it have to be like . . . ?" and then I gave seven excerpts from an attack on conventional university teaching methods by an English professor. Under the heading, "No, it doesn't have to be like that," more quotations from that attack, including this one:

> One day I broke [the Shakespeare class] into groups of four and said, "Go somewhere in the building and talk about what you think of Hamlet the man." They returned in thirty minutes and we had the best discussion I had ever heard in a literature class. With no cue from me, two groups squared off and let fly. Soon most of the students were saying something that counted for them. And it counted for me.

Then under the heading "Will this work in mathematics?" I quoted George Polya, author of *Mathematical Discovery*, saying,

> Students [should] *actively contribute to the formulation* of the problem that they have to solve afterwards. If the students have had a share in proposing the problem they will work at it much more actively afterwards.

And Morris Kline, author of *Mathematical Thought from Ancient to Modern Times*, saying,

The usual courses in mathematics are . . . deceptive in a basic respect.
They give an organized logical presentation which leaves the impression
that mathematicians go from theorem to theorem almost naturally, that
mathematicians can master any difficulty, and that the subjects are completely thrashed out and settled. The succession of theorems overwhelms
the student, especially if he is just learning the subject . . . The history, by
contrast, teaches us that the development of a subject is made bit by bit
with, results coming from various directions.

Then I went on to say in the handout:

Our structure: shall be made free enough to allow each student to carefully work out his or her own thoughts on a given topic *with the help of the
rest of the class* . . . The class will be broken down into groups of about four
people in much the same way the teacher did in the Shakespeare class. It's
a beautiful way of getting students to work with and for *each other*, not just
the *teacher*.

When I discussed the debilitating effect of grades upon individual
initiative, I quoted Daniel Bell, the sociologist, and Noam Chomsky, the
linguist, who said,

Even at the most advanced level of graduate education, the student is
discouraged by university regulations from working as any reasonable
person would certainly choose to do: individually, where his interests lead
him; collectively, when he can learn from the aid of his fellows. (*For
Reasons of State*)

There's a popular saying among math teachers that "Mathematics enters the body through the arm." I tell students that cooperative work is
allowed—and in fact encouraged—for the nine assignments that I give
during the term. Up to a point, that is. I ask them to work at first
individually on homework problems. After they've bounced the problems around a while themselves, they're free to get together with other
class members to arrive at complete solutions. The final write-ups are
then done individually.

I give no exams during the term, and no final. Grades are based
solely on the homework turned in during the term. I don't want students to feel pressured to show off in class. I put no grades on the
papers I turn back. Plenty of comments, just no grades. I keep internal
records on each student's progress and tell them they can have individual "interim evaluations" if they request them.

Although I'm trying to get students to make discoveries on their own
I sometimes ask leading questions of the groups. We proceed so slowly
that I can't afford to let a group go off on the wrong road for too long.

With the homework they can sample the educational benefits of wrong directions. I'm not there in their rooms to steer them with that.

I should say that withholding grades is not without problems. On the one hand, it *does* decrease grade consciousness during the term—that's almost universally agreed upon by the students. But many students come to the end of the term believing they have done better than I have judged from their written work. Nonetheless, I still think the advantages of the policy outweigh the disadvantages.

On the previous day one of Bill's students, David Cowhig, told me I would be interested in seeing a book on mathematics by Hadamard. He didn't remember the complete title. That night I found a note on my door that read: "Jacques Hadamard, The Psychology of Invention in the Mathematical Field *(Princeton University Press, 1945)." He was the second Bowdoin student to do that for me.*

Later that morning I ate breakfast in the cafeteria with John Sarkela, another of Bill's learners. I mentioned that I had heard mathematicians say that many of their courses are so abstract that they aren't useful in the immediate, practical world. I asked him if he saw any usefulness to his advanced math classes. John looked to be about eighteen.

Well, I feel a need for an abstract ordering of the world, for seeing a relation between the analogical and the concrete. Mathematics is the ultimate language of relations. Math has a hypnotic quality to it—when you see things come together. I relate Euclidean things to the math— the helix, snail hills, plants, galaxies.

At our next meeting, Bill said:

When as a student myself I had classes in Differential Geometry, it seemed very removed from reality—dealing with geometric objects in high dimensional spaces, and with properties of them that didn't seem applicable to anything. Since then I've come to realize that Differential Geometry is absolutely essential to the General Theory of Relativity. So recently I built the whole course around that. We did a lot of very abstract Differential Geometry but all along there was the idea that these things applied to General Relativity. We ended the course explaining some of the theory of Black Holes, one of those aspects of relativity which is seductively fascinating and mysterious. Sometimes Differential Geometry turns out to be a real dud because the notation is tedious and boring, and people don't get a feeling for how it's used. In terms of its content and reception by students I would say that that was the best and most successful course I ever taught. But it was still abstract in the sense that students aren't going to make use of the formulae in their own day-to-day lives.

When I taught Functional Analysis I tried to put it into a historical context. Why did people look at this question or that question? Well, historically it seems that very abstract questions tend to come out of questions that are somewhat less abstract, and those come from questions even less abstract, until they finally get back to something that leads the students to say, "Well, that's kind of a natural question, isn't it?" That class certainly wasn't 100 percent successful, but I was basically pleased with what came out of that historical thrust.

Mathematical textbooks don't give much in the way of historical context. Just the material—this derives from that theorem, and so on. A perfectly logical system that has no grounding in history. It eliminates the people who did the work. And also it eliminates the false turns that people have taken, the ideas that people worked on for a long time that were wrong. They're very rarely mentioned. I think this is more true of math textbooks than those in other sciences. The sad thing is that it makes the authorities seem so Godlike.

In comments on the class, most students are positive. One said, "The interaction in Math 32 is so good. In a regular class, you know, once you're taking notes, you stop thinking. Not in this class. It feels so good in a group." I'm pleased at his reaction. Many of these students are excited about math. It's not always common, you, know. Once a president of the Mathematical Association of America said, "Math is the one subject I know of that people are proud to be bad at."

After a couple of years I knew I was beginning to wonder if I was one of those math teachers that made people feel that way. My students were passive and docile. I felt I was perpetuating those attitudes in them. I wanted to devise a non-lecture teaching format, but I wasn't trained for such a search. They don't teach pedagogical techniques in mathematics graduate school. By sheer accident I ended up re-inventing what has for years become known as the "discovery method." For years at the University of Texas, R. L. Moore had students develop course material themselves, but the program was extremely individualistic and competitive, a characteristic I changed. Some of the best mathematicians of this century came out of Moore's program.

The conventional way to teach math is for the teacher to come in, write on the board for the whole hour, demonstrate to the class how to work through problems and questions, and then give students the job of taking their notes home and working out what they have just seen.

In only two and a half years of teaching this way I had become dissatisfied with the inherently passive nature of this traditional lecture approach. I had just completed a good semester by any of the standard measures, but in my course I felt there were vast reserves and abilities in my students that I wasn't reaching. These bright, lively, friendly, curious students didn't *die* in the classroom but they reclined into a passive role. I thought, "If the real power of this subject was in the *doing*, why not let the students *do it* right in the classroom? Let them learn from each other and by really thinking in the classroom." The details of the method then just seemed to fall into place.

I should mention another benefit of the discovery method. I've found out a great deal about how students learn and what can be expected of them. I discovered quickly that we mathematicians make too great an assumption about our students' level of "formal, logical thinking." Even in the best of students it was a far lower level than I expected. So that's why students always have such a hard time with proofs! But then I saw that it really was possible to teach these skills by the discovery method, and that gave the lie to a common belief among mathematicians: "You can't teach how to do proofs."

When I tried my new approach, I felt almost as if I had reinvented the wheel. At first I was concerned that group work might not be academically rigorous, but that's no longer a concern. If nothing else, the group-discovery method works better than the traditional method. I myself was always a loner in school. I needed a method like this that gets students dealing with other people and thinking logically. Often students can't do proofs because they don't understand the basic logic involved. Most of us use logic intuitively. Here are some points from the handout I give students working in groups:

> 1. Work closely together to achieve *group* solutions to the class problems; do *not* work separately in your own notebook and then present finished products at the chalk board. Listen to each other; we guarantee that the group is *more* than the sum of its individual members.
>
> 2. We feel that use of the chalk board is *by far* the best means in general . . . *As soon as* work is begun on a particular question, one group should go to the board and (a) write the question down; (b) draw a good picture (if appropriate).
>
> Then, if attempting to prove a result, any "obvious lines of argument" should be started . . . All subsequent work should then go thru the person at the board.
>
> 3. Make sure that *everyone* in your group understands what is being discussed. If you are confused, then speak up—never hang back. If a group-mate is confused, then offer assistance—just remember that simply giving the answer to a problem is not necessarily the best way to help a person's understanding.
>
> 4. Don't worry about the pace of other groups. Speed has little correlation with how "smart" a group is. Many a "slower group" has simply seen more in a given problem or has pursued some aspect in more depth.

In asking students to approach math in this unconventional way, I keep reminding them that they are following the beliefs of other people than just me. For example, I tell them that George Polya said in *Mathematical Discovery* that "What you have been obliged to discover by yourself leaves a path in your mind which you can use again when the need arises." And I tell them my favorite old Chinese proverb: "I hear, and I forget; I see, and I remember; I do, and I understand."

In a group, many of my students become sympathetic, more sensitive to each other. In traditional math classes, students seldom talk to each other at all. Here we get students fired up to do more, to care about getting results—even those that aren't exciting in themselves but may be important for something else.

I've had a few students for whom the method has not worked. They tended to be persons who lacked the confidence to speak up in their groups if they didn't understand something. Oftentimes other members of the group would sense this problem and attempt to handle it themselves. One of the beauties of the discovery method using small groups is the concern and responsibility that students feel for each other. But at times this was not enough.

One shy woman I remember was not able to handle the method. None of us could help. She came out of the course with less confidence than she entered it with. And yet, one year later she took a lecture course with me, and through diligence she earned Bowdoin's highest grade.

A school with all math courses taught in the discovery method might not be a whole lot better than a school which teaches everything in traditional lectures. I've become a believer in the advantages of a *variety* of teaching and learning experiences. Looking back at my own undergraduate and graduate education, it's not that I hated all lecture courses (I enjoyed college, so *hate* was never an appropriate word), but with only a few exceptions like Bill Transue's courses, that was *all* I got, and that, I believe, was stifling.

As I told you, perhaps the most successful course I've ever taught was that year-long sequence on Differential Geometry. I'm convinced that I couldn't have taught it by the discovery method. The math was at times extremely sophisticated and it took all my powers to simply explain the *meaning* of the results, let alone get through the proofs. So I gave a traditional lecture course. Maybe not traditional, for there was a great amount of give-and-take, certainly not ten stony faces staring blankly and students copying without enthusiasm. But the material carried the course: the students got caught up in this hard but seductively beautiful subject and were willing to follow me through hell and back to see how Differential Geometry could be used to mold a "curved four-dimensional space-time manifold."

One thing that disappoints me is that math students can't bring what's happening in their lives to bear on the class work, other than by calling up experience in other math courses. We need to show students flesh-and-blood, real-world applications, be they in the natural sciences, social sciences, or elsewhere. Max Schiffer, a Stanford math professor, has said that "Paper work can be related to the world we live in. With pen or pencil we can hitch a pair of scales to a star and weigh the moon."

I keep hunting through the literature for other people's ideas on teaching mathematics, hoping to find answers to doubts which still plague me, even with Math 32.

This summer I read *Why the Professor Can't Teach: Mathematics and the Dilemma of University Education* by Morris Kline. He attacks the highly abstract nature of math taught at all levels of our educational system. He says that math as it's presently taught is rarely *relevant* or *useful* to the majority of our students.

I'm excited to find other mathematicians who feel as I do. Steve Fisk, one of my Bowdoin colleagues, is plunging head-on into the discovery method this term. He went to a week-long conference in Pennsylvania on education change, where the small group discovery method was discussed. There he talked with Neil Davidson, the author with Frances Gulick of *Abstract Algebra: An Active Learning Approach,* published in 1976. Davidson has been working on this method in courses of all levels. He began in 1971. I have another friend, Phil Straffin, chairman of the Mathematics Department at Beloit College, who has recently taught Real Analysis with the discovery method. He wrote me: "I'm converted. Don't think I could ever do this material as lectures now."

Here are some of the responses to Math 32 written at the end of the semester by my students. One said:

> Lectures are boring—they always put me to sleep. I'm often only concerned with being able to do the problems and don't care especially for the theory. In this course that kind of attitude was impossible—which is good.

Another wrote:

> If you figure something out for yourself instead of just being told to remember it, most times you have a better understanding of the concept.

And still another said:

> I think students often blank out when a teacher does a proof in the regular lecture format course—it is much harder to actively follow it through. When you do the proof yourself, though, you have to think about it! This way you also retain it longer.

Another student wrote:

> The absence of exams was a very important part of the course. It removed all pressures, so that learning the material was fun.

These comments weren't careless, but considered. For example:

> I think exams help only in obscure courses where objectives and materials are unclearly presented—that was not the case in Math 32.

Another student wrote:

> . . . with lack of pressure to stuff into my head theorems, propositions and definitions, they seemed to just want to be there.

One student wrote:

> The professor could have been exerting a little control over his students. Sometimes we got away with hell.

And another:

> I am really not in love with this questionnaire. Its format is too restricted, and its questions too leading.

It occurs to me that too many instructors treat their students as morons or bores, or potential con artists or children. The Bowdoin faculty member who is perhaps the most popular with and most respected by students is the senior member of the math department, Dick Chittim. I was present when he was once asked why he was and is such a successful teacher. His answer was, "I treat each student with respect."

8

PETER KAKELA
Environmental Studies, University

In the summer of 1978 an associate professor of resource development at Michigan State University sent me this letter:

"Your books make me want to write better and to experience the helping circle [an audience of responders]. I would also like to get to know you better. Do you ever run writing workshops?"

A few months later I was standing in a 1920s house on Oak Street in Mason, Michigan, talking to a man standing six four, so well proportioned he looked too slim to have once been a starting defensive guard on one of Duffy Daughterty's championship football teams at Michigan State. It was Peter Kakela, who was saying, "I want to learn to write better myself. I'm teaching students how legislative action is influenced—and partly that's done by writing." I knew I was listening to an unusual teacher, so asked him to tell me how he got started in his work.

I applied for a job at Sangamon State University in Springfield, Illinois, because it was founded in 1970 to be "the public affairs university" in the country. There I set up a course in Citizens' Action in Environmental Affairs because I realized that you can talk forever about respecting the environment but if you don't get into the political workings of power, your talk will mean nothing.

I began the course by showing the students a dozen bills that Illinois legislators were going to consider while our course was in progress. We talked briefly about what directions the legislators might take, and then I asked the students what bills they'd like to work on. I had imagined they would form several groups and work on different projects, but they all wanted to study the Illinois Beverage Container Act, what we called "The Bottle Bill." One of the fellows was the host for the late show on the university radio station. He wanted to get something about the Bottle Bill on his program immediately, but I slowed him down. I wanted to train these students in thorough investigation.

At this time a public hearing in Chicago on the Bottle Bill was announced. That was two hundred miles away. "Can we go?" said several

Peter Kakela invites a student to take over.

students. "Sure," I said, and gave a tape recorder to those who were going and a couple of tapes I had bought. They went, and came back from Chicago all excited. In class they played some of the testimony they had heard. "That legislator didn't even know this—" said one student, mentioning a crucial point. I was determined that right from the start my students would know what they were talking about. They had strong opinions, but in this course they would have to get the data. They had to read journals and study the reason and logic behind all points of view.

As a group we worked to get the stuff together to make a Fact Sheet to present to legislators, lobbyists, and anyone else we were going to approach. I knew that otherwise the experts and the legislators would pay no attention to us. We took a month constructing the Fact Sheet. You see it's six pages long, single-spaced typewriter pages. For example, here's a table listing the BTUs of energy required for making and/or using six different types of containers, and summaries of bills passed in British Columbia, Alberta, Oregon, Vermont, South Dakota, Minnesota, and California. A fact sheet like that has to be concise and packed with solid material or it won't be read.

And the material has to be alive. For example, we used short key quotations, like this one from Milton Amdur, president of the United States Aluminum Corporation of Pennsylvania. He said, "Frankly, I feel the whole concept of using a valuable material like aluminum in the canning industry, when other cheaper materials are abundantly available, is a gigantic waste of our limited metal resources." This is the sort of selective quoting that isn't learned by most undergraduates. The students who wrote up this Fact Sheet knew they would send it to officials they wanted to talk to. If it wasn't strong, those people might not decide to see them. They had a payoff in mind while they were writing and compiling it.

At the end of the Fact Sheet was a list of thirty-seven documented sources. Legislators and businessmen who would read it might be skeptical. They would want to know where the facts and quotations came from. In university study, the common notion of *rigor* is that students taking up a topic will read everything on it, remember everything, and know the historical position of theorists and managers. If anyone could do that, a kind of *rigor mortis* would finally set in: nothing moves. I ask students to know a topic well because they are about to deal with persons not simply studying the topic but intending to come to decisions about it. The discipline required of these students is like that required of football players: they must perform, as well as know something about the game. Others on the field will resist them. Defenses and offenses change as the game proceeds.

Next we were going to meet with groups we had sent the Fact Sheet to, so we could hear from the lips of the advocates what their interests and arguments were. I was nervous about those meetings. For example, the assistant director of the Illinois Environmental Protection Agency and his administrative assistant arranged to meet us in a formal conference room. They walked in very dignified, with their files and note pads. One of my students was sitting there with his messy hair, another in a T-shirt. These men talked to us almost on an academic level, saying they had a stake in this matter and would have to take some responsibility in sponsoring this bill, so they were considering it carefully. They had had some bad run-ins with the public on a leaf burning ban. They brought out their numbers and graphs.

When we left their office in the school van, I said, "What do you think?" One student replied, "I feel like we just had an audience with the Pope." Another said, "Are *they* going to protect the environment?— they're so cautious." I said, "Maybe they need us to make statements for the environment. They're going to hear the other side from business, and then they can be in the middle." I found that even if we had only five minutes together after a hearing or meeting, the debriefing sessions—where we interpreted what had happened—were invaluable. I got students' real reactions. Their emotions and the emotions of the people they had met were present with us just as much as the ideas were. I was affected, too. I realized that some things about the bottle controversy I'd stopped seeing myself. I began to feel that maybe in my effort to be objective I'd bought into the bureaucracy. Usually we went into the field on class time. Our class met for two hours on Tuesday and Thursday. If some of the students could go to a soft drink plant, for example, in the afternoon, then maybe others could go the next morning. We were lucky. We lived in the state capital.

I must say that the students were getting an education. After the Environmental Protection Agency meeting, we met next with a legislator who sponsored the bill. Then with local bottlers. Another time, a labor lawyer for the store clerks was in town for negotiation. Him we met at 8 A.M. in a motel room—three guys waiting for us behind a bargaining table. Being on the other guy's turf was instructive for the students.

One man had had eighteen years' experience as a labor union lobbyist, more seniority than nine-tenths of the legislators. He was the classic stereotype of a lobbyist. We heard him say to a secretary of a legislator in the capitol, "I'm going to use John's office for a while." At our meeting he sat down, looked at one of our group with long hair, and said, "Now, are you a girl or a boy?"

These kids were contacting people in a work world in which the academic is looked down upon. In East Lansing, for example, where I'm teaching now at Michigan State, it seems that everyone in town is an *-ologist* of one kind or another. I myself use outside contacts to help keep me in balance. In Illinois the students wrote up such a good Fact Sheet that they often enlightened the experts they met with. I found that they can do things. But I don't just throw them unprepared into the world. We composed the Fact Sheet carefully and sent it ahead of us, asking, "What do you think of the matters taken up in this sheet?" The students had done a lot of reading and discussing before they went into action. It's like what happens before a football game. Now when I listen to a game on the radio I think of how much is not reported—how on the bus trip we talked, and then the tension in the dressing room, and maybe two minutes before we had to go on the field the quarterback would run to the john and barf. That and the practices were all part of playing. We had to get ready. Here's part of the handout I give senior majors in the Proseminar in Current Issues, Literature, and Professional Approaches in Resource Development. I begin by saying, "Let me start off by relating a true story—"

> Recently I asked my secretary to make a phone call. The Michigan Attorney General's office had referred me to an Oakland County court decision regarding the Michigan Bottle Law. I was rushed, so I asked Barb to phone for details about the Oakland County judge's decision. The next morning I found this note on my desk.
>
> >   F.Y.I.
> >   Re: Judge's decision in Oakland County.
> >   First called the Oakland County Courthouse: The operator connected me. The phone answerer at the Circuit Court said, "The computer is broken down and we would need the case number, anyway. But it doesn't sound like the kind of case we would handle. Try District Court."
> >   District Court: "It wasn't handled here. Anything to do with state is handled in Lansing. Or try Circuit Court."
> >   Tried County Extension Director: "Mr. 'CED' won't be in until May. I don't think he would know anything about it anyway. I'll connect you with the Prosecutor's office."
> >   Prosecutor's office secretary: "I don't know anything about it but it might be in Southfield. Jim Cherry is in charge of that area but his line is busy. Call back."
> >   Finally, Jim Cherry: "Sure, I handled that."
>
> Persistence paid off then but many people get frustrated, are hesitant to pay for one more long distance call, or end up waiting for days for the wrong person to return a call. Knowledge of the issue you are pursuing *plus* many other characteristics that you don't get out of books is required these days to get results from government bureaucracy.
>
> *Goals:* This course has two goals:
> 1. To help you learn what is not in books about how natural resource

policies originate, become implemented, or are interpreted. To start to learn this, you'll have to experience some part of government as it deals with a specific resource issue.

2. To help you think through and communicate your individual feelings on the progress of resource policy development. To begin here we will regularly do some free writing.

Methods: First you will have to select an issue and then pursue it, pursue it, pursue it. Doing the homework is the first effort; get the bill, find the report, read the material that specifically applies. But contacting the people involved is the most important aspect of this course. Find the staffers that are working on your issue. Listen to their inflection. Watch their eyebrows. Read their body language for the interpretation that doesn't get into the reports. To see people in their own offices, on their own turf, is always helpful to me.

First, we will form issue teams and I'll ask each team to give a 5-10 minute *briefing* to the class weekly. Report the news on your issue, tell truths and fabulous realities. Keep it brief but make it stick. Tell the class the new facts that you picked up this week that will score and be remembered by the class. We want to learn the latest details that are unfolding on your issue plus some of your experiences that will tell us what you are learning about the learning process.

Second, I want to help you identify the things that you are learning internally about the way government works. To do this we will regularly spend 15–20 minutes doing what I call free writing. Free writing is just keeping your pencil moving on paper and letting your intuitions about your resource policy experiences come out without worrying about spelling, grammar, or form. I believe that when you are able to tell your classmates a true-informed story they will remember you have more to say than someone who can spell, punctuate and compose "proper" boredom.

It may seem strange to try to learn the things that are not in books by writing, but I see it more as a discovery of those feelings and interpretations that you will begin to build as you study and pursue your policy issue. Contact the people intimately involved in your issue. Give credit to your own feelings and what your body is telling you about the situations you are experiencing. I also believe it takes both technical knowledge and interpretive feeling to develop the informed opinions needed to make resources policy and this society in general work . . .

Required Textbooks:
1. State of Michigan Government Telephone Directory.
2. Selected reprints handed out in class.

As I moved up in school I found learning getting more and more negative. I remember a course titled "Northern Lands" taught by a department chairman in a Canadian university I attended. He would walk into class with his gown on and dump his academic load onto ten students. Region after region he described—went on for a month detailing the coastal regions of Alaska. No questioning during all this time—just description. We went to this man and told him we'd like to ask some questions. He said if we wanted to question things we could write three papers during the semester, forty pages each. Well, that was better than just taking tests on the descriptions he was giving us. Such experiences unsettled me.

When as a new teacher I first looked at ninety faces before me, I thought, "My God, how do they learn?" I had all that content in my head and they didn't. It was staggering.

In that class in Illinois I found I had highly motivated students. For example, one fellow investigated the proportion of beverage containers to the rest of the garbage collected by the city he lived in. He wanted to put together a slide show to say that returnable bottles are best. "I want to say it in color," he told me. But I expected him to investigate before he presented. We went out to a bottle plant. It was closed, but later he visited it when it was functioning and came up with a script that was more objective than the one he had at first envisaged. In class we critiqued his project. When I saw the show I said, "I've got some more slides you could use." He was learning discipline in his work.

Early on in that class a student drafted some testimony on the bottle controversy that didn't make a point. The class helped him see that. Another student made a phone survey of attitudes towards the bottle bill. He presented a discussion of whether throwaway bottles or returnable are the cheapest in the long run. When he brought these studies into class for comment, he found he could improve them.

Now my students are learning in ways the conventional classroom doesn't provide. For example, one student made this written comment about a class: "Contacts can give insights into the workings of government or industry which could take an isolated stranger weeks of research to come up with." In teaching research papers I've found that book work by itself can be terribly time-consuming and sometimes dangerous, because the researcher may be blind to the biases of authors whom he has no chance of "reading" in the flesh.

I'm not against all of the traditional procedures in university classes. For example, I'm very specific about requirements. Let me paraphrase part of the announcement of one of my courses:

> In order to receive a grade in this course, you'll have to (1) keep a reading log book on the assigned reading plus specific materials that relate to your issue; (2) prepare a draft of testimony you feel is relevant and environmentally sound on your specific issue; (3) prepare an analysis of the legislative process, including anecdotes, personal reactions, revelations etc.; and (4) grade yourself and give reasons why you feel the grade is justified. If for some reason I strongly disagree with the grade you've given yourself, then we will have to get together and negotiate a reasonable settlement.

Now there in the grading, I depart from conventional teaching. When you send students out into the field and ask them to show initiative, and then come back and help each other by responding to each other's work, you can't give grades in the traditional way. That would break down the trust you're trying to create and destroy the basis for building responsibility in the learners. I know that some teachers think of their students as merely "empty buckets waiting to be filled," but I think that's like a doctor looking at patients and seeing only sick people.

The other day I received a letter from Peter along with a copy of an article from the Christian Science Monitor (*November 10, 1980*) *by Ann McCarroll about how most of us parents have engaged our children in family activities but forgotten to spend time talking with them "one on one." A daughter, Diane, reported that "We all go out for chicken—which is so-so to everyone. We compromise on something no one enjoys very much—but we're bored* together— *which seems to be the point." Her brother Jeff said, "We're supposed to share our problems over meat loaf at 6:15." Another daughter told of her father's "best gift." "My dad gives each of his children a special weekend each year. Each of us gets to choose and plan how we want to spend our weekend with him."*

In his letter, Peter said, "The article grabbed my fatherly instincts and I thought of all those meat loafs we've eaten while I was trying to get the kids to talk about how they felt about their day.

"I've had a second article accepted by the magazine Science, *which is published by the American Association for the Advancement of Science, but I still find revising the very hard work of writing. I keep telling myself to adopt a more cavalier approach. Those thoughts disappear as my knuckles turn white holding a pencil to scratch out one word here and add a new phrase in the margin over there. I want to become an easier writer."*

9

VERA MILZ
Reading, Elementary School

When I wanted to find a good teacher of reading, I called Professor Yetta Goodman of the School of Education at the University of Arizona. She said, "I know several, but the first person I think of is Vera Milz, who just finished up her doctoral work with us and works in the Bloomfield Hills School District near Detroit."

A few days later, Vera was saying to me,

As a beginning teacher in the early 1960s, I went into a school district where a basal reading text was handed me. It was Dick, Jane, and Sally. The old "Look, look! Run, run! See, see!" In workbooks the children were to search a page for the words they saw starting with "b." I was comfortable the first year trying things out, but by the third year of teaching I could see that the program just didn't meet the needs of all my children, and I was going over things that some of them already knew.

So I began to explore other alternatives. I went to lectures at nearby Oakland University. Quite a few reading experts came there from different parts of the country. Bill Martin was one of them. He was the author of the *Little Owl* books and collections of stories and poems in books and on tapes. Martin had one selection called *Brown Bear, Brown Bear, What Do You See?* that first graders absolutely loved. Even twenty years later, it's still one of their favorites. They would pick up that rhyme and begin to read, "Brown bear, brown bear, what do you see?" "I see a red bird looking at me." In their own writing at Hallowe'en it became "Orange pumpkin, orange pumpkin, what do you see?" "I see a white ghost looking at me." One year a mother came in with a little boy from Lebanon who spoke just Arabic and French. He was afraid to try English words in front of us. A couple weeks later his mother and aunt came in and said, "What's this brown bear?" The boy had come home chanting the lines. In class I noticed that he was really looking at the words in the book while he listened to Bill Martin say them on tape. Another person I learned from at that time was Roach Van Allen,

Vera Milz invites a beginning reader into a book.

from the University of Arizona. He came in and talked about children writing their own books, and then learning to read them. He also suggested having the children talk about a common experience, which could be written down by the teacher. That material would be easier for the children to read because familiar to them. At that time I heard Leland Jacobs from Teachers College in New York City. He opened up the whole world of children's literature to me. He taught a class at Oakland University, where every two weeks he brought a new author in. From these people I found there were a lot of good things available for teaching reading, but the school district I taught in said I had to follow one textbook and tuck in these other things in my spare time. I found my time was limited. Then I had an opportunity to visit another school. I observed a classroom set up to teach the Language-Experience approach with Van Allen's material. I got excited about what was going on in that room as I saw children making up stories that were typed into books which they read aloud. In sharing time, many of them read favorite poems. Or they charted and wrote up experiences such as a science experiment. In the meantime the person who set up the visit said that she thought I had a lot of potential as a teacher and so that very day they offered me a job in the Bloomfield Hills District. I ended up switching to that district, which through the years has been extremely supportive.

Early in the nineteen seventies when the Open School movement was beginning, I was able to see Open Schools in England. I was most impressed by young children at five and six years old doing very natural free writing in notebooks. When the children would take a walk around the grounds, they would be thinking as individuals. Their reading related very much to the writing they were doing. Back in Michigan, my children had been writing nothing like the English children were writing. When I got back to America, I handed out notebooks to my children to be used as daily journals because I thought they could probably write more individually than they had been doing. And they did.

Now when the children are ready to start school, I send them a written invitation. Here's a letter I used when I first started teaching at Way Elementary School:

> Dear Regina,
>   Guess what! Miss Jones tells me that I'm going to be your first grade teacher. I'm anxious to meet you. I just came home from Arizona. Last year I went to school there. And now I'm back in Michigan to be a teacher again. I'll be working in our room on Tuesday and I'm hoping you can stop by to meet me. If not, I'll see you on Wednesday, when school opens.
>
>   Love,
>   Miss Milz

That letter is rather long for a first-grader to read, but I'm assuming there'll be an older brother or sister or parent who will sit down and read it with the child. Children have had many experiences with print in their pre-school lives. When they come into my first grade, many are familiar with the letters of the alphabet. Even at two or three, many children notice signs such as "STOP" or "MCDONALD'S." When a child says, "I'm hungry, Mommy," even though she may not be saying, "That's McDonald's" and doesn't recognize the name, she's already beginning to control aspects of reading. When they receive my letter, children are having a school-related experience in reading that counts for them.

Many of the children do come in on Tuesday and visit with me and then I take them around the room. I usually put a lot of books out as I'm getting the room unpacked. I'll show them some of the books we're going to be using and some of my favorite stories. I'll also point out the mailbox in the room where they'll be able to get mail from me. And I tell them that I have a mailbox and when they want to send notes to me they can put them in there, and I'll read them by the next day. Not every child is going to bring me in a note. I never say to them, "You must write me something." However, usually by the first day of school I can say that my children are already writing to me. Several will come in clutching little notes they've written to me. Some have asked their parents, "How do you write this? How do you spell this?" The notes may be very conventional: "Dear Miss Milz. It was nice to meet you. Love, Caroline." One child will come in with a picture with a name written at the bottom, while another may say, "DEER MISS MILZ, I LK U, LV, TED."

At the end of each school day I clean out my mailbox and then the children get notes back from me the next morning. These notes provide a personalized reading text for each child. We both write to suit our own needs and purposes. If they need a menu for meals in the lunchroom, or something like that, they'll put notes in the box for me. If I have to be away from the classroom, or if I'm out sick, I'll come back to many notes saying that they've missed me. This letter writing often continues beyond the school year. Some children now in high school I still communicate with. It's been very gratifying to keep in touch with them, to know what's happening to them. Usually during the first week of school I give each child a notebook and ask them for a dated entry. If it comes in at the end of the day, I can read it after school or that evening. Some children will just draw pictures, and others will write quite a bit. They'll use Invented Spelling, so that they might write the word *car* and spell it *kr* yet they are already beginning to draw relationships with the conventional print in books. The children like to read their journals to each other, and frequently share them with the entire class.

On that first day I have them make a picture of themselves, and I can use that for a class book about the children. I go around while they're drawing their pictures and ask them something about themselves. I put that into the book, making it like riddles. Somebody might say, "I have three sisters," and I say as I write, "Who has three sisters?" and then on the back of the page I'll paste the child's picture. Initially when this book is published, they'll go through it and look for each other's pictures and be excited about them. Later they'll read what I wrote.

This is different from teaching children first a letter, then a sound, then a word, and expecting they'll put all the words together to make meaning. I want my students to read the whole world around them. Reading is not just connecting a number of words. As a reader, I don't take a bunch of words and string them together into something that makes sense. As I talk to you, I say things to create a *meaning* so you understand my message. I want to help children do this right from the beginning. A person learns to read in the midst of meaning, not in the midst of disconnected exercises. By the time I had finished my doctoral study with Ken and Yetta Goodman of the Program in Language and Literacy at the Center for Educational Research and Development at the University of Arizona, I was using their term "Whole Language Learning" along with "The Language Experience Approach" I knew from the past. For example, on the first day of school, when my children see that their coat hook needs to be labeled, they begin to write. They write because their notebook must have their name on it. They label their possessions and find that if they lose them, they get them back. Sometimes I'll hold up a note and say "I couldn't answer this person because I don't know who it is." In contrast, many teaching programs ask children to learn words such as *the* or *and*. There's no meaning in these words by themselves outside of the children's context. Instead, I ask them to look around their kitchen at all the things they can read there and bring into class. As they find meaningful print, they begin to learn many words. I really believe in the work of Michael Halliday of the University of Sydney, Australia. He says that language is learned in a social context. A baby says "Muh-muh," and Mother says, "Oh, you said *Momma!* What can Momma get for you?" or "Can Momma pick you up?" You begin to build a whole context around that sound *muh-muh* that has come out of that baby. The same thing should happen in children's reading and writing.

Once a nine-year-old boy came into my second-grade class with a record that said, "Cannot read *The Little Red Story Book*." He had repeated a class more than once. I said, "I think he's proven that he can't read it," and I asked him to write me about things that he liked. "Tell me about your house. What's your bedroom like? What's your favorite toy?" One story he wrote was about his dog. Up until then he had showed no progress on any reading test. But by the end of the year he had showed six months' growth in reading. He had been considered a total non-reader. People who came to the classroom were floored at the changes in that second-grade boy. He had been so negative. He felt really bad about himself. Now he's a child who's excited about reading.

Teachers have to start somewhere with each one of their children. Many will say, "We're supposed to teach *rhyme* in first grade." To spend time with that term can be totally irrelevant to a child trying to pull meaning out of a book. I'm more excited about the boy in my class who was learning English by saying "Brown bear, brown bear" to himself and finding all those different animals in a book that had meaning for him. He was having a great time. He was excited about the act of reading. Later he will discover the term *rhyme*. In my letters and notes to the children I write about things relevant to their lives. I'll ask them questions about themselves and tell them things about myself. I just bought a new puppy. It's become a part of the classroom through my writing. I have an advantage over the professional authors of the children's literature I give the kids to read: I'm sharing the same environment with them.

I've heard of my notes to the children being plastered all over the family refrigerator. Sometimes they're pasted into the little books the kids put together. However, I don't stop with just interacting with the children. I invite parents to become involved. I encourage them to write to their children, by putting notes in their lunch boxes. They can help by coming in and providing an extra pair of ears to listen to the children reading their stories. They also can sit down next to the children and read a story to an eager listener. During a parent-teacher meeting I ask parents to help me make blank books in which the students can write stories. It doesn't take us long to make covers. Parents will take ditto paper home and stitch it for me, to be inserted later. If each parent makes several books, it gives me a start of fifty or more books. And I'll let them keep a blank book so they can publish a book at home with their own child doing the writing. I've been in this school now for seven or eight years. There are a lot of trained parents now, and they make enough books for our whole building.

When our children write a story, they can come down to the school publishing area and pick out a cover and leave the manuscript. A book will be typed up, and usually in a week we can get the story back to the children. There's nothing like the effect on authors of seeing their writing in book form. The children want to read each other's stories because they are acquainted with the authors and want to know still more about them. Their stories become part of the reading program in our class. They write about events in their own lives, just as professional authors do. If I read the class a story by my favorite children's author, Tomie DePaola, I mention that he's writing of his own grand-mothers and other people in his family. They can do that too. I re-member Jenny in my class telling about her own dog, Maggie, that kept getting loose and would scoot out the door. One day the dog catcher picked it up. Then, like a professional writer, Jenny elaborated on her experience and turned it into a fictional story, just as professional writers do.

If the parents are too busy to help me out, I'll pull in fifth, sixth graders who are on a lunch break or study period to help me make books or do other things. They've also come in to listen to the children read. To get my kids interested in writing stories I like to invite children who've been in my class before to come in and bring some of their own books. They never throw them away. One girl in one previous year wrote twenty-eight books. Later on, she brought them back and left them in the room temporarily. Whenever she had a recess, she'd come in and read them aloud to my kids. Sometimes I'll ask a child, "Would you make a copy of that book for me? I love it dearly." I want a copy for my classes or for the Media Center, but I never ask for the original book. The children have ownership of that. The hardest year I ever had was when I went in to a new school and didn't have that backlog of books by older siblings or friends. There wasn't the personal touch that someone like the girl who wrote twenty-eight books provided.

When I go cross-country talking to teachers, I find many of them saying, "But I have to do this basal reading textbook with this check-sheet of skills, and I don't have time to let my students read." I think that's sad—if children aren't given enough time to read whole stories. In some schools, kids aren't even allowed to skip around in basal readers to fit their needs.

I've been able to use children's literature instead of basal readers. I've noticed that some of the publishers of basal readers have been able to contract with some of these good professional authors, but they often water down what they have written. The publishers will say, "I need a limited vocabulary. These words are too hard." However, I've taken the watered-down basal version of a story and also the original and had the kids read both of them. They had no difficulty handling the so-called "hard words" of the original stories. In one basal reader one publisher changed *fortunately* and *unfortunately* to *what good luck* and *what bad luck*. My children love to throw around big words. When I gave them the two books, they inevitably went to the one with *fortunately, unfortunately* in it. They love reading the book *Dinosaur Days*, and pronouncing all the long names like *Diplodocus* or *Brontosaurus*.

Some teachers tell their children that if they find five words on a page they don't know, they shouldn't read that book. They are sup-posed to count those words on their fingers until they reach five. Ken

Goodman calls that the "Dirty Fingers" technique. At times I've said to children, "Now maybe that book's a little too difficult for you. Can I read a part of it for you?" This helps them realize they're growing into it. But I don't stop them when they're reading something they're interested in. Our librarian will let children take out any books that relate to their interests. They'll say to her, "I've heard about such and such a book." Since it meets their needs, she'll get it for them if she can.

Ken and Yetta Goodman have been the greatest help to me in understanding fundamentals of the reading process. First, that children learn reading because they encounter it whole and within the context of meaningful use—not by looking at a bunch of individual words strung together. And second, that meaning must always be the key. I think on the whole adults don't understand the reading process because they remember only the things about reading that were difficult for them when they were learning. For example, many textbooks make a big thing of learning vowel sounds. But that's not one of the fundamentals in getting meaning out of a passage. I could take a book, black out every vowel, and by paying attention to the context, could read the entire book. Unfortunately kids in second grade across the country have been asked to learn these long and short vowel sounds, and they have stumbled. One teacher is saying "ett, ett" as in *pet,* and another teacher is saying the same sound slightly differently. The kids are confused. However, as their parents think back and say, "Oh, I had vowels, and I had those other things, and my kids are going to have to learn them or they won't be able to read," the chances are that those same adults were good readers at that point of instruction because they did a lot of overall reading when they were kids. In school they could take some of these things in isolation and give them back to the teacher. Sadly enough, they remember those irrelevant things because they were so hard, and they usually forget what they learned naturally at that time. Learning to read is complex and yet can be easy even for preschoolers.

I get excited about my neighbor's boy, who comes over and reads to me. What he's doing is so natural. Already, when he was two, he began to assume responsibility for parts of the reading act. He immediately began to turn the pages of the book *Where's Spot?* by Eric Hill that I was reading him. He saw that reading goes from left to right. He'd "read" me a Spot book. He couldn't say "Spot" at first. He'd say "Pot." The first word he read in those books was "No," which was a response found on each page. Now that he's four, he's continuing to move into reading gradually. He's becoming a reader—someone who loves books. We must bring up to consciousness these things that make us readers.

Children learn to read by taking risks, by reaching out. They make mistakes just as adults make mistakes in whatever they're doing.

Teachers must realize that. There's a series of books called *The Arthur Books* that Marc Brown has done. In one, Arthur has been chosen to be director of the Thanksgiving play. Nobody wants to play the turkey. Each of five people tells what he wants to be—the narrator, Governor Bradford, etc. The books says that "Arthur was so *desperate*" that he asked Binky Barnes, the class bully, to play the turkey. Every one of my second graders, who were pretty confident readers, said "Arthur was so *depressed*." Now that came very close in sound. And at that point the word *depressed* fit their needs far better than the word *desperate*. I was listening to several kids who were saying this was their favorite passage—where Arthur was searching around to find someone to play the turkey. They were identifying with Arthur. Now I could have said, "Oh-oh, it's *desperate*." I didn't because I didn't want to stop the children from staying with that story as it unfolded. Also, I felt that *depressed* was close phonetically to *desperate*, and the kids had chosen an appropriate meaning for it in the context. Later, when talking about some of the new words they had learned, I could bring up the point. But that would be a separate lesson.

Similar things happen when children are writing. For the word *you* they initially might write the letter *u*, but then they'll think, "There are more letters in here," and then write *yuo*. I can see that as a step forward. Children, if given many opportunities to write, will move toward conventional spelling steadily. They're not just putting down any old thing. They want to make sense out of their reading, and when they're writing, they want their reader to understand what they're saying. They're really beginning to make connections. They just need lots and lots of experience doing it.

Here [on the following page] is a response to reading that one of my first-graders turned in.

I've discovered that it's not dangerous to let children make a mistake and not correct it immediately. For one school year, I collected everything my children wrote. I found absolutely no evidence that children stayed with the same mistakes. Because of the new information they were picking up, they were constantly learning, and changing their spelling. It's through bad habits that people stop at the point of making a mistake. In their writings, high-frequency words move toward conventional spelling more quickly than a term you might use only once a year in your writing. One of my girls invented a spelling for *synchronized swimming*, and went on with her description of the show she was telling about in her journal. The same thing is true in reading—if reading is to make sense. Suppose they had learned the words *was* and *saw* in isolation, before coming to my class. They might confuse the two words. However, if I would constantly stop these children I would damage their progress in reading. I would rather they would come to

NOVember (6

I LiKE TO REED

I REED Los AV BOOKS

I HAV A NOO BOOK
it is CALLD THE VAIRY HAGRY

CATAPLR It's MAD BYE

ERIC CARle He OAS

LOS AV BUtifL PiKSHRSRs

I LikE TO RiH Storys

Too MY Pikchrs DRet iS

Good AiS His BAt I StL

Like Mt Pikches

iNE WAY GooD BY

Transcription of above: I like to read. I read lots of books. I have a new book.
It is called, *The Very Hungry Caterpillar*. It's made by Eric Carle. He does lots of
beautiful pictures. I like to write stories too. My pictures aren't as good as his,
but I still like my pictures anyway. Good-bye.

the point of saying to themselves, "Hey, this doesn't make sense—'I *was* a cat'—in this story. It should be 'I *saw* a cat.'" They have to learn to evaluate what they're reading on their own. No child just calls out words if she wants to make sense out of her reading. Being given reading matter so relevant to their lives, my children frequently don't have to deal with these problems.

Too many teachers fail to read aloud regularly to their students. With my first graders I read picture books that carry few words and also thick books that are all words. I'll read maybe for five or ten minutes and then put the book aside to go back to later. I don't feel a school day has been successful unless at some point I've read to the children. Some of the books I choose, the kids can't read by themselves and others they can. I introduce them to books they never would never hear of otherwise. When I begin a school year I read stories by one author. By the end of the first week my first-graders have appeared in the Media Center or Public Library and said, "I want the books by so and so"—the same author they've heard me read in class. If they like the book they want to read more by that writer—just as adults do.

I still read some books that were read to me as a child. I had an excellent teacher for children's literature as a child. I remember the Betsy books by Carolyn Haywood and the Dr. Seuss classic, *And to Think That*. When I began as a teacher I said to the kids, "These are books that I enjoyed." It's through the sharing of books like this that children catch the love of reading. Two or three years after, I often find children in the library in the section for books for older kids, and they say to me, "Oh, I remember you read that to me. I'm going to check that out. I can read it myself now."

When the children read aloud, they don't read in the sing-song, word-by-word manner so common in schools. What they read sounds like people talking. I think they get that from being read to so much. They may read it slower than I do, but not just like a bunch of words strung together. They put the meaning into it. I know some teachers will do lessons on reading with "expression," and they really enunciate, speaking in a sing-songy artificial voice. Parents who have several kids in the family have told me that this child who is in my class reads so it sounds like the kid is talking. They can't believe their child is reading.

I haven't mentioned reading across the curriculum. If we're doing science experiments or taking trips to a nature center, these things become the vehicles for learning to read and write throughout the year. It's the same with history and geography and cultural things such as how different families observe holidays. Children are also reading mathematics constantly, both words and symbols, in school and out. They are extending the ability to read gained while reading stories.

At my school we have a range of students, some that come from families economically very well off and some whose families qualify for title money. I don't think you can conclude anything by just knowing the name of a school district. Also, I'm not sure that economics is the great divider. Talking to some teachers in another school last week I heard of problems they were coping with. I could have related similar things that my students were experiencing. Society has always had many problems, and my kids are fighting these same problems. You find them in all school districts. For example, I have to look at myself growing up. I came from what I realize now as an adult was a poor section of Detroit. But then I wasn't poor. I couldn't afford to buy many books as a child. My major reading came from the Detroit Public Library. I had an adult card from the library when I was eleven because I had gone through all the kid books. I got interested in history. I can remember all those biographies. I had marvelous teachers. They didn't say, "Aw, these kids are too poor. They're never going to make it."

How are my children doing in reading? Standardized tests can't show that fully. For one thing, they fail to take children's logic into consideration. Standardized tests don't recognize such things. And in them there's no place for one of the girls in my class to put down that in one year she has read three of the Laura Ingalls Wilder books at an age when many children in conventionally taught classes are reading nothing but primers. Likewise a child who loves books but may be at a point of struggling to learn to read may be labeled a failure by the test. I learn a lot by listening to children in the act of reading, and I also observe what they're reading when they're away from me in the classroom.

I believe all children are reading—some perhaps on the simplest level, noticing words in signs or on cereal boxes—some more proficiently than others. Some children can read continuous text in books when I get them in first grade. Others can't. But they're all moving into reading, if we will just see that. In my class there are undeniable signs. Some of the story books that I keep there are very worn. They've been patched. They're not torn or marked in or damaged. They've been well handled. I can tell they're beloved books.

Right now we're living in a period when schools aren't looked upon as good places. When I think of evaluation, I know that if I wasn't doing something right, if my children weren't reading and writing, these parents would have a legitimate concern. But my children are enjoying reading and writing. They're learning and growing. They can begin to evaluate their own language learning. When I talk to parents I say, "You know I'm not going to be constantly correcting your children. I'm looking at how they're growing and I want to look at all the positive things that are happening." And these parents begin to observe, and they say, "Yes, our children are changing." Whole families begin to look at reading or writing in this supportive manner. For example, I've been in this school now seven years. Sometimes I've had a first grader who is now in fifth grade. His younger sister is in my present first grade. The older child still has his journal, and the little one brings her first one home. The older one says, "I used to write just like you did. You're really coming along."

The parents aren't critical. They're not saying to me, "You're doing things wrong." They're very excited about their children as learners. When children are learning, you don't hear people saying, "Why aren't you doing things differently?"

At this point in my life, I know I'll never be a skier. The top ski instructor at the school said, "If you didn't look so scared, maybe you could make it down the hill." And yet I can survive in this world not being very athletic. I'm not sure that in this day and age we can survive without reading and writing. We live in a very literate world.

Dave Curl and learners critique a photograph.

10

DAVID CURL
Photography, University

One day in 1976 I was sitting alone in the cafeteria at Western Michigan University and a handsome dark-haired man in his forties left his table, came up to me and said, "I teach photography here and I've been doing some things with my class like those your books say you do with writing students."

I thought that was an unlikely possibility but wanted to know more. So we had lunch together. A week later at David Curl's home in the woods I saw his darkroom and asked him how he got started in photography.

I was mainly self-taught. Got a B.F.A. in photography at a university, but that was later. I really began with an eighth-grade science teacher who was an amateur photographer, Herb Coon, at University School, Columbus, Ohio. He said to me, "Photography is something I do that's fun for me. You might want to learn how." It was that suggestion, more than anything he taught me, that changed my life. In ninth grade I sold activity and team pictures. In tenth grade, I worked for a local newspaper as a stringer, took pictures of all sports. When I was seventeen, I was substituting regularly for newspaper photographers on vacation—then I covered the whole range of assignments on the *Columbus Dispatch.*

I asked David how he conducted his class.

I divide the fifteen students into groups of three or four, ask them to get to know each other. Give them a big card on which they are to write their names and three good things about themselves. I have a camera set up on a tripod and each person is to photograph another one of the group. The camera is a 6 × 7 cm single-lens reflex with a Polaroid back.

While some students are taking pictures of one another, the others are discussing a photograph I have given them. I often show them this photograph of a stalk of celery with a new sprout inside. All groups are reacting to the same image although they don't know that at the time. I ask them to come up with as many thoughts and feelings as they can from looking at that photograph—symbolism, whatever it evokes. That and taking the pictures of one another require about an hour and a half. Then with a break, and a half hour for the small groups to report their reactions to the large group, that is the period, in a class that meets once a week.

When they come together in the large group, each person introduces a person they have photographed. They know something about each other because they have read the card on which they wrote three good things about themselves, and they have conversed while taking the picture.

Then they tell their reactions to the celery photograph. They discover that people see more in a photograph than the subject matter. They see different symbols, they read their own experiences into a photograph. For example, in the celery picture, they see protection, birth, a uterus when the picture is upside down, a landscape when it is sideways. The sprout also suggests to some students the latent possibility of becoming the full-grown stalk. Each group supplies distinctive responses, but there is about an 80 percent overlap. They find agreement in their diversity. They learn that the experience of the audience and the artist has to overlap to some extent before there is communication, so the artist has to provide some commonality for his audience.

At the end of the first meeting, I tell them, "Everyone will bring one mounted photograph each week, starting at the next meeting." And they do—almost everyone. By the third session everyone has a photograph for the group to discuss. These are new photographs, taken since they joined the class. Except maybe on the first week, I don't allow them to bring in any old works—no "golden oldies."

When they arrive for the second meeting, they put their photos up on the tackboard and mill around, talking. Then we all look at one photograph and I say, "How does this one make you feel?" If someone says, "I like it," I say, "What do you mean by *like?*" If someone says, "I don't like it. It makes me feel creepy," that's a successful photograph. It has got through to the viewer. So "like" is a copout. I don't want that. Someone may say, "That reminds me of—" That shows strong communication, if it can evoke other people's past experiences. This is especially important with photography. People who haven't had the experience may not be able to say anything except, "This is a vegetable."

Sometimes it's hard to get people started responding. But the small groups loosen up the critiques. You know I don't feel comfortable with "groupie" kinds of things. They're not my bag—get to know each other, play little games. But a few icebreakers help. Used to be that the semester would be halfway through before people loosened up. Now most of them start right away. Sometimes if people are reluctant to talk, I'll say, "Mary, pick a photograph and tell us your reaction to it."

At first students are backward about making negative remarks about the photographs. They don't have a list of arbitrary standards I've given them, so they're on their own. As we go along they pick up general rules that most photographers know, but we're not bound by them. "If there are scratches or dust spots on a photograph, does the scratch call attention away from the meaning of the image?" "How do technical problems affect how you see this photograph?" They are evolving standards together. I must always be careful not to make the first comment on a photograph in a critique session. I'm training them to be photographers on their own.

Some people come to my course afraid of the darkroom, but I don't let that become a problem. There's a young man in charge of the Learning Lab, which includes the darkroom, and the lab is open sixteen hours a day. We set up two or three demonstration sessions at the beginning of the semester and the students are left strictly on their own unless they ask for help. They quickly learn to solve problems by themselves and to work together with other students to master the techniques.

Many teachers make a big deal about the darkroom, fill students with awe, put formulae on the blackboard. I don't do that. I say, "I can teach you about photography, but I can't teach you to *become* a photographer. You have to learn by making mistakes and bringing the work to class to discuss it. But try not to make the same mistake twice." Very few students do. They have a good reference book that shows darkroom processes step by step, and I give them a few handouts, but then it's sink or swim. But I shouldn't say that, because nobody ever sinks. Most people think photography is more difficult than it is, but once they start doing it, they say, "That wasn't hard." When they come into class they don't believe they can do anything, but when they see the work of past students standing around the room, they realize they *can* do anything. They find out, for example, that they can produce technically a big picture that they thought could be obtained only by sending away somewhere to have it done. You know, I think the teachers who scare students are like some traditional religious leaders who teach people to fear God by saying, "What will happen to you if you don't toe the line?"

I ask students to bring in someone else's pictures that have communicated to them. I say, "Try to imagine how the photographer must have felt at the time of exposure." Then I tell them to make a photograph of a typical subject matter in the manner of some of the professional photographers they admire. This work should be *emulation*, not imitation. Here's an excerpt from a handout of "Self-Assignments" I give to my students:

> Don't simply copy something that you've seen published, but try to react
> to the subject matter as you imagine that particular photographer would

have reacted. Try to identify yourself with your chosen photographer, interpreting the subject matter as well as you can through his or her "eyes."

Self-Assignment 3 asks students to arrange with their instructor, their friends, or a cooperative photo dealer to examine several different types of cameras—to load them with film, operate the controls, and find out what each can do. Subsequent Self-Assignments ask students to make series of photographs that test the capabilities of their cameras—lens, aperture, shutter, contrast filters, flash techniques. Others require them to explore the difficulties and possibilities of photographing buildings, of making close-ups, and of copying. I ask them to illustrate a familiar household product so that it becomes tempting to buy or consume, to make several significant portraits of someone who is important to them. And to photograph the nude figure. One of my students made a remarkable photograph of two pelvises creating a sculptural effect that reminds me of the work of the great photographer Edward Weston.

Other assignments are to search for visual parallels or analogies, to treat a subject or theme both realistically and surrealistically, and to produce a visual paradox. Self-Assignments 19 and 20 ask for explorations and photographs of a junkyard and the learner's own backyard. Learners are asked to produce a series of photographs that have a common theme, to document an actual event or happening "so that essentials of the occurrence can be understood or felt by viewers." The last assignment is to "produce a series or sequence of from four to ten photographs which viewed either sequentially or simultaneously, elicit emotional reaction or communicate information more effectively than would have been achieved with fewer images." The course extends the learners' perceptions, and challenges them to find visual forms that demonstrate that extension.

I ask students to be honest about their own responses, their own emotions—to know them and respect them. But I also expect them to seek out several successful photographers and learn from them. My book *Photocommunication* [Macmillan, 1979], is full of short quotations from the masters and critics of photography; for example, Albert Szent-Györgyi's comment, "Discovery consists of seeing what everybody has seen and thinking what nobody has thought." In my class the work of both amateurs and professionals is taken on its own—looked at for what responses it calls up in the learners, not for what professional critics have said about it. The students may read the critics, but only after they have responded on their own to the work being discussed.

Right from the beginning, students see work around the room that was done by former students. At times I bring in a portfolio of work by a professional, and we discuss those photographs just as we do the students' work. The neatest thing is when students are critical of the masters' work because they know what they're talking about. Especially with some contemporary photographer, they often say, "I can understand how he did it, and where he's at, but that's *not me*."

I don't give lectures, but frequently bring in a slide presentation or a film showing a professional talking about his work. I find that a lot better than a third-person historical description—"When he lived in Paris, Jones did this—" Instead, maybe a guy like Bruce Davidson, who photographed juvenile gangs and the people who live on East 100th Street in Harlem, is saying, "When I was sixteen I was shy. I thought if girls could see my photographs and like them, then maybe they might like me." Through experiences like that students see that it's o.k. to be involved with subject matter when you're taking pictures. They view photographs in context and hear the photographer describe how he felt about subject matter. That brings in photographic history without appearing to.

In my introduction to *Photocommunication*, I said,

> For fifteen years I taught photography as if it were not an art form at all, but as if it were a scientific, academic subject. To my surprise, I discovered that some of my students were becoming effective communicators not so much because of what I had been teaching them, but because of their own terrific internal urge to create—to communicate. . . .

And I went on to say:

> I no longer teach the way I began teaching. Instead I have learned to encourage each student to photograph first and ask questions later. The technical processes I have included are merely means to an end—means to creating an image that communicates something to someone else or expresses the photographer's feelings or impressions of a situation or subject. Although technique—the *craft* of photography—is important enough to be stressed in this book and in my course, I believe it is a mistake to treat technique as if it were an end in itself.

In that book, I provided step by step descriptions of the process of taking and developing and printing pictures, with all the required materials and equipment shown in drawings or photographs, and many tips about what to do when something goes wrong or how to avoid common mistakes. The approach to photography is the fundamental thing, but the techniques are necessary, too. I believe in investigating things thoroughly. For example, in Self-Assignment 3, I say:

> Arrange with your instructor, your friends, or a cooperative photo dealer, to examine several different types of cameras. Obtain, if possible, one of each of the following types of cameras: 35mm single-lens reflex,

35mm rangefinder, 2¼ single-lens reflex, 2¼ twin-lens reflex, 4 × 5 or larger view camera.

With guidance from someone knowledgeable, practice handling camera and adjusting the controls. Pretend to take pictures. Sight through the viewfinder. Focus. Operate the shutter at various speeds. Learn how to load each camera with film. Answer the following questions about each of the cameras you have available: (1) name of camera; (2) size of negative; (3) types of film used; (4) focal length of standard lens; (5) other lenses available; (6) largest f/stop. . . .

In *Photocommunication* I tried to speak to my readers personally rather than give them a dry technical manual. For example, I said:

> When students are working together in a communal darkroom, the instructor or a humane and experienced assistant must be on hand to assuage anxieties, to alleviate technical crises, and to give on-the-spot praise and enlightened criticism. I used to think one had to master the fundamentals of technique before he or she would be able to communicate. But now I realize that was a very old-fashioned idea. It's like saying that before a young child can write an exciting story about something that interests him, he must first memorize all the rules of perfect punctuation, spelling, and grammar. I believe you should first get turned on to photography— or turned on to writing—by photographing or by writing. Once you get to doing a thing, you'll discover "how to" soon enough.

Take this photograph by one of my students. Most good prints are supposed to have some middle grey values. This one doesn't, but the peculiar lighting emphasizes the old man's figure even more, so we decided we could forget the general rule or principle in this case. Would following the rule strengthen the picture? That's the question. It really shows how an old man moves. The photograph seems to be a moving picture, doesn't it? Even though the light on the man is washed out and his figure lacks detail, I find it a telling photograph.

Mostly my students work in black and white. They shouldn't learn color first. In color the poorer photographs can pass just because of what the color does, but in black and white the underlying design elements must be there. I guess I often show my students the kind of photograph I associate with Edward Weston, Dorothea Lange, Walker Evans— people like that. It's not pretentious, and shows none of the current concern to be new for the sake of newness. The work is not "arty." This is what naturally is going to come out when you're thinking of observation and feeling, which we emphasize in critique sessions. Not so self-conscious as much work done today. And then I selected the photographs you've seen today—and my tendency is in that direction.

I call these lessons "Self-Assignments" because they're not requirements. I say, "Use these if you have trouble finding subject matter." I remember while I was getting my M.F.A. degree I was doing most of the photographs for Edgar Dale's book on audio-visual communication. That was while I was taking a course in photography. So I did the photographs, professional, you know, for a book by a leader in the field. I chose to do them instead of the regular assignments like "A still life object with inside light," etc. At the end of the semester the teacher said to me, "I'm sorry but I'm going to have to give you a B. What you did was fine, but you didn't do the regular assignments." It was the only B I got in that graduate school. Almost no one in my classes lacks ideas once they get into taking photographs and seeing what others are doing, but it's reassuring to have such a list of assignments to fall back on. The ongoing work consists of a student exposing at least one roll of film every week, developing it, then making and mounting one or more enlargements to bring to class and display.

The students come into the room, study the photographs out of their own curiosity. Get some coffee, cookies. We start a little late, the students gab and get reacquainted. But I tell them, "The one thing I want you to do in this class is talk about the photographs." I vary the format of critiquing once in a while. I may pass a photograph around and ask for one word to describe the image. Sometimes a student will start the class by pointing at a photograph on display and say, "How did he do that one?" and we're off.

At the beginning of the semester a student may make a gesture toward a print and say, "I could never do anything that good." Then I pick one done by a rank beginner and say, "That one there was done by a girl who had never taken a photograph with anything but an Instamatic camera before she came to this class." And the present student says, "Oh wow! I could do that." It happens every time. Half of the people in this course have done no serious photography. A few are experienced. Many of the M.F.A. art majors take this course, which is offered in the College of Education. In the comments made in the class at the end of the semester, both novices and experienced people say they learned from one another. The experienced especially talk about the new possibilities they learned from the naïve beginners—who weren't aware of what they were supposed to be unable to do.

Until you got me talking about my students' work, I don't think I've fully realized how good it is. We have an exhibit of students' photographs every semester, and a few are selling their work and having their own shows. Most textbooks use as models the work of famous people like Alfred Stieglitz, Edward Weston, or Ansel Adams. When I put together my 304-page, 8 × 11 inch book for Macmillan, all the photographs I used were done by my students.

Steve Urkowitz vivifies *The Odyssey* for merchant mariners.

11

STEVEN URKOWITZ
Literature, College

In 1977 when Steven Urkowitz wrote me that his teaching and a book of mine spoke to each other, we began a correspondence. Eventually I interviewed him on a stairwell of La Guardia Airport in New York City and over the phone from New Mexico.

I found that when he was teaching at Baruch College of the City University of New York he had succeeded in engaging night-school students with the classic plays of Euripides and Shakespeare. In his courses there were Korean sophisticates, Haitian villagers, Chinatown tough guys, a few native Chinese kids who had marched in Peking with the Red Guards, black kids from New York's Harlem and Bedford-Stuyvesant areas, and Caribbean islanders. Students who spoke Spanish included people born and raised in New York City, one from Madrid, one from Peru, and one from the Philippines whose first language was Tagalog. Most of them rode the subway to school. Later, he taught literary classics to young men and women at the Maritime College of the State University of New York who were preparing to enter the Merchant Marine.

I said his was an unlikely accomplishment for an English teacher, and he replied:

I always thought that students do best when they're responding to the best possible material. I used to try "socially relevant" literature, and they got all messed up in confusions of social identity and in defining what was relevant for them. I figured they could read Euripides and Shakespeare because those writers took up universal experiences—life and death, the relationships between parents and children, love, and the war between the sexes.the sexes.

That comment still didn't explain to me how he could gain the sympathy of people so unlike him and bring them to reading and understanding such difficult works as Greek and Elizabethan tragedies. I asked him to attempt to explain this apparent miracle.

I think I could relate to people to whom school seemed a foreign place because I had had so much difficulty there myself. As a student I was always late, and confused. I barely made a C average in high school and college, and later I flunked out of graduate school. My father was a mailman who loved to read ancient history—the classic Greeks and Egyptians. I grew up liking science. I was going to beat the Russians to the moon. I spent a year in engineering school and got a summer job in a radio-manufacturing plant. The people there showed me you didn't have to put on professional airs to be a good person. Then I spent two years studying physics before finishing a degree in literature. I taught science and math in junior high school and eventually finished course work in English for a doctorate. But when I came to writing a dissertation on the texts of Shakespeare's *King Lear,* I found I had a block on writing. At first I'd sit down at my typewriter alone at 9 A.M., and at 9:20 I'd be sweating, too nervous to go on any further. My wife quit a job, went back to school so she had more hours to be at home with me. After a month or so, I could write for two hours. Then later I could write through a twelve-hour day. I learned the craft, and subsequently I made the thesis into a book, *Shakespeare's Revision of "King Lear,"* which was published by Princeton University Press in 1980. Later, when I was teaching "remedial" students, I knew what they were experiencing. I asked them to put down on paper what they actually did when they were reading Euripides, how successful they felt the activity was, what was most satisfying about the experience and most frustrating.

In the years before that I had done some directing in the theater and served as a dramatic coach to a professional vocal group named the Western Wind, which has performed in Alice Tully Hall at Lincoln Center. And my wife was working in theater.

I began my remedial course at Baruch College with intensive assignments from a writing text. I started my drama section with a very short talk on the shape of Greek theaters and the way an entire community got involved in a play. For example, I said a Greek chorus is often like a bunch of our neighbors commenting on an event, and that helped students recognize individual voices and contradictory actions in the play's choral passages. Then I told them quickly the plot of the first play we were to read, Euripides' *Alcestis.* The form of the drama, in its speech-headings, dialogue, and stage directions, makes the story confusing to any readers. My summarizing of the plot didn't lessen the power of the play for them when they read it because its important quality isn't surprise, but rather the way the experience is articulated. In giving the synopsis of the play I purposely allowed myself to move from the formal poetic diction I was quoting from the play to my native Bronx street-talk. I was excited, because I feel *Alcestis* is one of Euripides' outrageously daring dramatic plots and I had the chance to re-tell a wild story.

Then I sent the students home with the admonition that they should read the entire play in a single sitting. In the next class their writings reported how they were confused and disturbed by the play, as Euripides almost certainly meant them to be. They tried to find easy answers where none was available, but they liked the play. Next I asked each student to select and prepare for reading aloud in class a single speech or part of a speech of ten to twenty lines. I outlined the techniques of dividing up a dramatic speech according to the "actions" found within it. It's crucial to know in a speech, for example, who is being addressed, where each sentence begins and ends, and what motives might underlie each sentence or action.

I had the students write brief introductions for their readings, place their speeches very simply in the dramatic context and then describe the initial action, the people being addressed, and any dramatic turn or change of address within the speech. They read their rehearsed passages to the class. The group was arranged around the perimeter of the room, so no one had to get up or come to the front of the room to read. We all listened, as politely as possible, and I offered no criticism of any kind for the readings. Simply by hearing how the more successful readers held the attention of the class, even the most frightened ones were getting something from the experience.

Then I divided the class into four "production groups," each responsible for a quarter of the play. I appointed a director for each group, although later I realized that often the students would have done a better job choosing their own leaders. They held rehearsals outside of class. For some, these tasks were easy, for others too difficult or at first not sufficiently interesting. At the first classroom performance, several readers came unprepared and had to fake their way through the material. The experience of having to sight-read complex verse proved to be a chastening awakening to them. Few came unprepared more than once.

I get students to perform scenes from plays or books in class by just telling them to do it. They keep surprising me with imaginative classroom presentations. The exercise is not to get great acting, but to have students feel the rehearsal and repetition processes. My performance standards are very high and sometimes I step in to direct the students' work when I should find ways for them to do it themselves. But I'm working on this and expect to do better next year.

When I was teaching a Shakespeare play at Rutgers University, I distributed a handout at the beginning of the course. Here's an excerpt from it:

> When I was in my first graduate school course in Shakespeare, I kept falling asleep over the plays. I just couldn't get through more than a few dozen lines before my eyelids got very heavy. I tried reading aloud; I tried reading while standing up; I tried reading in my room, or in a car, or in busy cafeterias. Nothing worked. I asked Albert Schwartz, one of the guys

I was living with, a real Shakespeare nut, what to do. He said: "Always remember who is talking, who is listening, who else is on the stage, and who just left the stage." Then I got hooked on reading Shakespeare. When you look for the *action* that the words demand, then you catch fire.

The thing I push for, that I put my time on, is the recovery of the immediate moment of the apprehension of the work of art. That's when all my training, all my library work, all the languages, all the graduate study pays off. In my handout to the students I said:

> Aristotle, an old teacher of mine, once dissected plays into manageable aspects that he could then talk about rationally. His labor is valuable, thorough, and immensely appealing to the academic mind. I'll be taking many ideas from him. But beware. Aristotle was an academic, not a theater man. He divided a play up into its parts, but then couldn't put them back together. Students who examine any single aspect of a play, such as "plot" or "thought," learn much about plots and thoughts, but they almost always lose the play itself . . . With this warning, here are Aristotle's "parts" of a play; I'll use them as a way to organize my own presentation.

But the students, they still initially find the drama, especially Shakespeare, "foreign" in form and language. I try to prepare them for the shock in my handouts:

> Most editors of the texts you're reading know little or nothing about plays. Don't look to them for help on visualizing what you're reading. I think they, as a class, are embarrassed that their author wasn't a novelist.

I say to them, "You're on your own as a reader. I'll try to help, but it's like learning to ride a bike. You just do it."

The biggest thing in asking the kids to read the classics is coaxing them, gentling them, encouraging them. The material, this great literature, is very, very hard. One reason that we define it as the greatest is that it's so challenging. The worst thing that happened to me when I was a kid was that the stuff was thrown at us very aggressively. "You're a dumb little kid, you must appreciate this on our terms." The teachers would give us all their abstracted, graduate-school topics that they thought were important—"What is the theme? What are the central image clusters here?" And they would talk about books as if they were the raw material for writing papers. "Well, this is a wonderful example of iambic pentameter." "This is an example of the Baroque," or "This is a Greek tragedy." But no one knows what an ideal Greek tragedy was supposed to be. No one should use *Macbeth* only as an example of some greater class. That reduces it to "Oh yes, that's tragedy. Ho hum. Now let's look at a comedy." It's like going to Florence and saying, "Oh yes, that's an Italian city."

I fight for the integrity of the experience of encountering the work of art rather than the meanings of the work or the general ideal class of the work. When I find passages that make me cry, that send chills up my spine—those are the ones I bring to class and read out. I say, "Hey look, this made me cry." I'm searching basically for experience. This is the main reason why I can't work with bad translations. I don't respond. The kids don't respond. To help this effort along, I spend a lot of time finding good editions. I first read the *Odyssey* in a bad prose translation and got to the end of it and thought, "Oh, all right, that's like a great book huh?" and wasn't at all impressed. But now I use the Fitzgerald verse translation, which is vibrant and tough.

I try to read the stuff every time as a naive reader, sit down with the book the evening or day before and go through it to renew my own responses, so that I can offer students one person's pattern of feelings. What the kids are looking for is a way to respond to the disorienting experience of art. If they are given a placid, safe, intellectual, predigested pablum response, they're going to model their own responses in the same way. I think a lot of teachers are too scared. When they're in front of a class they're defending their authority. They don't want to show their vulnerability to artistic or intellectual challenges. They don't want to say, "I get excited about this," any more than they would like to sit down in front of the class and say, "I really groove on hot dogs." Instead they don't let people know. Rather than being responsive members of the culture, they stand up there as the abstracted agents of it. That's the trap. It's built into our schools and their classroom structures.

A great book will set up expectations for you and then pull the rug out from under them. Artists design surprising experiences, and they delight in the audience's perception of that surprise. When you have teachers and students who are scared of surprises, when they're looking for short answers instead of intense experience, then they're in trouble when confronted by art. So I work with students on feeling, on experiencing the poem or the play. In my world literature course I begin with the *Odyssey*. At the end of the first day of class I get up and read the opening of the first book of the *Odyssey*. It's thrilling. I try to achieve that wild sensual experience of hearing that poet's voice come across. It's the sensory experience of a work of art that I want kids to get. I'm pushing for visceral response. It may seem as if this is highly anti-intellectual, but it's not. What I try to do is use all the training I've had in order to discover what those potential responses are and then work up my classroom performance. When I've provided them with a model and analytic tools, I say to the kids, "Now *you* have to find what is alive in this work and put it on for us." So they present a scene from the book. With the *Odyssey* I have them read passages to one another in small groups. They are to look for the sound of a genuine storyteller.

They already know what that thing sounds like, and when they try, they can see how daringly I've thrown myself into those things in order to act them out.

I've gotten very undirective about the writing I ask them to do. I say, "O.K., find a passage, a line, an image, a character, whatever—in the reading you do tonight, and respond to it. Talk about why this bites you or how it connects to something in your own life." But I push hard to get from students connections and responses as vivid and honest as the works we're reading. I feel very unwilling to be bored in class. I can't do anything that's boring. If someone tells me, "Look, you have to teach this or that because it's necessary for the kids' ultimate maturity," or something else, I say that's nonsense. There's no excuse. If something's important, then it has to be interesting. If it isn't interesting, then it isn't important.

In one of the seduction scenes in *Madame Bovary*, which my students at the Maritime College were reading last year, you have two actions going on at once—the seduction inside the town hall and the agricultural fair downstairs, where they're presenting awards to the best farmers. Just as the arch-seducer is throwing his heaviest lines at Emma Bovary and she's about to fall in his clutches, the guy announcing the awards says, "And now for the best manure . . ." The first time I read the book I didn't see the joke at all. I thought the presentations of the awards were dull and the seduction uneventful. But when I was preparing it for a class and looking for surprises, I found that surprise, that juxtaposition. It's that creation of an expectation and then hitting you with cold water to make you wake up—that's what I feel the great life of art is all about. It's to enrich, to broaden your experience, your appreciation of simultaneous experiences. What I don't understand is why teachers let themselves collapse into boredom.

The opposite of boredom is a gut response. Recently I used a new anthology of poems and said to the kids, "Now look, I've picked out the things I responded to. If you want to read more, do so. If you find things you like, tell me, but I didn't respond to other things in this book. I'm telling you about things I reacted to." I was surprised by Ezra Pound's translation of an Anglo-Saxon poem called "The Seafarer." Even in translation it was hard reading. He made it immensely difficult. I read it and was challenged. I felt it dealt with the tough-mindedness of this seafarer who despises the soft life of cultured society. He chooses the painfully heroic life of the Viking seaman. I had the kids read it, and I read it through in class, explaining grammatical connections, annotating references. That took about thirty-five minutes. Then I read it through straight. Later, when I gave them the chance to write about anything they wanted to choose from the forty-odd poems we had worked on, more than half the class wrote on "The Seafarer." Like him, high-school and college kids want challenge. They're excited by the potentialities they see. But if the literary material is presented to them as "classic," as "perfect," as nothing they can add to themselves, then they turn it off. Because that's what they're rejecting—the authority of predigested experience. That's the best thing about that age—searching for raw adventure.

People who present literature by saying, "This is the mainline culture. You have to accept it" are walking into the age trap. In my class they liked "The Seafarer" because they shared his desire to be tough, to choose the difficult life, to self-consciously avoid the soft life. One of the reasons I think spectator sports are so incredibly important to most of us is that if we could, we would choose the path of excellence, of rigor, of strength and toughness. I think I would find that attitude in a monastery or a girls' conservatory as well as in the Maritime College I'm teaching in. The poets are like the athletes, sharing an honorable way to live in the world.

The reason we can respond to distant authors like Homer so well is that the patterns of behavior that he's trying to teach are so often the things we all are trying to teach. The values of high culture, the values of familial integrity, the values of hospitality. These are trans-cultural values and they're tied into heroism. I could see that when I was reading cultural anthropology and history, and then when I looked at Greek drama and Anglo-Saxon epics, and novels of 19th-century France—material that is not as readily accessible to me—I went in with the willingness to say, "O.K., somewhere in there is a human being that has gone through the same experiences I've gone through." That kind of training and willingness to read outside of conventional literary criticism led me to this kind of openness in the classroom. The conventional structures of literary study are valuable, but primarily for my understanding the work, not for transmitting the experience of the work to students. That line from Swift I think of—"I saw a woman flayed the other day. You can't imagine how it altered her appearance for the worse." That's the sense the kids have—"Oh well, are we going to analyze a poem, slice it up, flay the thing?"

Experience and meaning—that's a basic opposition in Western society from the Greeks on. There's a pressure to idealize things and to find what their meaning is, to extract the essence. "What is the essence of Macbeth?" "What is the essence of Emily Dickinson?" Now that's one of the great potentials of language—it's an abstracting medium. Certainly English, and the other languages I know about, encourage abstraction. It's very heady, exciting stuff. I've lived on it for a long time now. "Romantic Love" is essentially the worship of abstraction. And patriotism is often the worship of the abstract virtue of the country. But the lesson of experience, of wise men, of old men, of great books, of politicians, of old teachers I've known, is that the ideal is a trap. It fools you, and ultimately pays nothing. Anyone who's been in an idealized love affair knows that. What I think happens is that literary students often fall in love with the idea of the book and then when they become teachers want to carry on that idealized relationship. The book becomes the Holy Grail, the gorgeous girl they looked at from afar. But when you actually marry that person, or actually go to war and live through the disguise, you realize, "Hey, this war is not something to go into the way so many patriots think it should be." "This marriage is not what my fantasy told me to expect." "This class doesn't love *Jude the Obscure* the way it should."

I look at a book and say, "This is not something abstract. It made me cry. It's not a meaning." *Macbeth* is a gut-wrenching feeling. If you try to say, "Well, *Macbeth* means, 'Don't kill your king,' " nobody's going to respond to that. Nobody's going to care. If Shakespeare just wanted to say, "Don't kill your king," then he would have written, "Look, don't kill your king." Instead, what he did was write this play in order to give audiences an experience so they will know—they won't necessarily understand—they will know in their guts that king-killing is a poor business, while they sympathize with Macbeth's terrible fall.

When I was teaching at Medgar Evers College, one class had read through the last scene of *Lear*. I had them write about the one character they had paid most attention to in the scene, connecting the character to someone from their own experience. They read what they wrote in small groups, and there was a lot of steam and arguing going on. Evelyne Armand had written about her Grandpa Justin, thinking of the sometimes magnificent, petulant, and senile figure of King Lear, a man trying to work out his relationships with his children.

REACTION PAPER

... He made most of his own furniture at home. I remember a sofa he made for Grandma for their twenty-fifth wedding anniversary. It was a beautiful piece of furniture made of mahogany. He had worked many Sundays putting it together.

He was very persistent in his work; he would do something over and over until he got it right. I used to watch him work with delight. One day he was making a rocking chair for me and I stood by him all day until it was finished.

Usually he would work in the back yard under a straw roof. Because of the tropical climate he wore no shirt. His biceps would bulge under the strain and shined with sweat while moving the sharp saw into the piece of wood.

Sometimes I had to sponge his large forehead just like a nurse sponges a surgeon in the operating room. Then he would wink his dark brown eyes at me, and he stroked his bushy eyebrows with one finger to let me know I had missed a spot. . . .

He never visited with his children, they came to see him. I never saw him even once in my home. In spite of that extreme shyness, he was devoted to his family. He gave an allowance to every grandchild of his, all ten of us he had at that time. . . .

Sometime around Christmas, I remember, Grandpa came home with a co-worker two hours after leaving for work. Something terrible had happened. He was not a very talkative man. He just whispered, "I can't see."

The word spread around that Papa had become blind. It was so sad everybody cried. A doctor was brought to the house to examine him. The diagnosis was bilateral cataracts. Surgery was out of the question because he refused to even budge out of his room. Every member of the family tried to persuade him to go to the hospital. Finally he was left alone with his handicap.

At first he was depressed, but gradually he became accustomed to darkness, and he accepted his condition with courage. He spent the rest of his life in solitary confinement. He died peacefully at home, in his room, on his bed, at the age of ninety-two.

In that class I read my own writing done for that same assignment:

REACTION PAPER

No, no, no life?
Why should a dog, a horse, a rat have life
And thou no breath at all? Thou'lt come no more.

I put off writing about *King Lear* myself. I know that when I move into the experience of the play my whole being begins to vibrate. But some things should be said, and the very effort at saying them brings about a brave feeling of renewal, sobriety, and peace.

I was one of three brothers. My father was a kind man, but he didn't know how to deal with his anger at his sons when they didn't meet his standards. I remember how he would rage at my older brother when he did badly in school or when he got into trouble in the street. For what I remember as years and years, my older brother would taunt my father, and they would burn insults back and forth between them. Sometimes my father would grab his son to shake him. Michael, who was very small, would swing punches at my father, who was a big man.

The household steamed for years. When he was about twenty-two, Michael took off for California, and except for about half a dozen short visits, he's been there since. Now, twenty years later, he's married, calmer, easier with my father.

My younger brother Paul was a big, handsome kid. Unlike Michael and me, he was a ballplayer. He had good hands and eyes, and he would push in a game where I instead would back off. Like all of us he had a lot of bravado, and he got into trouble in school, too. He was stubborn, and he wouldn't try different ways to solve any problem. Just his way, right or wrong.

He never did learn to drive very well. He had an odd way of aiming rather than driving a car. In the winter of 1968 he crashed during a snowstorm. His skull was crushed when he was thrown from the VW bus he was driving. More than anyone else in the family, my father was shaken. Though for years he hadn't been in a synagogue, we would go together every morning to recite the Kaddish—the prayer for the dead. For the first weeks he couldn't get through the prayer without stopping to weep. For two years he went, every morning.

I'm not sure what goes next in the story. Much happened. Both my children were born while we were in Chicago during the next two years. My father came and stayed with us, longer than either my mother or my wife's mother. One day he said to me that he had stopped going to the synagogue. He said, "It gets me down."

Over the last six or seven years he's grown very wise. He cracks jokes a lot and they're very funny. When we go to the cemetery around the High Holy Days, he'll pray and weep and say to me, "Years, Stevie. If you ain't got years, it's nothin'." And he seems to treasure my brother in California, visits him, and sends him money that he has squirreled away without my mother knowing.

There's a quality that I can only describe as "density" in my father now. It's maybe the joy that Lear felt inventing the life he and his daughter Cordelia might lead in prison. Lear deserved more years at what my father is celebrating now. But it's a state reached only after terrible pain. You don't "learn" it. You suffer and endure and then become it.

When I was dramatic supervisor of the singing group, I asked singers to do what I ask students to do in responding to literature. "Find something in your experience that resonates with the text, and work with that." This is classic acting technique which has been discovered over and over again. Think of the debate between the Sophists and the Philosophers in classic Greek times. The Sophists were Method Acting teachers. They taught people to argue cases as if they were their own, to put themselves in the shoes of their clients. Their training was a series of exercises in sympathetic responsiveness like those Stanislavsky developed in our century. This was also the basic rhetorical training that Elizabethan boys had. "You are Julius Caesar at the Rubicon. Write a speech justifying crossing the Rubicon." And in the meditative tradition that the poet John Donne carried on as a preacher in the 17th century. It was "Feel yourself carrying Christ's cross." A meditation for Easter. "Now here, feel this. Watch this. What is the weather around? What else do you see? What are the details from your own life you distill into this image?" The big fight was between the idealizing philosophers like Socrates and Plato and the pragmatic, experiential Sophists. This same debate is still fundamental in western society. You find it in the structure of schools and colleges. In an American college you take abstracted courses in which you learn the *Principles* of Psychology. Introduction to Literature. Fundamentals of Physics, whatever. That's why the courses are so deadly dull. "The horse. The horse is a four-legged animal." God forbid you should jump on one. But the necessity is to use both approaches. But really to be a learner, you must play from a full deck, use all the tools available, all the analytic *and* experiential tools.

When I'm asking students to experience literature in my course, I must remember to make that classroom safe. Safe from humiliation, safe from outside nastiness. One of the things that surprised me when I started teaching was how nasty students and teachers can be to one another. Now I know I have to make this classroom a safe place where people giving honest responses to literature and to ideas will be protected. If people are nasty, if especially the teacher is nasty, then all the good ideas and methods will go to naught because the kid will leave burned. More than anything else, I cannot hurt a student. I have no business, in the classroom if I do. I remember when I first started teaching in junior high school. Given my own frustrations, my own lack of preparation, my own background, things didn't work. I was dull, and the kids were bored, so they acted badly, so I humiliated them. I remember one, smart black kid from the Bronx—his father was in jail. One time I just tore into him and said things that make me blush now. He took a pencil off one of the kids' desks and I said, "Do you want to go to jail like your father?" His face turned grey and I still see the hurt in his eyes. Like too many young teachers, I was without resources, or rather, I didn't know how to *use* the humane tradition I had studied for so long.

Now I'm saying different kinds of things, and so are my students. The fourth or fifth day of the semester last year we were working on Homer. After class, walking out, one of the kids said to me, "You know, I really like this book! I can't put it down. I thought it was going to be terrible, I thought it was going to be like Shakespeare."

And then later, when we were reading *Madame Bovary* I noticed that one of the kids who had been responding vividly all through the course looked glum, long-faced, awful. After class I went up and said, "Hey, what's the matter." He said, "I don't like this book." I said, "It's a great book. It's funny. It has all these great parts. Come on, read the book!" And after the next class he said to me, "The reason I don't like the book is that *I'm* Charles Bovary. I'm going through this."

Charles Van Riper crams stories into his pipe for telling.

12

CHARLES VAN RIPER
Speech Therapy, University

When I taught at Western Michigan University, I belonged to a little group of faculty members interested in the study of communication. We met several times a year for dinner. One night the speech pathologist Charles Van Riper talked to us. Remembering some of his cases, he told us of a successful businessman I'll call "Edward Russell," who had suddenly lost the ability to speak. After conversing with Russell and observing him closely for fifteen minutes, Charles moved nearer and said, "Oh, so you can't make any sound, Mr. Russell?" The man nodded his head in the affirmative and Charles placed the hot bowl of his lighted pipe on Russell's arm. "Ow!" he yelled. "You damned fool! What do you think you're doing?"

"I thought you could talk," said Charles. "Now let's try to find out what you've been hiding from."

After telling the story, Charles looked around the table at us and said, "I've learned to do whatever is necessary in my job."

I had heard that Charles had clients from as far as China and India who wanted help with their speech difficulties. He was irresistible, talking in his relaxed humorous way at that dinner, or later, walking on his land up in the northern region of lower Michigan looking for deer. In my classes I frequently mentioned him and sometimes said to my students, "In this university works one of the great teachers in the world. If I were you I wouldn't graduate until I had taken a class with him, no matter what my major field of study was."

A week later one of the young women in my class told me that she had gone to Professor Van Riper's office to find out what course she could take from him. Nobody was there. Apparently the secretary was out for lunch, but a door to an inner room was ajar, and my student heard a series of strange growlings. She looked inside and there was a little girl walking around on all fours on the rug followed by a middle-aged man also walking on all fours. Both were growling loudly. Just as my student turned to leave, the man's eyes fell upon her and he said, "We're playing bear. Can I help you?" That was the way she found out which class she should take from the older bear, who was Charles Van Riper, at work with a client.

One of the founders of the profession of speech pathology, Charles was born in 1905 in the Upper Peninsula of Michigan, and at the age of one began to stutter, eventually so violently that he avoided human contact when he could and almost became a recluse. Since then, he has written twenty-eight books, three of which are stories about the "zany" characters he knew in Champion, Michigan, as a child, and one, Speech Correction: Principles and Methods, *that has sold a half million copies. Always in his professional career Charles has been concerned that his writing should not be pedantic, but straightforward and lively. Here, for example, in his popular textbook, Charles is telling how "some children when completely immersed in some other person's role, can speak almost perfectly the same sentences that they cannot possibly say without error in any other situation." He goes on to say,*

We use fantasy, children's theater, and creative dramatics to establish these roles and much suggestion and coaching to make them vivid enough so that the child can throw himself completely into them. . . .

> CLINICIAN: Don't shoot me when you come in.
> CHILD: Oh hoh. I'll thcare you. You be thcared now when I come in.
> CLINICIAN (*lifts two fingers*): Like this?
> CHILD (*returning to his own role*): Naw. Look, when I thay "Stick 'em," up you've got to thtick 'em up like thith. (*Demonstrates.*)
> CLINICIAN: Oh, I understand. Let's start again.
> CHILD: Stick 'em up now!

Writing in The Western Michigan University Journal of Speech, Language and Hearing *in 1978, Charles spoke of the "wretched prose" in most speech pathology journals:*

In retirement I still read them from cover to cover but with a growing sense of outrage as I picture the furrowed brows of students trying to decode their jargon. The information is always useful, but why must we have to dig so hard for it? Why is it so hard for specialists in the disorders of communication to communicate? It isn't difficult to write if you really hunger to have your reader understand.

This is the way Charles wrote in a handout to prospective students in speech therapy in 1966 when he was a department head:

Speech therapy is a new profession, now barely thirty years old. You will be prepared academically and in casework to join this profession whose official organization is the American Speech and Hearing Association. You will be expected to adhere to its code of ethics. We will do our utmost to see that you become a credit to this profession and we will scrutinize you and your work to that end. At the same time, you will find here helpfulness and permissiveness, for we are therapists too. You will get tired but you won't get bored. You will get frustrated by the challenges we will give you and you may fail at times. We like students who fail but learn from that failure. If you show a desire to master your professional skills and knowledge, you'll have a fine time here. If you don't, we'll heave you out. You see, we keep thinking of the many children and handicapped adults who may sometime be dependent upon you for their lives, lives which will be either full of tragedy or lives rich and rewarding. You may be the only chance they may have, and you must be worthy of their need.

Here are excerpts from a statement Charles Van Riper wrote to his staff in 1967 or thereabouts:

Our duty to our students, to our cases, to all our fellows, is to set them free. We must not bind with our chains their potentials, for our own selfish needs for ego status or in revenge for our own enslavement. We must guard ourselves constantly lest we make them dependent upon us for our own ego-needs. This is hard to do, for many of our cases and students will seduce us into the master's role, thereby absolving themselves of the burden of responsibility for their own failure to fulfill themselves. We must not blame them, for this is all they have known but we should not aid them in their folly. Each of us is responsible for the fulfillment of his potential. . . .

How then can we help our cases and students to realize these truths, if truths they be? First of all we must hunt hard in each of them for every small sign of potential, focus upon it our spotlight of faith, reward its confrontation by our own pleasure in the insight. Next we must help them to search for alternative modes of action and *insist that they choose* the one most promising in the long run. To do this, of course, they must gather and scan the available information and do some predicting. This they will resist because of the labor and the responsibility involved. They should be encouraged in every way to get this and do this. We must not get it for them and do it for them though we can make it easier. But we must not say to them: "This is what you should do or try." The moment we do this, we assume the role of master; we make them dependent. Always they should choose. We must help them learn to hunt for ideas and activities from any source, from books, from other members of the staff, from their own cortical convolutions or glands—but they should choose and we should not tell them which one they should use. Let them find out!

All men should be their teachers and supervisors. A supervisor should be a companion, not a comptroller, he must not be a yes-no man, a good-bad man. We can control by praise as well as punishment. Accordingly, we must as teachers, therapists and supervisors, be permissive, giving absolution for comprehended errors of judgment, but always helping our students to grow tall. Our responsibility is to make them responsible.

In 1965, when I was teaching at Western Michigan University, students launched a supplement to the university newspaper called The Western Re-

view and asked Charles Van Riper if they could interview him for one of their early issues. Charles said he didn't like interviews, but would be glad to write some comments on teaching. A few weeks later he gave the editor, Barry Guitar, the following article. Barry was majoring in speech pathology at the time, and working with Charles. Later he became a professor at the University of Vermont.

Dr. Charles Van Riper Reflects
upon His Philosophy of Education

I have just made the horrible discovery that I have taught the same undergraduate course, Introduction to Speech Pathology, fifty-nine times and will teach it again next semester. The shudder is more of shock than revulsion. Incredibly, I contemplate this sixtieth performance, if that is what it is, with real enthusiasm. I like to teach that course! But surely this is a time for pause and self examination. Is it masochism? Should I resign my professorship and join the Peace Corps or is it already too late for this Ancient Mariner to discard his academic albatross? Must I teach Introduction to Speech Pathology throughout eternity?

Since most instructors must offer the same course several times, it is possible that the scrutiny of this, the extreme case, may provide some illumination concerning the murky influence which repetitive teaching has upon the teacher and his students. Without much hope that I can be entirely honest, let me attempt the analysis of how I try to cope.

We have known the stereotype of the old professor whose lectures followed his yellowed notes from year to year so closely that his students knew that Academic Joke Number Nine would be emitted at precisely twenty-three minutes after eleven on the fourth day of the class. While I admit that a few of my favorite anecdotes seem unduly familiar to me if not to my students, I think I can deny that I fit that stereotype completely. For one thing I never use notes. When I first began to teach the course, long before these present students were born, I prepared every lecture with utmost care and each new semester I revised my outline and my notes. But I soon found that they began to bore me utterly. So I re-worked them into a text so I could forget them. This is not to say that I no longer prepare for each day's class session.

Very rarely have I ever come to class without having mulled at some length, and when I have not, my teaching was dull and uninspired. I have found this incubation period absolutely necessary if I am to generate that excitement in my students which is my goal. Since I know them and what they have been reading in the texts and references and I know what I have told them in earlier sessions, I begin the mulling incubation process by asking myself what can I give them that will focus, illustrate or amplify the topics we are investigating together. In this, I try to avoid any repetition or review of what presumably they all have read. I'm not a book reviewer. I will not belabor their ears with what they can get through their eyes.

Instead I scan and search my past experience in research and therapy and knowledge of the literature and observation of my fellow-man for material which will open windows through which they may desire to peer. And, as I grow older, I find myself seeking constantly to relate the information to their lives and their futures. I fear I'm now expressing my own philosophy of the essential dignity of man's existence a bit too often. But these students are searching for identity and for values, and I cannot deny their hunger. Sparks begin to shoot when the discussion moves in these directions.

Oddly enough I find that all the topics we discuss seem to lead eventually to the scrutiny of the self and the culture. This may be due to the fact that since speech is the unique feature of man's existence, I find in my subject, speech pathology, all the evidences of man's frailty both as an individual and as a member of society. At any rate, in my preparatory mulling before each new session, I find myself anticipating what the students' questions and thoughts might be and hunting for material which might serve as tentative or provocative answers. Finally, I make some attempt, usually a feeble one, to organize some sequence to the presentation but often it seems to organize itself there in the lecture hall, the feedback from the students creating its own new pattern and often to my astonishment.

These mulling periods are so essential that I jealously guard the time they require. One of the maddening and saddening things about these last thirty years in higher education is the continuing constriction of a professor's leisure. We have so very little time to think. Always there is the demand for research and writing and especially those damned committee assignments that plague us so in this country. I protest the whole committee function! Only a misanthropic camel could have ever invented a committee.

Trying to be cooperative in my early years at the university, I found myself being appointed to one committee after another, and with each my own small cup of time was drained. Finally in sheer desperation I sought the aid of an older colleague who apparently never had a committee assignment. "I have a formula for beating the system," he said with a grin in his beard, "but do not divulge it to the Dean. I used to be on a lot of committees too, but I learned to remain absolutely quiet throughout all the discussion and wrangling and speeches and to wait until everyone was exhausted and bored and ready to tell the chairman to do what he had long intended anyway. Then, and only then, I would reopen the question with vehemence and many objections and challenges. Since I had not spoken before, they had to hear me out. The word soon got out that I was a lousy man to have on a committee and I've had time to think and read ever since."

I applied his formula and lo! it has worked well. As a small contribution to the current administrative chaos, I now reveal his secret. The product of a committee is in inverse proportion to the square of its membership.

As a committee of one, I soon learned that the effectiveness of my teaching depended directly upon my understanding of my students' needs. When I failed to teach well, I repeatedly discovered that I had misjudged them. The clarity or vividness of my lectures played only an ancillary role. I have heard a few of my colleagues over their coffee cups declaiming that they "laid the stuff out and the students could jolly well remember it or flunk." Some others have boasted, I think guiltily, that they rarely had a conference with an individual student, never permitted questions in class, and viewed themselves as fonts of knowledge from which those who wished could fill their pitchers and to hell with the rest of them.

Another one said, "To cope with the faceless individuals that sit before me, I just assume that all of them will be fascinated by hearing me talk to myself on the topic at hand. To maintain this belief I insulate myself so far as possible from the students. I don't want to know how stupid or uninterested they really are."

These reactions are not wholly due to the frailty of instructor sapiens. In part they arise from the evils of the mass teaching imposed upon us. Our classes are far too large to enable us to know our students. Yet I have said that this student contact and understanding are absolutely essential if I am to teach well. Perhaps my own struggle to cope with this sad necessity may be revealing. In 1936 my class consisted of six students, all of whom had possessed enough curiosity to enroll in a course with the strange name of "Speech Pathology." We explored the subject together, a *modus operandi* which still constitutes the basic structure of the course. But then we could talk informally with much commentary, prediction and recall as well as nonsense.

They used to refer to it as their "sharing time." Usually it was more of a septalogue than a dialogue, but the mutual identification of student and teacher was always present. We examined patients together, did therapy and research together, and then shared our thoughts and feelings with each other. I knew these students intimately and they knew me.

As the years have passed, this optimal teaching situation has gone forever, except in my graduate seminars. In the last ten years I have never had less than one hundred unknowns cramped and crowded in the amphitheatre before me. I now make no effort to know all their names; I remember the professor of ichthyology who said that every time he memorized a student's name he forgot a fish. Nevertheless, I have an illusion, and believe my students share it, that I have a fairly clear appreciation of their thinking, attitudes and needs. Over the years I have developed a technique of sampling which at least sustains that illusion.

Early in the course I give the students a set of assigned readings and projects on which they are to report by writing not an abstract of the content or experience but an account of the personal reactions, thoughts and feelings which these generate. I read these papers myself—a tremendous task usually requiring fifteen hours—write a few personal comments on each and then invite selected individuals alone or in groups to visit me either at the office or at my farmhouse on a Sunday evening. I resist selecting only the brightest or most interesting ones but seek a representative sample.

In our conferences the talk roams widely since I use my professional skills to make sure that they do most of the talking. I may do this two times a semester, more often if I feel I am out of contact with them during my lectures. But the impression that I care to know my students seems to travel swiftly and other students who urgently need me manage to overcome the barrier reef of my secretary, a wise, perceptive woman, who knows how to screen out the apple-polishers.

In the class sessions I encourage any interruption of my lectures to ask a question or to make a comment. I do this by invitation but also by suddenly stopping my presentations and roaming up the aisles to hold a brief spontaneous dialogue with some class member. Or I may turn out the lights and ask them in the darkness to think a bit about what I have been saying and to tell me when the lights come on again. Or I may select a panel to come to the platform to discuss my discussion. Or I may send a young man and an attractive girl out into the hall to explore "How differently you would teach your future parrot or baby to talk," and then to share with the class their thinking. Or I might select one student at random by using my *ictus*, the forefinger, which I aim blindly over my back, and devote the session just to teaching him alone as the others eavesdrop.

Occasionally I will have an "Instruct the Instructor" assignment in which the students write an unassigned paper which will teach me something that I don't know but should. I collect the papers, then use my *ictus*. Surprisingly most of them take this very seriously and I have learned much from them, though there are always the few who insist upon educating me concerning the positions of Arabian intercourse, or some such vital matter.

I should say here that only rarely has a student ever exploited the permissive relationship in the class itself by wisecracking or inappropriate discourse and when it has occurred I have always found that the person has been badly hurt by some teacher in the past. Students seem to sense my respect for them and their potential growth and they appreciate it.

In regarding the above, I hope I have not conveyed the impression that I always operate in this manner. Different classes require different approaches even though I teach the same course. There are days when I lecture throughout the hour but I am always conscious that in the mass of heads before me there are important individual human beings. I find myself scanning constantly. I talk first to one student, then another, not to the amorphous horde. I try to get through the masks some of them wear. When a girl yawns, I know she was probably up late helling around, but I cannot help but redouble my efforts to interest her. Sometimes I feel like a sheep herder. There are certain students whose faces can be used as sensors, but I try not to address them only. The real joy of teaching comes when you can see the lightning of intellectual excitement emerge from what looks like a clod. I've found that there are no clods, only unresponsive human beings.

But the upshot of all this interaction is that I have come to realize that each new class presents a different challenge because it is composed of different individuals. The mix varies widely from semester to semester. As in wines, there are also vintage years for students. Some of the best years came when the veterans returned from World War II or Korea but there have also been good ones before and since. Perhaps my sampling is faulty or my skull computer poorly programmed, but I have never been able to envisage the average student. I cannot teach the same course twice in the same way because I just don't have the same students.

A similar necessity for variation stems from the nature of the course itself. When I began to teach, speech pathology was an infant field with a tiny literature and less research. In these thirty years, it has grown tremendously and now the input overload of information is almost overwhelming to one who must interpret it. Yet this very flood creates the need to design a new course each semester.

For years I have recorded a lecture or two for my own private benefit or trauma so I could have some objective evidence of what the devil I was doing. I kept those recordings and a week ago I listened again to some of the earlier ones—scratched into aluminum discs, for we had neither wire nor tape then—and I was amazed and bit sickened to hear the many bits of misinformation I had inflicted on the unsuspecting.

Another change in the nature of the course has come with the increasing number of students. Except for their texts, they do not, cannot, read the same things at the same time in the literature because of limited library offerings of the same reference. When I first began teaching I could assume a common background that all possessed, but now I am frequently forced to abstract and summarize the basic information for the students instead of sending them to the original sources. This is always a real loss since distortion always creeps in. Students still read much but they read different things and I'm sure many of them miss much significant source material.

We are thus forced to rely too much on the standard texts, a few of which I have written. With respect to the latter, let me say that I feel every instructor should use a text he himself has written. I have used the text of my colleagues and never teach as well when I do so, mainly because I find myself arguing with their authors too much or restating their material. My own texts I know to the point of nausea so I do not duplicate their contents in class and also I find their author surprisingly reasonable. Writing a text frees one from depending upon it.

I am also able to keep out of ruts because I routinely use the presentation of actual cases who tell their sad tales of communicative frustration. By working with them before the students, I always meet new problems which demand new commentary and explanation. It is impossible to teach the course in the same way when these living illustrations vary so much. We also use films and tapes and other audiovisual material but I get jaded easily after I've seen or heard them a time or two even when they are very good.

Finally, of course, I have changed. This change is the most difficult to assess since I cannot remember that callow youth who presided over the course so long ago. I have aged but have I grown wiser? I fear that illusion. At any rate I certainly now have more experience and knowledge to share. Throughout the years I have constantly been a working speech therapist, doing diagnosis and therapy with the people who comprise the subject matter of my course: the stutterers, the lispers, lallers, voice cases, aphasic victims of brain injury, the deaf and hard of hearing. I have been an intimate part of many lives and I must have learned something from so many troubled souls.

And so I return to the hard fact that soon I shall teach "Introduction to Speech Pathology" for the sixtieth time. Has all this been but the pumping of a tired balloon? Perhaps so, but I know that next fall semester when I walk into that amphitheatre, I shall hear the sound of trumpets.

Stan Vukovich listens with friends to a student paper.

13

STANYAN VUKOVICH
Social Studies, High School

I learned about Stan Vukovich, an Alameda County Teacher of the Year, through Jim Gray, the director of the National Writing Project (formerly the Bay Area Writing Project), a program for enabling English teachers to write better themselves and enable their students to do the same.

I began teaching at McClymonds High School in Oakland, California, in 1968. McClymonds is the only regular high school in west Oakland, historically one of the poorest areas in all of Oakland. Immigrants from eastern and southern Europe and China lived in the area before blacks moved in during World War II. During my fifteen years there I've taught about ten whites, ten Asians, and ten Latinos. The rest have all been blacks, and I'm white. We've never had any racial disturbances at Mack. Even during the worst days of the late sixties and early seventies, the students were peaceful. The school's ethnic homogeneity and relative small size, 750 to 1,000 students, have kept things relatively placid. According to district records, about 70 percent of the students' families are on some sort of welfare.

In 1979 one of the English teachers at McClymonds came back in the fall with high praise for the Bay Area Writing Project. She never described what went on, but would always coo and say that BAWP was "marvelous." That year I attended a workshop conducted by Mary K. Healy, one of the associate directors of BAWP for the California Council for the Social Studies. Her presentation was indeed marvelous, and I signed up for the BAWP summer session at Berkeley that year. I've been a BAWPer ever since. Later the entire social science department at Mack participated. I regard this as a sign of the department's recognition of the need to teach more writing. Our school administration vigorously supports our efforts to introduce more writing into our courses.

When I began teaching at Mack I had high hopes that all my students would become scholars entering four-year institutions so that they could become leaders in the struggle for black liberation. Then I found that some of my students didn't know where the Pacific Ocean was in relation to Oakland. One boy in a college prep class in U.S. history answered a question on the causes of the Civil War by writing, "Slavery it bad. I don't like it. It cause the war." This was his answer on an hour-long test.

With much trial and many errors, I bumbled along until I got involved with the Bay Area Writing Project. I determined to use some of the techniques I had learned during the summer session. While doing a unit on the pre-Civil War period, I prepared a newspaper project for my students. I divided the class into two newspaper staffs, one for the pro-slavery *Charleston Mercury* staff and the other for the abolitionist *North Star* newspaper that had been run by the former slave, Frederick Douglass.

These newspapers are four-page, five-column publications with front-page banner headlines, and illustrations. Here in the *Charleston Mercury* is an advertisement for a runaway slave, typical of the period:

$ REWARD!!! $

[portrait drawing]

WANTED: Ray Jules runaway slave. Seen heading North. He is a light skinned Negro, possibly passing as a white. Twenty-five year old. 6'3" in height; brown eyes, golden brown hair. Reward $4,000 alive. Notify Sir Walter Jules c/o *The Mercury*.

On the third page of this edition of the *Charleston Mercury* for April 12, 1861, appeared in the "Interview of the Week" column, this article:

Charleston, S.C. April, 1861. Duncan Clinch Heyward, a slaveowner of the Palmetto State, was interviewed by a *Mercury* reporter. He was asked a number of questions relating to slavery.

REPORTER: Now that abolitionists and freedmen are joining together to fight against the institution of slavery, do you think it will be ended? Will slaves be happier free?

ANSWER: Being a slaveowner, son, I can surely inform you on the life of slaves, young and old alike. They are happier on my plantation than they would be free. As for those meddling Northern abolitionists and crazy free darkies there is a powerful dislike on my part for them and their kind.

REPORTER: Yes, sir. Why do you suggest that the slaves would be less likely to take a fondness to freedom as opposed to slavery? And why are abolitionists and freedmen so disliked by you and men like yourself?

ANSWER: Because, being slaves and having masters is the best thing in the world to happen to darkies. They have it made much to their advantage over freedmen and poor whites. Free food, a place to sleep, shoes, clothes, and guaranteed jobs. The so-called free Blacks are in a constant struggle to stay alive in the Northern and Western states. Slaves even get free medical care, while the freedman doesn't.

Abolitionists, Quakers and all others meddling in our affairs are disliked something powerful here in South Carolina, because they tend to try to destroy our economic and political system. In a sense, they are jealous-hearted at our success with the institution of slavery and our great supply of cotton and our free labor to work with it. . . .

In my instructions to students working on that newspaper, I said: "Remember that you are writing from a Southern white point of view. This is an academic exercise only. It is not intended that slavery is at all defensible."

In another article in that issue, a student wrote this article headlined "Massa-Slave Relations":

Plains, Ga. 1861. Abolitionists don't want to read it. But our roving reporter has just returned from Plains, Ga., where he interviewed a slave on the Carswell estate.

REPORTER: What is your name, boy?
ANSWER: I'se called Jebdiah, suh.
REPORTER: How long have you been a slave?
ANSWER: Don't reckon how long, suh.
REPORTER: Did your master give you your name?
ANSWER: Yes, suh.
REPORTER: Does your master ever whip you, Jebdiah?
ANSWER: Massa only whips me when I ax for it, suh.
REPORTER: Do you mean to say when you do something wrong, you tell him?
ANSWER: Yes, suh. Cuz I loves my massa and don't want to be sold.
REPORTER: Did you master ever feed you out of pig's trough?
ANSWER: No, suh. Massa feed us out of wooden bowls.
REPORTER: Do you say you have a good master?
ANSWER: Yes, yes in deedie. I got me a very good massa, suh.
REPORTER: How do you feel about slaves that run away?
ANSWER: I'se feel that they crazier than a loon, suh.
REPORTER: Why?
ANSWER: Cuz massas are the best people in the world and when you got a massa like mine, you don't need to be free, suh.
REPORTER: Thank you, Jebdiah. Here's a piece of candy.
ANSWER: Thank you, suh. Thank you, suh. Thank you, suh.

Behind the finished newspapers done by these students lay a great effort of discipline and planning. I chose as editors two students who were super achievers, people who were rarely absent from school. I let them know their responsibilities. They were to assign articles, editorials, commentaries, artwork, want ads, and other tasks to the other students. Usually the "reporters" selected their own topics from those suggested by the teacher, but this was a newspaper. It had to go together and focus. It couldn't be the outcome of the whims of a group of students. It couldn't repeat itself in its articles.

The student editors had hounded their staff to meet deadlines. They saw that reporters met in editing groups to check the articles for content, shape, and correctness. The editors helped me lay out the dummy sheets, write headlines, and make up the final version of the paper.

The reporters read from assigned readings or materials in the library in order to get their "stories." At the bottom of their reports they had to list the sources they had used, although those "footnotes" would not appear in the newspaper. They wrote in ink and double-spaced all articles so they could be easily revised. They agreed to revise all their articles when asked to do so by the editor or teacher. When they were finished with an article, they read it aloud to the class for responses. Not only was their work published in printed form but during its creation they made it public to their peers. They didn't simply hand it in to me and get it back with corrections and a grade. For some of the students, reading their work revealed to them as well as their peers their weaknesses as readers and writers. It was test of fire. The writing was headed toward publication. Reading aloud early drafts of reports generated other topics in the minds of the listeners, and excitement about the project rose.

When the students worked on a newspaper, they read primary sources, the original words of participants in the now "historical" events they were studying. Often those documents were written in highly formal style, but I asked them to write their reports in fresh, vivid prose. In producing newspapers written in the pre–Civil War period, for certain articles they had to imagine what Black dialect of the period might have been. They are not experts in language but they took on different voices far in the past, which allowed them to show that most slaves were uneducated and yet not stupid. Their newspaper articles carry the freshness that I asked for. For example, for the *North Star* for April 12, 1861, one student created this article:

MURDER BY SPIDERS

Boston, Mass. March 1, 1860. The following interview came to us from a reporter who just interviewed a woman who escaped from bondage in the state of Tennessee.

REPORTER: What is your name?
ANSWER: Tanga.
REPORTER: Are you a slave?
ANSWER: No, I escaped.
REPORTER: How did you get free?

ANSWER: I killed my massa.

REPORTER: How did you kill him?

ANSWER: I put some spiders in his buttermilk. Then I took that there whip and I hit him, and I hit him, over and over.

REPORTER: Why did you kill your master?

ANSWER: He got me pregnant and he killed my young'un and he beat me everyday. One day my massa even bedded my little brudder.

REPORTER: How many brothers do you have?

ANSWER: Lord know! My daddy split up; my mamma split up. Ain't no telling how many kids they have. . . .

In the same issue an editorial begins with entirely different language: "We the people of the North don't want to disparage the South with words. All we want to do is to state the facts. . . . " Another article is written again in dialect:

SECRET TESTIMONY
by: Prosser

The following is an excerpt from a long unpublished interview with Gabriel Prosser before he was executed for conspiring to free slaves in Virginia.

I's a very religious man and don't think my people shall be held in bondage any mo'.

I's guess bein' a religious man I's can see visions and dreams. I dreams bout my peoples one night. I dreams I see my people on top of a hill. Round dem at da' bottom of dat very hill is wader and overseers is in da wader with guns, shouting "Work, Niggras, work." I's would somehow get close 'nuff to see dem, soon as I's try to do somethin', they'd see me and come after me. I's start makin' tracks. I's be really runnin' and all of a sudden there would be a cannon in da bush and I's blow 'em all away. I'd wake up shoutin' "my peoples is free; my peoples is free!"

According to proficiency tests, a good number of the learners in my classes read far below their grade level and many of them have done little writing in school or elsewhere, but in the newspaper project I ask them to deal with sophisticated problems of language. They have their difficulties doing that, as any of us would, but they are becoming aware of subtleties of language because they have a reason for making up someone else's language. And behind and beyond this classroom task they are remembering they are Blacks, members of a minority in White America. This is fun, this newspaper project, but it's connected to their reality.

My students have been taught Standard English since Day One when they entered school, but many of them still haven't mastered it. Especially the verb endings and spelling. They have to learn Standard English if they're going to apply for a job, if they're going to go off to college, if they're going into technical school, if they're going to write a business letter.

In U.S. history, I taught a group of kids who had low skills scores and had them write about what it was like being black in the South during the 1920s and 1930s. I said, "I want you to imagine yourself back about thirty years ago where there's a beautiful park with a beautiful swimming pool and it's a summer afternoon and you want to go swimming. Write a letter to a friend telling why you can't use your community swimming pool." I told them to be as expressive as possible. "And if you use black dialect, go ahead and write it." Some of the papers were really good.

One or two of my students in a class will get annoyed and say, "Why do we always have to have black this or black that?' I understand where they are coming from, but I also feel that for some of our students the more information they have of the black experience the better off they are. On the final examination in Government I gave them two court cases to analyze, one was *Dick Gregory* vs. *Chicago,* where he and his followers went into Cicero after picketing in front of Mayor Daley's house in Chicago and were arrested for disturbing the peace. A group of white spectators came by with rocks. I gave my students some tests on the First Amendment, the clear and present danger time, and the Eighth and Fourteenth Amendments, and one girl wrote on her paper, "I get annoyed reading about blacks," and I said, "You can't get this annoyed. This is part of reality." But most students enjoy the units dealing with blacks, and too often they aren't given enough about black history. Many of them don't get it at home. Many of our Oakland teachers complain that in the South there's more black history incorporated into the school work and parents are more knowledgeable about black history there.

I also asked students to produce newspapers in the World History class—*The Roman Forum* and *The New Roman Times.* Two girls, the Prosser twins, decided to do articles on the life of a country girl and a city slicker. They did them on their own, using some imagination. I had some books they were able to use, they went to them, and wrote up their own accounts. I wanted every student to write three articles, and most kids did that. For *The Roman Forum,* one girl wrote a gossip column:

ROMAN WHISPERS

Alexandria.
   Did you know Cleopatra is King Ptolemy's wife and sister? Isn't this a remarkable situation: two young people, brother and sister as well as husband and wife. In addition they both hate each other. Each is eager to kill the other so the survivor can rule alone in Egypt.

Ptolemy's chamberlain Pathinius is arranging for Cleopatra to be expelled from the royal palace where she has lived all her life. You'll never guess why!!! Ptol and Pathi feel that Cleo thinks too much for herself!!! . . .

Here's one of my students summarizing the fall of the Roman Empire in the West in language that belongs to him, that suggests he has made this material his:

STEP-BY-STEP DECLINE

For those of you who wonder what has become of the Roman Empire in the West, I have summarized the events leading to the present disaster.

With the end of the Pax Romana in the year 180, our empire was taken over by soldier-emperors. Within the next one hundred years there were twenty-nine emperors. Most were murdered by the army or rivals. It got to the point where the office of emperor was sold to the highest bidder. For fifty years constant civil wars were fought for the throne. In 270 A.D. Aurelian was able to restore order to the empire. . . .

I also had students do a number of I-Search papers—a form of searching that goes beyond library sources. To publish them, we got support from the Marcus A. Foster Educational Institute to reproduce papers written in his American Government class. The institute was dedicated to perpetuate the ideas of Foster, who was killed by members of the Symbionese Liberation Army in 1973.

One girl, Sharee Embry, wanted to understand the arguments for and against abortion, so she talked to people at the Oakland Mormon Temple and to a Catholic supporter of the Pro-Choice Movement. Here's part of what she wrote in her I-Search paper:

I gave myself a tour of the Oakland Mormon Temple grounds. I felt like I was the prey being stalked in the jungle, the only one of my kind as far as the eye could see. The view from the mountain top was spectacular as I walked through the beautiful garden of multicolored flowers and water fountains, trying to dodge the eyes of everyone in the parking lot and find my way safely to the visitors center and await my interview. Relief echoed throughout my entire body as I saw the road that lead to my destination. Being an hour early and since he wasn't there, I bought a few post cards and listened to two movies which explained to me how and why the Mormon belief started. . . .

Here are excerpts from her interview with an official of the church:

Could you tell me some of the issues of Pro-Life?
O.K. Well, we definitely don't approve of abortion. We think that to destroy a fetus is really destroying another human being and therefore we

think abortion is a pretty religious issue. Therefore, we don't approve of it.

What about in cases of incest or rape?

Of course there are some exceptions to everything. We think that each case would have to be studied. Abortion, is proper, we think in the early stages of pregnancy if the health or welfare of the mother is seriously going to be challenged or threatened, and I would think that as soon as you know of the pregnancy take care of it if there has been rape or incest. . . .

What advice would you give a teenager who wanted to keep her baby but knew she couldn't support it?

Well, knowing that every case is different, you'd have to examine the family stand point and the support of siblings, having come to this situation, I'd advise her to keep it. Soliciting family help when you can, keep the child. Unless again there are grounds like if the father is unknown. Because sometime in the balance of her life, she'll wonder about that child. I think she could make a way if she makes an effort and isn't promiscuous and having children all the time.

What about a woman who has been informed by the doctors that her baby will be born retarded? What do you think she should do?

Well, if she's planned on running a full term pregnancy, and none of the other grounds we've talked about are present, given chance, I don't think she has the right to terminate a life.

You said she didn't have the right to terminate a life, but it's her baby and her body, doesn't that give her a right? I mean it's her life she'll have to spend in anguish?

It's true. We're involved in the process, but life itself comes from God and again I don't think we have those rights. You take that statement and stretch it to its logical conclusion. You start with the mother, the closest, does she have the right to terminate this baby, then you go a little further to the family do they have the right? Less but some? Extend it beyond that to the community and then to the nation. Where do we decide other people have the right to terminate life?

But, how does Congress or the people for Pro-Life have the right to say you can't terminate your pregnancy? Where does their right come from?

Well, that's a tough issue, not only in our city, but all over the world. We have always been a people who honor life. I think it's only in our modern day discussion that we get caught up or trapped. If you partake in the actions that make li.e you should go through all the way, and I don't agree that the anti people have a good issue. . . .

What is so sinful about pre-marital sex?

We think that is, well our Scriptures tell us that fornication which is really pre-marital sex is a sin of great gravity in the eyes of God, and that He has told us that sin is next to murder in its seriousness before His eyes. He made men and women like they are, but He also perscribed that there is marriage, the way for people to come to The Fountain Of Life and that we are not supposed to give in to all our base appetites. He teaches us to obey the Ten Commandments and other refine teaching comes no where

near permitting sex permisciously. They should only be in the proper
bonds of marriage. . . .

And then this girl searching for an answer about abortion interviewed in her home a Catholic woman employed as a Licensed Visiting
Nurse at a local hospital. After several questions, Sharee asked the
woman:

> *Do you think child abuse will increase if women are forced to keep these un-*
> *wanted children?*
> Yes I do. If a woman has to keep a child she doesn't want, for any
> reason, she'll start to abuse it for any reason. All her life she'll be forced to
> support him and sooner or late she'll forget it and give up. . . .
> *Were you always for abortion?*
> No. When I first entered nursing school, I thought that that was the
> most sinful thing that a woman could do. The fact that a baby was being
> brutely killed just made me sick.
> *What made you change your mind?*
> Well, around nine years ago, after abortions were legalized, my neigh-
> bor's youngest daughter became pregnant. Since she was only thirteen I
> told them that she could have an abortion at the hospital and I'd stick by
> her side the entire way. But, being Catholic they refused and made her
> keep the baby. Because the girl was an anemic, the doctor even suggested
> an abortion, but being stupid they refused. Well, one Sunday while her
> parents went to church, Linda went into labor. She called me and said that
> the pains had started around 3 hours ago and that her parents wasn't
> home and she'd started bleeding. Well, I rushed over there and when I
> opened the door, she was just curled on the floor whimpering. I called the
> ambulance and they arrived quickly. Linda made it to the hospital in time
> to save the baby, but not herself. To this day her parents, still raising their
> grandson, blame themselves, and so do I.
> (At this moment I decided to leave and come back the next day because
> Linda was one of my friends and until this day I didn't know how she'd
> died.) . . .

So there was an I-Search done in that class. I kept the misspellings
and typographical errors to remind readers that correctness is not the
first thing in good writing. This paper shows preparation, persistence,
intelligence, and courage. It's remarkably objective.

Whatever is close to the students, they will get more mileage out of.
Just because it's immediate. I think this is a real key. Prior to discover-
ing and working out a program for students to do I-Search papers, I
found the research papers being written in my class weren't good and
that all I was really teaching them was plagiarism. I remember a classic
case. I taught tenth grade for eight years—World Studies. One kid
decided he wanted to do Buddhism and I said go to it. I suggested he

start with a particular encyclopedia and read all the references to Buddhism. Anything dealing with Buddha. Then when it refers to another volume, read the statements in that. The kid wanted to impress the teacher. So he went to the *Encyclopaedia Britannica*. The child couldn't read, so he looked up Buddhism but instead found Buddhist Art in Korea. So I got this beautifully plagiarized paper on Buddhist Art in Korea. That was the last straw for research papers.

Eventually I went to the Bay Area Writing Project and Mary K. Healy showed us how to get students to do an honest modest research paper and later Jim Gray told me about the I-Search format. So I combined the two, and now my students are searching in ways that count for them and for others.

I usually start I-Search papers in March and I have the students give progress reports to the class in which they have to read their starts to the paper or explain what they're doing. I have to do the same sort of thing when they're putting out newspapers. They need time. Some of them just sit on their duffs. I have to constantly monitor their progress. Sometimes I find they're not doing anything.

Then their first draft is due around the first of May, and the final draft at the end of May. I require them to interview three people. I don't care who they are, but they have to interview three. I had this one kid who was doing a report on the CIA. I said, "Call San Francisco and ask for the CIA office." He told me he had called. "They won't give me any answer." I said, "Well, wait a minute, we'll call together." So I called San Francisco and they said, "Well, we can't provide you with any information but call the CIA office in Washington, D.C., and your student can interview somebody at the Information Office." So after we got the address of the main CIA office, I took the student down to the principal's office and introduced him to the principal and said, "May we have your phone"—this was before 8:00 o'clock when school began—"for this student to call Washington?" And the principal said yes, and then the student refused to do it. He was just too shy and bashful to get on the phone. It really irked me, because many of our students are really competent on the phone in an all-black setting. Once they are in the all-white setting, they're like the fly in the milk, you know. They really get shy and reticent. I try to encourage them to develop poise and confidence in their own abilities, but this kid absolutely refused.

I break the I-Search project down into four steps:

I have them tell me what they know about their subject. In some instances students have a lot of misinformation that sort of justifies the project to them.

Then they describe how they went about gathering their material, how they conducted their interview.

Then they write the actual report and include the notes.

And then they tell what they learned from the entire project.

That girl who wrote on abortion did some preliminary reading on the Pro-Life movement and so she had some objectives. And then she set off on her own. Some students did the reading but never got to the point of doing the interviews. Their papers didn't become as personal or as immediate, and consequently the quality wasn't as good.

I had another student who was writing on McCarthyism. Paul Robeson's son was speaking at the Oakland Museum, so she went there and interviewed him after he gave his talk. She was able to get information that made her paper a great deal stronger than it would have been otherwise.

When a student brings in material like that, the teacher looks at it in a different way from the way he does when the material has all come from books he has read or could read if he wanted to. It's a sharing of information and ideas then. I've only been in the Oakland Mormon Tabernacle once in my life and then I was just sightseeing, but when that girl went in and met with someone from the Pro-Life movement, and then with a Catholic who's Pro-Choice, the paper became more meaningful for me. It really became a discovery paper rather than just something taken from books. The important thing is that information discovered that way is internalized. It's not something memorized and regurgitated for a test. That subject matter will be with the student for life. That's the hardest thing to accomplish as a teacher.

I use role-playing also. It entices students. They regard it as a fun situation. It's the bait, the candy, that gets them to eat the rest of the meal. For example, last month I gave them four cases from American history: *Gideon* vs. *Wainwright; Miranda* vs. *Arizona; Rabinowitz* vs. *U.S.,* the Fourth Amendment, search and seizure; and *Terminello* vs. *Chicago,* which is a First Amendment case. I set them up in teams. They have to argue cases before our Supreme Court—three or four students acting as the court. And then I give them the tests for the Amendments. Go over all the amendments thoroughly. And the judges give the verdicts. One interesting case, a seventeen-year-old black man was convicted of murder in Louisiana and was to be electrocuted. But the electric chair malfunctioned and he survived. His lawyer said "You can't re-execute him because that would be cruel and unusual punishment as well as double jeopardy." And so the students have to decide those two points. That means they have to go back over the Amendments and make certain what they're arguing in the case according to the Constitution. I tell them you have to take this side or that on a particular issue. And if there's time, I usually allow them to argue on the opposite side. It's a great exercise. They have to really marshal their facts because they know what they did when they argued the other side.

I should tell you about the Street Law Foundation. It started out in Washington, D.C., in predominantly inner-city schools. In the Bay Area it operates out of the University of San Francisco. The Foundation provides us with a set of instructions and sends in law students from schools in the Bay Area. They come into our classrooms and teach three days out of five for about two-thirds of a semester. The course is called Street Law. In the unit on Family Law they take up separation, child abuse, divorce, dissolution, communal property and how it can be divided, and then the requirements for getting a marriage license. Some of the students are thinking of getting married, or have already started marriage, and they find out what their legal rights are.

There's another unit in Street Law called Consumer Law. If you buy a product and sign a contract, what are your obligations? your rights? How can you break the contract? Under what circumstances?

Again the kids do a lot of role-playing. The law students come in three times a week and the regular teachers conduct the class the other two days. I use that time for writing assignments, for clarifying what they've found difficult. And then there's Housing Law. Signing a lease. What's involved? How can you break a lease? What happens if the heater isn't working or the water is turned off—through no fault of your own? The students bring in a lot of their own experiences from the community. They'll talk about an aunt or brother or sister who's been involved with something about a rental unit or something they've purchased.

And then there's Criminal Law. Very often the law students and I will arrange to have speakers come in. We've had people from the Rape Crisis switchboard in Berkeley. Some of the boys in my class were very immature on that occasion. But most of the students were interested because they didn't know what it was like to be a rape victim.

Last year Street Law arranged competitions. Each school would have to take a case and prepare both the state's and defense's side. And then about two or three days before the trial, the school would be told which side they would have to take. Then the case was argued down at the local municipal court before an absolutely fabulous young black man, Judge Barranco. I guess he's in his thirties, He's really a nice guy, wonderful with the students. We lost in the first round, but it was a great experience for the kids. Witnesses had to learn their parts. The lawyers had to learn to question witnesses in order to bring out all the information. And they had to be prepared for challenges from the other schools. The competition went all the way up to the state level.

Yesterday I went to an in-service session of the National Writing Project in Berkeley, and a woman from an affluent suburban school was talking about teaching literature. I don't teach literature but I see some applications for my courses. She has students select three books that are tied together by a theme—child-parent relationships, maybe, or Western writing in the United States. The students keep a reading log and when they find something in the book that touches the theme they note that and put down their response to it. Later they look over the log and draw a paper from their notes in it. I could do that in my classes.

For example, I usually have students read Frederick Douglass's *Narrative of My Life*, Howard Fast's *Freedom Road*, Horatio Alger's *Mark the Matchboy*, and if time permits, Upton Sinclair's *The Jungle*. One of the themes I use is success. The American Dream as seen from different points of view is portrayed in all those books. When the students respond with experience from their own lives, they're not only understanding the books better, but they're validating their experience.

I think it's incumbent on education, and especially social science, to teach citizenship. If the students, for example, could understand the Bill of Rights in relationship to their own lives, that would be one of the greatest things the schools could do for any citizen. But I think that school boards' idea of citizenship is often nothing more than good behavior. That is part of it, but that's not voting or becoming involved. We have to prepare students so they can go out and vote, and we have to acquaint them with newspapers so they can understand the issues. There's so much ignorance the students bring with them from home. So many of my students have these preconceived ideas about Ronald Reagan as a bad president. But I want them to be able to substantiate such an opinion with facts from newspapers, television, and radio, or not hold it. They say, "I don't like so-and-so," and I say "Why?" and they say, "I just don't like him." That's no reason. That's not citizenship.

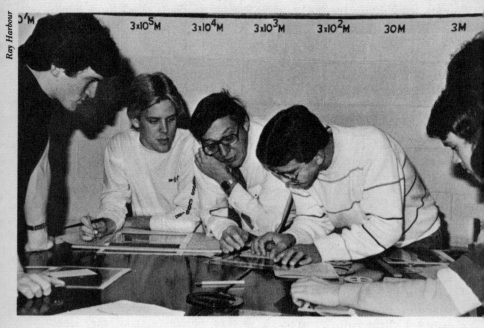

Don Campbell, cheek in hand, studies a learner at work.

14

DON CAMPBELL
Physics, High School

Professor Carl Berger of the College of Education at the University of Michigan had told me there was a good physics teacher at Central High School in Portage, Michigan, a suburban community of 40,000 people. I phoned Don Campbell, and he said he was pleased to be singled out by Professor Berger, but insisted that in his own physics classes he simply did the customary things, took up the usual physics units—"nothing very original."

"Do you lecture?" I asked.

"Oh, no," he said, "I would never do that. I teach physics pretty much as a laboratory course."

I asked what had given him that idea.

I don't know. I guess I've always thought students learned science best in the lab. I try to start from the laboratory and go to the classroom, whenever possible. Let them do some observing, get a functional background to base their theories on. Then take it back to the classroom. That seems to work best for me. We have fifty-five-minute classes that meet five days a week, and my classroom and laboratory are in adjoining rooms, so I can take a group from class to lab or from lab to class. I can structure my teaching time to fit the lesson needs.

I don't think there was any one thing that made me believe in the laboratory approach. It was just the way I perceived physics. You explain the natural universe while you're looking at it. The laboratory is a good place to see what's going on.

In many science courses the kids are supposed to read what to do in the lab manual, do it, and then be graded on the answer. I just talked to a man who in a geology class at a college in Ohio was handed a card with eight rock samples glued to it and was expected to identify them later in a test. He and the rest of the students never looked at the rocks in that area of Ohio in their natural setting and were never asked to think about the geology of the region they had been raised in. This fellow said that he had grown up on the Mississippi River in Illinois, and he had never known much about the place and power of that great river valley except what he had learned from a film called "The River" by Pare Lorentz that was shown in his American history course. In my course the kids walk in on the first day and some are interested and some couldn't care less.

I structure the course around two texts, the PSSC, which was produced by the Physical Science Study Committee for the National Science Foundation course back in 1960, and the texts produced for Project Physics developed by the Harvard Study Committee.

We start the course with the study of Optics. Rather than tell the students what light is, I ask them to observe a number of different phenomena of light. Then, only after they have observed *how* light behaves, is it time to ask the question, "What is light?" One of the nicest things about starting with Optics is that some of the early experiments require simple measurements and the students don't have to use complex equipment. They can focus on their observations. During this phase of the course I introduce such matters as lab reports, graphing, and analysis of the data the students have collected.

I have five sections of physics this year. I'll tell you what I did in class on the first day. I saw the students for just fifteen minutes. I told them what physics is—a way of understanding one's natural universe by codifying five aspects of it. We try to measure length, mass, time, electric fields and magnetic fields.

The next day I told them we were going to start this class out with a movie by Dr. Richard Little of the Massachusetts Institute of Technology, who put it together for the old Physical Science Committee Study Program sponsored by the National Science Foundation. In the film he does some rather simple experiments that would be difficult to perform in the classroom. The students go along with most of these and some of them begin to get caught up in the ideas. Then with the use of the camera he demonstrates refraction. The viewers of the film are placed in a swimming pool, down there underneath the water looking up at the feet of a swimmer hanging over the edge of the pool. When those feet separate from the swimmer, who seems to float in the air above the water, the film is demonstrating internal reflection and refraction. Dr. Little doesn't say what that is right away. Suddenly, my students want to see that part of the film again to check what they're seeing. Then they begin to think about the explanation, and I tell them that as we go along in this course, we're going to look at a lot of phenomena and then try to pull them together and explain them. Dr. Little makes that pitch, too.

While the film is running, I stop it, run it back, and we talk about a point. Very quickly the kids realize they can ask questions, and some of them do. The film, which was meant to be part of the PSSC course, runs for 20 minutes, but we take the whole hour to go through it. The discussion becomes free flowing. Sometimes I initiate it, sometimes they do. When they start to ask, "Why did that happen?" or "What's going on there?" I tell them to remember the question and we'll take a look at it later. Maybe they will be able to answer it themselves. I start off giving students a chance to respond.

Let me illustrate how I work from the lab to the classroom. In the study of the reflection of light, I have students measure the angle of incidence and the angle of reflection and locate where an image forms with a plane mirror. You know that if you stand six feet in front of a mirror, for example, your image looks as if it's coming to you from six feet behind the mirror. Then I introduce a curved, parabolic mirror. When the students are up close to it their image is right side up and enlarged, but when they move away, the image is small and upside down. I demonstrate that if all the incoming light *rays* are parallel, they will be reflected to a point called the *focus*. The focal length is then the distance from the mirror to the focus. Then I have them find this point using sunlight. Now we go into the lab to take some data. Each of the eight lab stations is equipped with some modeling clay to hold the mirror, a long strip of ticker tape paper, a clear filament flashlight bulb, a source of electricity, a 3 × 5 card, and a meter stick. The students are instructed to place the light bulb about one and a half focal lengths from the mirror and to turn on the light bulb. They are to move the 3 × 5 card in the reflected light until an image, the real image of the light bulb, appears on the card.

Visualize a lab filled with twenty-four senior and junior men and women who are used to thinking they're quite sophisticated. Oohs and aahs can be heard all over as they begin to see the real image for the first time. There it is, the picture of the light bulb, right on the card. Move the card and it is just light, but at that point, and only that point, there is the image! They mark both points of the paper and move the light bulb. A new image at a different spot. "Here it is!" someone will say. Until the students have a hands-on experience with reflection, they don't have much real understanding of such a phenomenon.

I try to stay away from the cookbook approach to lab. I give the students some direction and get them started in observing and making measurements. I show them how to analyze the data, which in this case is measurements done in a systematic way. Analyzing the graph they have drawn for their data, they can come up with an equation that will allow them to make predictions about what they're studying.

Next we study refraction and lenses and do the same kind of thing. After they've gathered data and they've looked at a number of different phenomena of light, I start asking the question, "Well, what do you think light is?" The students try to construct a model of what they think it is. In the old days we would have called this a *theory* of light.

I don't tell them what light is. I just let their ideas develop, but I give them something to look at first. The notion is to try to develop a model after they have made enough observations that it will be meaningful to them. They're juniors and seniors. They've read science books. They very quickly come up with "Light is a wave." Some aren't so sure. "What about a particle?" they say. I ask, "If light were a particle, how would it reflect? How can we test this?" And we talk about the bending of light as it passes from one medium to another, the refraction, and they learn that Newton predicted it would be a particle, and that light would travel faster in glass. When measured, light was found to travel more slowly in glass. I take them through the logic used in an experiment to predict what will happen. I show that a model has to be tested some time in history, and must give the correct answer to be valid. This model was not verified. So now, the students were all assured that light was a wave!

Now I go through some wave theory and have the students look at waves. What do waves do? How can you use waves to explain the phenomena we've looked at? Many of them are convinced that light is a wave, but some still like light as a particle. Then I bring out the photoelectric effect and show that here was Albert Einstein looking at light somewhat like a particle again, calling light a *photon*. Students then want to say, "Well, it must be a particle that travels in waves." And they come up with a pretty good model of light. I don't tell them this is right or wrong. They'll find that out later in the course. It's a pretty dirty trick to play on them, perhaps, but it makes them think.

I use some of the Project Physics materials that were done by the Harvard Study Committee. They take a historical approach to science. After we've studied Optics, we take up a unit which asks the question, "Where is the earth in the universe, and how do we think we know where it is?" D. C. Heath and Holt, Rinehart and Winston put out some of the material I use. This starts out with the Greek answer to that question and goes through the work of Ptolemy, Copernicus, Tycho Brahe, Galileo, and Newton. When students look at what these people did, they begin to get the feeling that each person or group stands on the shoulders of the people who have gone before. They find that all the astronomers didn't start out with the correct answers—like Brahe thinking as he worked that Copernicus was absolutely wrong. Yet his own data helped Kepler later show that Copernicus was on the right track! Do you know that I can bring in Carl Sagan to do an entire lecture on Kepler and Brahe for me by using the video tape of the TV program *Cosmos* that we have? The students get the book's slant, my slant, and then Sagan's. They identify with Tycho Brahe closely. He was quite a character, you know. He had a nose made of gold to replace the one he lost in a duel he fought as a young man. Students begin to sense the reality of people who did these studies. I then try to bring them to where we are today, and they take a modern look at the question of where we think we are in the universe.

In school I memorized Kepler's three laws of the universe. I didn't have any idea of how they were applied. Now I ask students to use some of the data from the Project Course that allows them to plot the orbit of Mars from information supplied by Harvard University. From the data, the students make a plot and then try to apply Kepler's law to the orbit they draw. Then the laws begin to make some sense to them. They can see that the orbit of Mars is not a circle. They understand why Kepler had troubles with plotting this orbit, and why we say the orbit is an ellipse.

In the lab I don't assign partners. Students choose them. Sometimes I'll say, "This experiment requires two people. No more than two can work together on it." At times I'll say, "We'll divide the class up in half. Let's just number off." I try to make sure that the same people working together early in the year aren't later always working together. During the last period of time, when we're doing the mass of the electron no more than four students may work on one set of equipment. The group they choose then must remain the same throughout the time period. For other experiments they're free to move from one group to another at their own choosing. So, if students feel they could work better with someone else, they're free to move.

In the study of motion, or *kinematics*, we again start in the lab. To record motion, students use a ticker tape and a simple timer that prints dots on a paper tape. They pull the tape through with their hands. If they pull with a steady motion, the dots are equidistant. If they speed up or slow down, the distance varies. By counting the number of dots they can make three types of graphs from this information. They can study distance versus time, speed versus time, and acceleration versus time. They come to see how distance, speed, and acceleration are related. I don't have them work with formulas at that point. You probably remember as a high-school physics student being told "Speed equals this." "Acceleration equals this." We try to relate this information, and using graphs, solve problems before ever seeing a formula.

There's no other way around learning kinematics but through solving problems. At this point in the course I use what's commonly called a *contract* method. We can't call it that in our district because *contract* is a legal term. So we call it a *project*. The agreement says, "Every student will solve these problems." I list the critical problems every student must do and at the bottom put in some materials they may choose additionally. But the problems in the top part everyone must do. From work in other classes, students are used to turning something in, getting it corrected, and taking their A, B, C, or D. When they turn the problems in, I circle those they have wrong and say, "Now go do this right. If you want the answers, here they are, but I want you to do the problems and come up and tell me how you have done them." I check this in a one-on-one basis and don't accept the work until all the answers are right. For students who've never had that happen before, it's discouraging at first, because they have to go back and correct their own materials or get zero points. They can't get a C or D and accept that. They have to get the problems right. They have to understand the material. It's a hard two weeks for me. The first year I tried it, I swore I would never do it again, but when I tested these students, they tested so much higher than those who weren't asked to do this. I think it's because they've got to hang in there till they get it done. We just keep working at the problems. Some of them do those problems four or five times before they get them right.

"Well, what if my friend helps me?" a student asks me.

I say, "O.K., as long as you know how to do it."

"Isn't that cheating?"

"No, I don't care if you stand on your head if that's how you learn how to do them, as long as you get them right." It takes some convincing for some of them to see that they can learn to solve this type of problem. I may go overboard against the conventional notion of making each student work entirely on his or her own. I say, "If your friend knows how and can teach you, that's great. That means there's more teachers in the room helping us." There are problems on the student choice part of the project statement that challenge the better students. They struggle with these and sometimes decide, "If we organize this work, we can learn to do all of these problems." And then they help each other. In each section I have about twenty-three to twenty-eight students, and I have five sections.

I've been trying to figure out why I emphasize the laboratory so much in my teaching, and that question has taken me way back in my memory. I was born in 1934, right at the end of the Depression and grew up in a lumber camp in the Upper Peninsula of Michigan. If you go from the Two-Hearted River west about sixty-five or seventy miles, you come to a little town called Munising. We lived fifteen miles away. The Pictured Rocks are there. Back in the country. We were UPanites. Some of my teachers were deplorable. We studied physics the way you talked about it. My math teacher was extremely limited in her ability. I didn't know that at the time, but I sure learned that later. In the service I ran into some very good people who were instructors in the Air Force, very well educated. I was an instructor and taught math to basic trainees. I was one of the few people in the section who had had only a year of college. That was at the end of the Korean war. Those instructors really knew what they were about. And they've done some fabulous things since they've left the service.

My father-in-law was a big influence on me. He was also my early music teacher, in the high-school band, long before I dated the woman who became my wife. He taught me by example to respect people. Quite a few of the students he had are now teachers.

I did my schooling up at Northern Michigan University. In those days it was a smaller school, and some of those teachers went out of their way for me. One of the nicest things that happened was that I volunteered to wash bottles—for pay, of course—for a chemistry professor, Dr. Hunt. He needed a lab assistant, so I became a bottle washer and stocker of chemicals in my freshman year. I wasn't a great chemist—although I teach chemistry as well as physics—but I learned how to take care of a chemistry lab. I went into the U.S. Air Force for four years and when I came back Professor Hunt caught me walking down the hall and said, "Where did you put those ignition tubes?" I went in the lab and they were right where I had put them. And he said, "You want your job back?" I was married and we had two children at the time, so I said, "Sure." and I worked for him for three years more as a laboratory assistant. I was coming back from the service and he put me in a freshman chemistry lab as a helper and I had to relearn all my chemistry. I had taught in the service and I knew a bit about teaching, but that helped me see how to work in a lab with those college freshmen. I began to know when to ask a question of a student and when to answer one. I learned to have the chemicals and equipment ready when they were needed.

In lab sessions you give students enough information so they can make some decisions on their own and try some things, and then you can ask them some questions that lead but don't give answers. Let them work things out for themselves whenever possible. Nine sets of students working on a problem get a straight line and the tenth set gets a curved line. Is the curved line wrong? I never deal with it as if it's wrong. Their "wrong" answer is a point of departure—to find out what happened there. If the technique was wrong, then we'll deal with that. But maybe they were the ones who found the thing that's right. I tell students about some of my own experience in research. For example, about the time when I was working in a summer institute and was checking a Geiger tube. Everyone knows that the Geiger tube calibration curve goes out in plateaus and then the line turns and goes up. Well, mine ran up, plateaued, and came down. I reported it in class as a coming down, and everybody laughed. I challenged them to test it in the lab. When they did that they found the line graph for my tube went down instead of up. It didn't go up as they had plotted it. The thing was that they hadn't followed the matter through to the end. They didn't know these tubes had a flaw. In my own classes at a moment like that I point out that sometimes in nature you think that something is supposed to work one way, but it doesn't. I tell them, *"You report what you find out,* not what you think it should be. If someone else said it was ten and when you measured it you found twenty, put twenty down, and we'll find out later whether it was right or wrong. Then we'll deal with that."

But if you take that attitude as a teacher, you have to be willing to accept what the students observe as worthwhile information, and grade them accordingly. Don't knock them down because they didn't get the preconceived answer. I don't grade my labs that way. If students have something different in their lab from the others and interpret it according to the data they have, their data may be wrong and the interpretation right. If so, they get credit.

The physical action has a lot to do with learning. In the study of kinematics, kids in my lab may feel they're not capable of graphing motion, but to go into the lab and pull the tape that prints dots and registers motion is a fun thing to do. Everybody's doing it and having a good time, and the reluctant ones get right in there and do it, too. I've never had a kid block at that.

And then, what student isn't interested in how his or her car goes down the road—speeding up or slowing down? You have to relate the motion studies to the real world. When I step on the gas, what's going on in my car? They can relate that back to the tape moving. And then they get excited. Once one of my students got a ticket for speeding and went down to the police station to find out how his speed was measured with Vascar, which the police were using at the time. Then he invited the policeman—checking with me first and the school—to our classroom. This was back in the early seventies when the policemen were called "pigs," as you know. This fellow came into the classroom, a nice, personable young man, and did a bangup job. He convinced the kids that he was an all right kind of guy, that policemen were human beings. He discussed how radar worked and how Vascar worked, and we went to the front of the school building where his traffic car was. We monitored traffic for a while. The policeman could look and see who the driver was in a car and tell us what that driver was going to do. He was right almost every time. Good experience for the kids. The policeman took us through one driver. "When this person gets down the hill, she's going to step it up to 45 or 50." And boy! she did it! He did that again and again. We'd say, "How do you know that?" He said, "That's just the way people act. She thinks she's out of my radar range."

Occasionally my students do physics projects on their own. In the kinematics project I encourage them to do outside experimentation on that part of the assignment where they have choices. One is to use the information to make some measurements or build a cell. We give them a number of options. Some kids might take equipment home and measure the toy racing cars on their model trains. There have been a few students who carried on an experiment over periods of time. One boy who had taken physics from me took the electricity course and we found some independent study time for him. He did some digital electronics. I said, "We need to build a timer that will turn on when an object goes through a starting gate and turn off when the object goes through the second gate. Do you think you could do that?" "Sure," he said. I wasn't sure, but he was, and did it. He's a sophomore or junior at the University of Michigan now and he came back to school and wrote me out the manual this spring so we could use the timer he was able to get together for us. He finished it after he had left our school. Those cases are rare when someone does something like that, but I guess you can say we have an open enough curriculum that we can allow some of that kind of thing to take place that's beyond the regular physics class.

Some kids who are blocked on math and science soon find them boring because they never had any good experiences with them in school. For them the work of physics can be frightening. But things can be done to lessen those feelings. For example, I try to gauge what is the right time for things. When students need to make the graph, that's the time we start stressing how to make one. When they have to analyze a graph, that's the time we stress how to analyze one. By this time in the year, right now, about six weeks from the end, we are doing an experiment where they calibrate the field strength of a coil in fundamental units. They measure the magnetic field strength, then make a graph of it, and plot the field strength versus the current through the coil. Very few students were having any problems yet with that. Then on Friday, they started to measure the mass of an electron and refer that to the graph they had made of the magnetic field strength of the coil. We had a nice big equation on the board and I asked them, "If I had put that on the board early in the course and asked how many of you would try it, what would you have done?" Most of the students said, "I would have walked out." But by the end of the year they can handle it pretty well and they begin to realize that. When they can actually do what's being asked of them—and it's quite sophisticated—they're proud of it.

I think there's enough inherent joy in physics—to open doors of understanding that haven't been there before. It's fun to see the kids stand back and look at the world from an entirely different perspective, so they see something they haven't seen before. It's kind of like looking at a painting you've seen a hundred times and somebody points out a piece in that painting that's beautiful that you've missed. A brand new idea to you.

And then there's always the pull that comes from taking up things that are part of the students' daily lives. When we're talking about momentum and energy, we use the automobile a lot as a frame of reference. We talk about what happens in accidents. Why a seat belt is important. We calculate the forces on a person wearing a seat belt during an accident. We do some supposing, a thought experiment, and get some data and make a problem based on that. We talk about a skier landing on a tree, and what happens in that interaction—what the forces are. The kids can sure see why their bones get broken in accidents. We do those kinds of things as well as just study a particle flying down a table and hitting another particle.

In one of the very minor experiments we do a study of electricity, series in parallel resistances. In the lab, we study how lights are wired in a house. It's very practical kind of thing. We can calculate power in terms of watts and watt hours. We work with appliances the kids use and calculate how much it costs to run each one. They can figure out that very quickly. When a parent says, "You know the stereo is on and it costs us a lot of money to run it," the kid can point out—without being smarty, I hope—that "The stereo is costing a half cent or two cents an hour to run, but that other machine downstairs that's running is costing us quite a bit." They look at air conditioners, refrigerators, stoves, and such things. They soon learn that turning off lights means saving a few dollars. The parents react very favorably to that project. The students can take an electric bill and figure how much an appliance costs to operate per hour by reading the little plate on the back of the device.

I recall one young man having a real bad time with his stepmother because he was doing an experiment and she was complaining about the electricity bill and he didn't think it was costing that much. When the boy told me about that we sat down in my office and figured out that the cost was about $10 or $11 a month. He was shocked that it was that much and went home and told his stepmother he would be willing to give her that much toward the electric bill. And that cleared up the problem in that home. He got a little insight into her problem. I think she saw his problem, too.

One thing that impressed me with this age group of kids—maybe it's because they're suburban kids, I don't know—is that some of them don't even know how water gets heated in their house. That's something Dad takes care of. I have about 50 percent girls in my classes. Sometimes they haven't bothered to ask anyone about things like that. Through physics they start asking questions and get a little more control over their environment.

We talk about these practical things a lot, but all the time we're walking the students through the different areas of physics and at the end of the year we do some nuclear physics to wind up the course. It reviews everything we've been doing. At that point most of them can see that this is a study that man has worked his way through. That's the main thing.

Today is May First. School will be over in six weeks, but I'm not yearning for that. We've got a lot of stuff to do. We're just getting into atomic and nuclear energy. We're going to have a lot to get done in that section. Right now, these things interact with the students' lives. Whenever you talk about nuclear physics, you're touching what's being done in the world today, what decisions are being made about nuclear power or disarmament. I'm going to ask the students to bring in clippings from the newspaper for the magnetic blackboard I have. Do that for four weeks or so. See what's in the paper about the topic we're studying. Just to see what happens. I did that with energy once. The six weeks I chose turned out to be when the Arabs shut off the oil. We had that blackboard filled up each day. We made a scrapbook. The group must have had twenty-five to thirty pages on 2×3 feet cardboard covered with nothing but articles out of the newspaper. That year they got the idea that energy was really important.

But in the long run, it's not the material or current events that count the most. It's the students. One year I was working with this boy who had been a D student all the way through. I could hardly keep him in his seat. He was just a rascally boy. He never stepped over the line completely, but he was a thorn in my side all year long. In the lab he would always do something offbeat. By the end of the year he was coming along in his work O.K. I didn't see him after that for two or three years. Then one day here was this young man coming down the hallway dressed in a smart business suit, and lo and behold, it was that fellow. I said, "Well, what have you been doing?" and he said, "I've been in the Marines and I came back to thank you."

I said, "What for?" because I thought I'd never taught that boy any science.

And he said, "It's not for the science. It's because but you taught me to be honest and to say what I observed. That was really important to me."

I'll carry that with me forever.

Marcia Umland, teaching in England, reads to one and many.

15

MARCIA UMLAND
Writing, Elementary School

On July 10, 1979, in a room in Tolman Hall at the University of California, Berkeley, Jim Gray from a back corner seat watched his teacher-students in the Bay Area Writing Project (now the National Writing Project) present ideas and methods that worked for their students in classrooms. The first "presenter" announced herself as Marcia Umland of Vista School in Albany, California, and stood nervously before the tables around which we were all seated. She began talking about enabling first and second graders to write things that matter to them in school, where ordinarily they do no more than copy what the teacher puts on the board, practice spelling, and compose sentences like "Tomorrow will be Thanksgiving Day. On the first Thanksgiving Day the Pilgrims and the Indians ate dinner together."

Marcia is strong-looking woman—lean, olive-complexioned, with black hair and an aquiline nose, but there was an uncertainty about her first sentences and stance. She said, "One of the kids reported that her locker door was off its hinges. I said, 'Write a note to the janitor, why don't you?' After school the janitor found this note: 'Dear Tom, pleze fix this lokr door.' "

Marcia said that one of the reasons kids don't learn to write is that in classrooms writing isn't used for communication, and she went on talking and showing us the writing of her students until I wanted to hear her talk for a week; but as a visitor, I had to catch a plane. Later I wrote her and arranged a meeting on Thanksgiving morning in San Francisco.

When we sat down in a bed-sitting room at the St. Francis, where below us in larger rooms hundreds of others were meeting at the annual conference of the National Council of Teachers of English, Marcia began to talk with none of the diffidence she had shown before her peers in Tolman Hall.

I was born on October 28, 1942, in Washington, D.C., where we were living because my father was in the service. I don't know exactly what he was doing there. We lived in Washington only six months. We moved a lot, New York, Virginia, Southern California, Nebraska—six months here, six months there. I remember Father studied at Cornell to become an entomologist, so Mother did secretarial work there. Dad was the first in his family to go to college. His father died when he was a teenager. A lot of pride revolved around his Ph.D. from Cornell University both before and after he got it. He finished school when I was in the first grade. I felt his pride in me when I gained academic and leadership recognition in college. I was not expected to do well in college. It was pleasing to surprise everyone, but most of all, my father.

By the time I was in eighth grade I had been in eight schools. I remember being new all the time. I made a very poor adjustment at first up in New York. But for three years we lived in a tiny town in Virginia called Holland, where I went to second, third, and fourth grade. I was very shy. I remember the teachers. On the first day there a girl brought me an ice cream bar, and across the classroom sat an Indian boy. We eyed each other a lot. I felt an identity with him because I had been mistaken for an Indian myself. I even made a close friend, Elizabeth Ann Felton—I don't remember whether she spelled *Ann* with or without an "e"—I think she became a minister. I remember going to her farm and loving her family. They seemed so stable.

In Virginia I wrote a sentimental story. It was the first time a teacher paid attention to me. She told me she wanted me to read it at the PTA meeting. I was very shy, but I did it. As I began reading the paper aloud I got caught up in it and read it well. It was called "The Littlest Star in the Milky Way." It started out something like this. It would soon be Christmas Eve. Christ was about to be born on earth. The heavens were bustling with sounds and activity. The angels were busy practicing their carols. The stars were all very excited, for that night the largest, shiniest and most beautiful would be chosen to be the star of Bethlehem. Over in a corner of the Milky Way the littlest star began to polish and shine some of the bigger stars. Although he was a little sad that he would not appear before God for the selecting of the Star of Bethlehem, he was glad he could help in some way to get ready for Jesus (I said it was a sentimental story but I guess *sweet* would be a better word.) The little star was working on polishing the other stars. And a message came from God to join the group. God had decided the little star would be the halo for Jesus. I guess that was the most religious time of my life. And that was in Virginia before the church-school separation was made clear.

What was literature for me at the time? I remember *The Littlest Angel* was popular. In preschool days I liked a story about a lost penny, which kept falling out of the pockets of six different children, and one about kittens. Albert Payson Terhune intrigued me with his stories about dogs. But it was *Understood Betsy* which meant the most to me. Her aunts had started taking care of her—she was a very fearful child—and she had to leave them and live with distant relatives who didn't understand a child afraid of animals. They were very warm people who felt that life is life and we're going to live it. They asked her to do jobs and she learned to do them. At the end of the story she's changed and helps the aunts when they visit her at the home of her new family. The aunts were clearly the fearful sickly ones projecting this onto the child. A child helping grownups to understand grown-up things—that impressed me.

In my family I felt trapped because of all the moving. My parents didn't often bring other people into our home, so Betsy was a good model for me. I was a mystery child to my parents. Did a lot of taking care of my brothers, the one, a year and a half younger than I, and the other, ten years younger. I liked the idea of taking care of my brothers. I wasn't shy with younger people as I was with my peers. When my brother was four I built a rocket ship for him and trained a dog to jump in our wagon and my brother would pull him. I found my little brother entertaining. I didn't have a heavy peer group thing going.

Our family was an isolated unit, but in college, when I moved away, things changed. I majored in elementary education and was encouraged. While I was getting my high-school diploma, Mother was getting her teaching degree. And while I was in college she taught six years of elementary school. I remember making bulletin boards or display things for her classes. I was considered non-musical but artistic. I drew a lot. The greeting cards I made for relatives pleased my family. I was much appreciated by both my parents—when I was in a place to be noticed and feeling open enough to respond to them. I was a daughter in the sixties. I was encouraged to become a nurturing person. I'm not married now but have boys ten and twelve. I think of being ten—saw my outgoing younger boy the other day coming home from school. The girls have found him and he was arm-in-arm with two girls, the three of them dancing and skipping down the walk toward home.

Mother read a lot, played word games, enjoyed puns, was a stickler for grammar. She was a "look-it-up-in-the-dictionary" person. My younger brother was very verbal. He'd invent expressions, "Freddy-isms," we called them. One that we all adopted was "Whobody at the door?" Of course, all children invent language like this. When people laugh at them and correct them, that unique English disappears. The response of adults influences whether children will continue to be fascinated with language or simply accept it as it is given to them. When we were kids we wrote letters to grandparents, not just thank-you notes at Christmas, but telling about what we had been doing. We were expected to write.

I taught in public schools in Southern California for a few years, had my own children, tutored and subbed, taught full time in the pre-primary program in Richmond, dropped out to set up a day-care nursery school—child care was both a personal and professional concern of mine. Three years later I burned out doing that.

I subbed and worked various jobs while madly seeking to get back into public schools. I taught in a beautiful private school and continued vacation time jobs and job hunting, then began teaching in Albany, where I am now.

In the day-care center I served children from two through ten, full and part-time. I liked the cross-age educational opportunities, the intimate, creative atmosphere, and the feeling of being self-employed and meeting important social problems head-on. I had the children of clowns, dancers, filmmakers, professors, students, waitresses, editors, writers, researchers, and craftspeople. In my home I watched and helped them grow in their formative years and was helped myself by this diverse community of parents who chose me and my methods, avoiding the institutional barriers between teachers and parents which so affect children and education.

I devised and collected materials I thought appropriate—I was influenced by Montessori and Sylvia Ashton Warner—and scheduled the day to include instructional time for both the group and individuals. Each day I wrote a newspaper and I also had an album of pictures which included captions. Most of the children were too young to read or write but they made attempts and pretended they were reading and writing.

The group was multi-racial and included a deaf girl I knew when I had subbed for six months in a class of aurally handicapped children. Della made a lot of odd sounds which were indeed words and recognizable after you got used to them. But the hearing children—though they gradually began to understand both her oral and sign language to a limited degree—were more intrigued with mimicking her, as if it were a game. Gradually, they all, including Della, discriminated between talking and making noises for fun. Della's pet sound for fun was a rapid "Duh, duh, duh," one of the first sounds she probably learned to make, considering her first name.

All the children learned some sign language and we sang songs using actions or AMSLAN (American Sign Language). I still use some sign in the classroom, though I've forgotten much of the little I knew. It's an extraordinarily expressive language, which for me has revealed the limitations of oral language. For example, think of the poetry of a literally superimposed or overlapping message uttered with the hands. Think of the convenience of being able to communicate in a crowded room or over distances without shouting. With a few simple signs I'm able to tell someone to sit down or to go ahead without interrupting myself or others. I recently talked to a very busy and successful gynecologist who, with an interpreter, had given a one-hour talk to a deaf audience and ended up staying two more hours for the question period because his audience was so responsive and direct. That's another characteristic of signing people. They haven't much use for our -isms and -ibles because their language is so inherently graphic and explicit.

In the day-care class I posted a sheet of paper on the door to the room, and the kids would tell me their news and I wrote it there. We added what had been done during the day. I could bring the parents to the sheet and show them what we had done. Little kids don't have any time framework. They bring up two-months-ago happenings as if they happened today, so this sheet helped them order things in their lives. Pictures and writing both. When we ate our oranges and smiled, we all looked like oranges and they drew themselves. I wrote on the paper for them. They could only write their names.

At home I have a photograph of a child on my lap. A new child came to the school and as soon as his father left, he ran out the door after him because he was so upset that his father hadn't said goodbye. This happened when a reporter was visiting the school. I took the boy on my lap and said, "Let's write a letter to your father." He said the words to me, what had bothered him, and I wrote it. Rather than trying to talk him out of the fear, I got him to describe it.

In second and third grade when I write notes to parents, I read as I'm writing, with the kids standing next to me. The kids don't like the mystery of people writing things about them without knowing what it is. Whenever I write about kids, I let them know what I'm writing. "What should I tell the principal about your behavior? Weren't you the one who kicked five people and bit four?" "Oh, no!" Then they tell what really happened without all the self-justification. The principal at our school is good, can be trusted. They're aware he'll be fair when they go to see him. But when I talk to them first, by the time they get to see the principal and are confronted with his question, "What's another way to solve the problem you had?" they're prepared to think about that. Sometimes when two kids complain to me about each other and have different stories, I say, "Go outside in the hall, talk to each other, figure out how it could have been done differently, and come back and tell me." Generally kids don't have a great animosity toward each other. They just lose the sense of themselves and the alternatives to a violent reaction. They're always expecting me to see who's at fault when I don't witness an incident. I won't do that. I tell them I'm not writing things down to make a judgment, but to get their versions of what happened.

So much teaching of writing in elementary school is simply an avenue to teaching the days of the week, or copying off the board, answering questions on dittoes in complete sentences, and in third grade, a little bit of book reporting that's very directive. Teachers ask, "What would happen if you were small enough to fit in a teacup?" That kind of lead works only with a few children, and generally the ones who could and would write on anything. Another problem I've run into is the spelling hang-up of writing in school. That affects a substantial minority of potentially fluent child writers. Kids are always asking questions. They come in from other classes and line up at my desk and ask, "How do you spell this?" They want an answer and then they're satisfied. I gave out boxes of words written on slips of paper for the kids to invent things with, and that didn't work. It seemed to some like such an enormous task to write a sentence. I typed words at the top of the blank sheets of paper for them to use in writing something. But I prefer getting kids to brainstorm themselves to get words they might use.

After I had taught for a while I realized that even the poorest student can make a word I can read. They don't have to have the words perfect before I can figure out what they're saying. I can read them if they're misspelled. I use a spelling program based on word families and four to six levels of grouping students. It is with a dictated test that I've found my way of getting children to learn from errors within a context. By correcting all spelling, mechanical, and neatness problems on their returned tests, my students are learning both the value and use of conventions. At first nearly everyone has many marks on their test papers. I never mark their own compositions. But by March, perfect papers are gloated over frequently, and I begin to see some carry-over in their own compositions. I've completely eliminated word lists and generally don't supply spelling, responding to those who ask, "Spell it the best you can," or "Where do you think find out?" The whole room becomes a resource—bulletin boards, globes, maps, other children, books, a variety of dictionaries—because they often can find a word faster where they remember seeing it before.

I've always been influenced by students. They surprise me and I tuck that surprising information away and use it later. I had a first grader who could write. He brought things into class that he had written at home. I saw I was holding students back from their own ability.

I think of my own children growing up. I once taught a preschool equivalent of Head Start. Watching really little kids trying to write out words—they leave out vowels all the time. I found it was more important that they were trying. When they had built a block structure that at the end of the day was important to them, and yet it had to be taken down, I would draw a picture of it and say, "So and so's built this wonderful structure on————(a certain day)." And we'd keep that picture. When I began using their own words in making such records, that made a difference. Not "Joe and Terry built this *tower*"—which would be *my* word, but "Joe and Terry built this *hotel*," which was *their* word.

I've not always been very organized. I hated school as a kid. I never admired teachers except a couple of real experimenters I had. But in college in the sixties things began to change for me. I was in the YWCA—not just the organization. You know then it was a movement. We dealt with social issues in our own lives. In class when I was majoring in elementary education every course seemed to spend six weeks trying to define what a child is. I already knew—from working with my little brother. This was intellectualizing what I knew, by people who had lost touch with children. I was bored. The idea was to devise lessons that were foolproof and tight. An attractive bulletin board was really something super.

At the University of Nebraska in Lincoln, I became very active on campus, and I elected to take an ethics course from Professor Jere Jones. He was colorful in those pre-hippy days. He had recently married a woman, with two kids, who was a former student of his in Colorado. He always had an unlit stub of a cigar in his mouth and wore beat-up, paint-spattered boots in class. He was from Arkansas and somehow talked fast with a drawl. He asked a lot of important questions about values, stood right in front of you and asked them so you felt they counted. Some students found him too strong, but he was right for me. I remember the final exam question had some philosophers like Descartes, Spinoza, and some characters from Robert Penn Warren's *All the King's Men* sitting around a table in some purgatory. The world has just blown up—human causes. One person says, "How did this happen?" Our task as students was to finish the conversation in two and a half hours of exam time.

Jones asked me to be his reader assistant. "There is one other girl," he said, "I don't know why all my best students this year are female. She has as much intuition about what I'm trying to teach as you do, but I decided on you because you seem more articulate. You can put it in words better, and therefore will be able to write better remarks on student papers." And that is what I did. Twice a week I picked up a stack of papers and responded to them. I didn't grade them. He had a little three-point scale. I was to give these short papers a zero, plus, or minus, but had to respond with a few written comments on most of them. I learned a lot about writing and teaching from this. The ironic thing was that as an elementary ed major I was almost prevented from taking a philosophy class because my advisor thought it might adversely affect my grades. They tried to convince me to take first aid because that counted as an academic elective and was "what many of our students do."

Teaching in elementary school can be isolating. A teacher can always do badly—just assign things and get the kids to say them back and then make a good presentation when the principal visits the room. When I wanted to spend all that time with those little people in class, I found that the intimacy I had shared with my peers in college in the sixties was carried over into my classroom. I cared about the students and couldn't stand to sit in the teachers' lounge where they were gossiping about their students. I was happy to switch schools frequently so I wouldn't have to become close to such teachers. I felt so protective and connected that I couldn't stand to see my students change grades and move into someone else's hands. It's egotistical, I know. When you see the worst kids changing—that doesn't happen until April and May often—then you can't stand to leave them. And you think of what kids have to put up with in school. One in third grade, the son of a friend—I'll call him John—was taking a math test in which the problem was to "Name these coins." He wanted to play *Willing to Suffer,* but the temptation was too much, and he wrote down, "Tom, Joe, Dicky, Harry." He said he had to spend the next recess doing it over. It's easy to forget your sense of humor as a teacher, but I have a feeling that innumerable little incidents like that one, if handled with a sense of humor, encourage a sense of word play, which is so often born young. And it can be done without diminishing the importance of taking tests or behaving appropriately. Reading and writing are not areas where John has found success in school though he and his mother have a great knack for storytelling, conversation, and humor. She's a lawyer and writes well, but John is struggling with writing in high school. He's beginning to learn what he should have been helped to learn long ago.

I try to teach practical writing. When something's wrong in the room, I get the kids to write about it. One girl says, "I have to call my mom because she has my lunch money." And I say, "Write a note for the school secretary explaining the matter so she can call your mom, and we'll send it to the office with the roll call." I have a statement here from Jimmy Britton, the British educator, who says, "At a certain point a child discovers that writing is an efficient way for an individual to contribute to a group effort." I would add, "And for a group to contribute to an individual's effort." Although I'm ultimately in control in the classrooms at all times, I must have children help me in my efforts to teach them all. I think we wait too long to expose children to this reality. They can use writing as one means of doing that through active participation. There is usually an uncomfortable imbalance in which the teacher is active and the children learn that the only way they can help is by being passive—quiet, waiting, cooperating with requests.

When I talk to teachers I ask them what ways they have used writing in the last three weeks of their own lives. Mostly it turns out to be notes to themselves. What to do, errands to remember. It's not expository writing as we think of it. It's not correcting a sentence. In one class a little girl was not joining in with what we were doing. She looked so unhappy that I approached her and asked what was the matter. "You having a bad day?" "Yes." "Why don't you write to me about it now while the rest of the class is doing this work, and I'll talk to you at recess, because I'm going to have to go on with class." She wrote:

to marsha

Today when I whs eating my sadwich one of my sadiwchs fell on the
grownd. And Jenny and ilsibith siad ew. And I siad it was it fanny. And
when I was playing freez tag. And sarah was it and I said tims she taged
me. And when she taged me it was clos to my arm it skrap me and it hert.
And avre persun tught me. And I din'd like it

Writing that note pulled her together and she rejoined the class. That
little note had universal appeal. Later when I asked the kids to pull
something out of their writing folders and expand it into a larger
writing, I said to that girl, "How about the note you wrote me? You
could make a little book—about your awful day. Because everybody has
awful days and other people would like to read about yours." "No," she
said, "That's mine. It's not for other people."

I get notes from kids of all kinds. One kid whose family was going to
move wrote me goodbye notes for three months. "I guess I will be no
more." It was heavy duty. Here's a note written on a day I was absent:

Dear Miss Umland.

I don't like it when you are gone it isen't fun.

And then a drawing of an upside-down animal/human figure crying
"boo boo" and "RIP rest in peace."

I get so many gifts of pictures. I accept a picture and tell them what I
liked about it. And I say, "It would be nice to have some writing about
the picture, too." The kids choose what they think are their best pictures and put them in a looseleaf binder for the whole class. Then
when they have time, they go to the binder and pull out someone's
picture that they like and write about it. They write letters to the artist
or describe what is in it, or what they like about it. I let them know it
would please me to have their pictures and writing soon—a contribution. When someone wrote a story out of someone else's picture the
child was flattered. Others were reading the story and enjoying it. The
children weren't afraid that others wouldn't enjoy their stories.

At that age they're just beginning to get a subtle understanding of
what they want to say in writing, but they don't think much about how
they're going to say it or how anyone else has said something. An
appropriate way to get that is from professional authors. I read them a
professional piece and ask, "Who can tell what sentence in that says
why John felt happy?" I ask them to pull out their writing folders and
look in their own writing for a sentence where there's no capital letter.
"I can't find any like that," one child says, disappointed. I ask another
to help a writer look for such sentences and if they don't find any,

assure the writer that it's good they can find no sentences without capital letters. They have difficulty thinking about each other's work, especially about its style or form, what makes it work. Sometimes they're inattentive when the writing of other kids is being read aloud. They're building their egos. They can't think too much about other kids' work in a helpful way.

But I'm getting better at response groups with second and third graders. I simply include others in my conferencing with a student about a composition. A few times a year I ask all children to redraft a piece of writing. Some do it on their own at other times, too. When the first draft is ready, the child signs up for a conference. Three to five children who are ready also attend. The child reads the composition and after a few positive, specific remarks, I ask the child, "Do you have any ideas for this?" Often while reading to the audience, the child has discovered some revision possibilities, revealed by interspersed "oops" and subsequent pauses to erase or insert. Young kids have to do that immediately. If the child has more ideas, I make a few notes for reminders.

Next, I ask if the writer wants ideas from the group. If so, the paper is read again. This is necessary for the distractable audience and offers the writer a new distance from the work. Then I take notes again on the ideas that are offered, including my own, but I scratch out the ones that the writer is not receptive to. The students are enthusiastic about this. They aren't required to say anything or take ideas at all, but most do. Some get as many ideas as they need just by reading their work aloud. Best of all, the children are involved both as conferee and conferencer, and their ideas get better and more specific as we go along. They pick up the language of analyzing and constructively criticizing writing through my full participation. I'm hoping to use this method more often and refine it a bit next year.

I get kids working on words by giving them two words like *witch* and *itch* and ask them to make a drawing to accompany them. I draw lines on a big sheet of paper, boxed out like spaces for newspaper articles, and ask them to fill it in with things like those they've seen in newspapers.

Working with kids as individuals or in small groups can be chaos. One class may take longer to learn to work with me instead of against me than another. In my present class it may be spring before we'll be the kind of class I'd like to be in. I've had to pull back and tighten up at times and give certain kids more options than others until they get their energies channeled and capitalize on their powers. I have twenty-eight students, a whole range of backgrounds, and two grades in the one room, kids from seven to ten in age, some who know English only as a second language, some who're identified as learning handicapped children.

I learn different things working with individual students and with small groups. For example, here's a record I made of a second-grader working through what was for her a long composition. She was one of the least experienced writers in the class. In her first draft she wrote:

> Once upon a time, there was king.
> In a thick wood trees lived a witch.
> She put spells on evrething.
> One day the witch put a spell on the
> King and the little gril melted the
> witch and they were happy now.

In a conference I asked Carly to read her story to me. I said I was confused about the thick wood trees. She answered that the witch lived in the thick, wood tree. She was convinced that this was clear except for the "s" on the word *tree*. Then I asked her to list the main events which occurred after the witch put the spell on the king, including what kind of spell it was. Before she came to see me the second time, she wrote out this list of events:

1. The spell put the king to sleep.
2. For a long time he slep.
3. She melted the witch when she dide all her spells would come off so it did.

I told Carly how pleased I was that she had put all the main events on her list. I said she made it possible for me to understand what had really happened to the king. I asked her then to write the story using both her first draft and the list. Her second draft went like this:

> Once apone a time there was a king.
> In a thick, wood tree lived a witch.
> She put spells on evrything.
> One day the witch put a spell on the King.
> The spell put the king to sleep.
> For a long time he slep. She melted the
> witch when she dide all the spells would
> come off so it did. The end!

Carly read the story again. I was content with the changes she'd made even though she had left out the reference to the little girl. But when she asked, "Any questions?" I couldn't resist.

"Why did the witch put a spell on the king?" I said.

"Because that's what witches do!" Carly replied.

"Who was the little girl and how did she melt the witch?" I asked.

Carly went back to her desk and wrote this third version:

Once upon a time there was a king. In a thick, wood tree lived a witch. She put spells on evreything. one day the witch put a spell on the king. The spell put the king to sleep. For a long time he slept. The king's daughter was very brave, so one day Lily, who was the king's daughter, took a pail of water and threw it on her and she died. When witches die all there spells come off. And so the king and Lily where happy.
                                   The end!

In the list and the second draft she had left out "and they were happy," but included it in the final draft. She made some spelling changes, some of them after asking other people how to spell the words. In her last draft she no longer confined herself to one sentence per line.

Carly wanted to tell this story. I believe that's why she was able to improve it. Children write for lots of reasons, to satisfy the teacher, prevent punishment or disapproval, keep up with their peers, or to reach some other goal that requires writing. Or to create art, what James Britton calls "adding to the world's store of good things." If teachers learn to be observing enough and are sensitive and curious enough, they can make some headway in getting children to write a lot and for real purposes—their own. Children have to start out being effective writers in order to become effective writers. Our job is to help with the sophistication and discrimination, watch the timing of our criticism or "laugh" while exposing the kids to the variety of purposes, audiences, and infinite possibilities of the craft. Whobody can do this is a teacher of writing rather than an espouser or assigner.

A teacher can't get kids to write one way or another by just announcing that's the task for the day. I remember at one point I stopped giving out lined paper so that kids could both draw and write on the same sheet. I asked them to write in factual areas, make a chart about fish, with columns for what fish eat, where they live, etc., and the kids filled them in. "These are things we will not make up or guess at," I say. And they look up the facts and we go over them to see that they're right because there are times in life when they're going to have to be factual. And they create a fill-in-the-blank spelling exercise with each other.

But I don't want to make instruction too rigid. I like it when they write a poem in an answer instead of just a word or sentence. Kids have little respect for writing. They don't see us adults writing much. I don't want them to think of writing as just a skill they'll use later or when they get more connected with life.

When the time came to part, I asked Marcia, "Isn't this kind of teaching exhausting? Don't you sometimes want to quit? Like the little girl whose sandwich fell on the ground, don't you have your awful days?" She said:

Of course. When I'm ill-prepared or afraid or just forcing stuff on kids because "It has to be done," I'm quite capable of projecting all my anxieties on them. There have been non-productive writing periods followed by panic that I'm on the wrong track entirely. Recently the whole district had a writing assessment hour—all the kids wrote on the same topic. It was a good one and broad enough. But my class was unaccustomed to an assigned topic and the quiet required for the whole period. After looking over all the papers from the other classes I was sure that my class as a whole didn't do as well as some of the others who had had more practice. And occasionally there's a parent conference in which I want to avoid bringing out the writing folder because the child has written as little as possible and there are just a few tattered, miserable scraps.

I despair when I work with people who don't understand or support what I take personal pride in. I quit public school teaching once partly because of that. I've had two or three marvelous principals to work under. I think I've been unusually lucky—two out of about ten.

I get exhausted, but not burned out. Sometimes I'm dropping my dream for a day or two, but most days I'm on, and stunned by the kids. Lately I've realized that in setting up a classroom at last I've given myself permission to form a society I'd like to live in. But I wasn't always adequate to the task.

I said to Marcia, "I wish I had been in your class when I was a kid." And Marcia answered, "I wish I had, too."

Carol Elliott delights at two learners playing the Mirroring Game.

16

CAROL ELLIOTT
Acting, University

While teaching summer writing courses at Bread Loaf Graduate School of English at Middlebury College in Vermont, I kept hearing my students talk about the acting class they were taking from Carol Elliott, who during the school year teaches at Princeton University. They spoke of how they were finding acting different from what they had supposed. It was not putting on a mask, they said, but rather peeling off masks to get down to truth. Their main resource as actors was themselves. One of them said, "Carol has very high standards, but she makes you feel you can reach them."

I began conversations with Carol, who was living in the same faculty rooming house as I was. In the second summer of our acquaintance, I took my writing class to the semester-end presentation of dramatic monologues done by her students from professional plays. Almost without exception they were superbly acted—richly humorous, commanding. My students were amazed at this high quality of performance by their peers, all of whom were English teachers, and many of whom had had no previous acting experience.

I asked Carol Elliott how she conducted her classes.

At the beginning of the course, I allow students to make all their own choices about a scene. Who they are. Where they are. In the early part of the course I urge them to be themselves, not to play a seventy-year-old physicist or some character outside themselves. Because they know most about themselves. They will come in with a scene, having made up imaginary circumstances. And then they'll make choices about how they want the scene to go. I have to be careful that I help them realize the choices *they've* made. It's so easy for a teacher to say, "God, the scene would be so much better if they had made *this* choice. If only he would've exited on that line instead of the way they ended it." I have to remind myself that I'm not there to present a scene that I would do but to help them actualize the choices they've made and communicate them to an audience. Sometimes I champ at the bit. "Why don't you do it this way?" I mean by that "my way." If I do that, then the whole business becomes a matter of pleasing the teacher. I tell them, "If I work on a scene with you and you find me insinuating my ideas into it, just say, 'Well, Carol, that's not what we intended.' " They have to be able to do that. And then I learn, "Hey, there's another way to do this thing."

Last week I read an unpublished essay by Peter Elbow [who was also teaching at Bread Loaf] about what he calls "The Doubting and Believing Games." At one point he's talking about the fact that most of the time as readers we approach in a very critical way our peers who are presenting their work for our responses in a writing class. He says that perhaps we should try to believe in the work instead of coming at it negatively. We should try to assume the view of the writer when we encounter the text. Then we may be able to help him clarify some perspective he wasn't aware that he had. We can help him improve the writing instead of make him feel defeated and confused. As actors, that's what we're trying to do all the time in helping an actor create a role.

Today the student who gave this Peter Elbow article to me was involved in such a situation. I'd given the class ten lines of dialogue for two people and said, "Now you construct your own scenario, your own character, and justify these lines. You can bring in anything you want. Basically you'll be improvising the scene. The one restriction is that you're to use the words of the text." They're fairly ambiguous—"Do you want some more coffee?" "Well, why don't we go for a walk?" "I don't feel like it right now."

One woman was playing the scene with a very attractive younger man. They had decided that their scenario would be that they had been at Bread Loaf one summer and had had an affair and were saying goodbye. This was their farewell.

After the scene was over we spent some time thinking about what that really meant—being involved in an affair for the summer. At the end of the discussion this woman said, "I didn't want anybody in this class to think I would have an affair. And so I never believed in it myself. I never put myself in that situation. I was afraid they would look at me—because my husband and children are here—and say, 'Look at that woman!' I didn't believe it myself."

And that's the whole point. If the actress doesn't believe it, how can you expect the audience to believe it? And we didn't. We just knew it wasn't real. Whatever dynamic, whatever appeal or magnetism happens between two people in that sort of situation, it's not like just two friends or roommates saying good-bye. Earlier we had talked about how difficult it was for both of them, and she had just given me this Peter Elbow article because she was feeling very uncomfortable with the class. She was scared. In her first exercise she had done well, and had said, "My, I'm surprised. It was so simple, and in the critique session I didn't get any negative comments." What she had done was simple. It had defied all the rules or principles but still was very good. Then when she did this scene with the young man, she had put up some sort of barrier. She was implicitly saying to the group, "Go ahead and say whatever you want because it's not going to bother me." But she knew she hadn't had any stake in it.

When students finish a scene, the question I have the class address is "What did you see?" I learned that from Viola Spolin, the author of *Improvisation for the Theater*. I caution students against putting their response in terms of Did I like it? What was good? What was better? Was it a flop? To eliminate that kind of absolute, I ask, "What did she do?" So they say, "Well, I saw a woman very depressed. She was grappling with some sort of problem or something was weighing on her." Or "I saw someone who was absolutely disgusted with another person, who was so apologetic, so willing to try to mend whatever had wrenched the situation." That's a beginning which allows actors to hear if what they intended to communicate actually was communicated.

In acting, part of our job is to help actors make their own choices. I want them to try to realize those choices, not make another set of choices, unless they're totally wrong. So if they decide, "I want to end this relationship," that can be their choice. And we just try to help them realize this choice rather than say, "Oh, you should stay with her." I'm talking about a scene in which the lines don't say what choice has been made. Let's suppose say that an actor is involved with just sitting somewhere thinking about something that worries her, and she makes a decision. In the middle of that deciding she begins to laugh. That's quite possible, and it's an interesting choice on her part. Rather than say, "You're in the middle of a problem, and gee, I wouldn't laugh," if we're playing the Believing Game we accept what the actor has outlined for herself and say, "Let's see if we can help her realize that."

Of course, when an actor's working on an exercise, that's different from when she's being directed in a play. The director has a general interpretation of the play—I say *general* because it can't be absolute. No one knows fully what the character is really about except the actor portraying the part. You're in there and you're living it moment to moment. You have a sense of it that the director just doesn't have. I think the actor knows much more about it as the rehearsal process goes on, and in a sense has more authority about it than the director. You talk about the main line of the play together. The director has a sense of that. But the actor is out there engaging with the other characters and that's doing something to him. Line by line the actor is the authority.

I ask my acting students to keep journals of what they're experiencing in class. Record impressions and feelings, ask questions, whatever. I'm having an interesting dialogue in the journal of one student. She's one of these dynamic persons, just terrific. I'm fond of her. She's got enough restraint and she's sharp and very sensitive. She's grappling with the problem of how to be a good English teacher. I think she's learning that as an actor when you're working up there with someone else you share the responsibility of the scene with your partner. You have to work together. You don't speak your lines, wait for the other person to speak his, and then say your next one. That's not true acting, which is a collaborative act. If your partner on stage doesn't collaborate with you, it's impossible to create a genuine exchange. This is true in teaching also. This woman has been teaching only a couple of years, but I know she's got the potential to be a great teacher. But from her journal entries, right now I can tell she's been assuming all the responsibility for the learning that goes on in her classroom. If the students fail, it's all her fault. The other day in class she did a wonderful scene, very moving. That's what's hard about acting, you know, because there she is, putting her emotions on the line, reliving some event in her life and investing herself in the moment. She was crying in front of the whole class and they said, "Ohhh, great!" And it was great emotion but not great acting. She was working by herself, acting by herself, trying to build this emotion, instead of using the person who was with her to create the scene. Basically, whether she was aware of it or not, she had assumed the total responsibility. We had reworked the scene in such a way that the actors couldn't use words, just touch, a little touch. They had to deal with each other, pay attention to each other. When you say a word, you often don't really hear what comes back to you. I think most of the time good playwrights are giving you two people. They're not going to have two people up there who don't affect each other. There's no dynamic.

As a basic step in acting I use the Mirror Game, which Viola Spolin and others have employed. One person, A, is the initiator and B is the mirrorer. The purpose of the game is for two people to work together so that one person is moving and the other is mirroring those movements exactly. We don't say that the purpose of the game is for B to reflect all the motions that A makes. The responsibility is on both persons working together. The first time around, people tend to want to trick each other. There's lots of giggling, people having a grand old time, but not much working together. After about two minutes I stop the game and talk about it and people begin to realize that the responsibility belongs to both persons. If I'm moving and I can see that you're not following me, I know I have to make some adjustment, and that's one of the key principles. It's that adaptability that an actor has to have to anything new that happens, to be aware of that newness.

The Mirror Game is about communion with another person. It's about letting go. Letting go with my own rhythms and trying to adjust. Not feeling I have to abdicate myself, who I am, to become you. It's an

adjustment of our kinds of energies that will create the energy that
makes the specific, the dynamic. If I'm working with another partner
from the one I began with, it will be different. She will create a different
dynamic. It happens on the stage that way. You work with one actor and
she gives you a certain kind of energy, and you deal with that instead of
wishing it were otherwise. And this actor I'm working with—"Goddam-
mit, why doesn't she say the line this way? Why doesn't she give me more
emotion?" If you react that way, you're spending a lot of energy trying to
find the cause of the problem instead of solving it. The mirroring game
is about solving problems. You get someone who isn't following you.
How do you work together? The focus then becomes the work, not the
ego. Can I do clever movements? Gee, can I follow this other person?
No, not that, but how can we two work together?

Now the secret of playing the Mirror Game is not to watch the hands
or arms or feet of the person you're mirroring, but to look into their
eyes and see their movements peripherally. What Viola Spolin calls
having a *point of concentration*. If you look at each movement of the
person in front of you, you'll be all over the place and a step behind.
You have to have a center of control and then you'll find yourself
magically catching the rhythms of the movements of the other person,
not just mechanically following them a second later. Then you'll mirror
the movements in a way that gives an onlooker the impression that the
two of you are actually one.

I'm fascinated to see how Peter Elbow's Believing Game is on a thinking level much like the Mirror Game on a physical level. I had a student this year who wrote in his journal that he had a professor who put
him off. He didn't like the way the man lectured, the way he approached the works, the kind of papers he assigned. So just at the most
frustrating moment, when he thought of going to the professor and
telling him how he disliked everything he was doing, he read Peter
Elbow's article and instead told himself that he would play the Believing Game. He would try to go along with everything the professor was
doing, try to see what motivations and reasons the professor might
have for doing what he was doing. And he began to get a great deal
more out of the class.

We're learning a lot from the journal writing. In the acting class
where I meet students only twice a week, many of them are experiencing shock. It's important for them to have a conduit that reaches me. In
class their scene is critiqued and sometimes what they want to say is,
"You know Carol, it went so much better in rehearsal," but that isn't
appropriate when they're supposed to be receiving suggestions and
criticism from the rest of the class. They might want to say, "I thought
I had it, and I didn't." Or "It was just horrible." I got one journal entry
last week that said, "Oh, I was so angry at myself after it was over. I

had allowed myself to become self-indulgent in the scene. And I just wanted you to know that I wasn't angry at you. I was angry at myself."

In journals they can write, "You know I didn't agree with what you said. I thought I did a really good job." Sometimes they're not willing to say that in front of a class. Or there are comments they want to make about other people's scenes. It's difficult to criticize your peers. I'll reach the point in class where I want them to critique each other. Sometimes they'll not only applaud but say, "That moment was terrific. Great choice!" Or "Too ambiguous. I didn't understand what was going on there. Why did you make that choice?" But sometimes it's risky for them to say, "I think the whole scene was over-dramatic," which is one thing that was said a few days ago. I thought that was an act of courage when a student said that in class. The journals allow for such comments to be made more privately. There are many things left unsaid in acting class. You don't have time to go over every single moment in a scene, and sometimes one moment that the actors have worked on for a long time played beautifully but took them lots of energy to get there, to solve the problem. It's important for them to have a way of telling me that. The scene lasted two minutes but they spent five hours working on it. They ask me questions in their journals. "Can you tell me why Sheryl and Joan's scene was so good? You said it was good, but I didn't understand why. And why was it that my scene didn't work?"

I don't want to imply that everything is easy in teaching acting. I've been a student in classes where I had a guru as a teacher. I just needed that teacher to tell me whether my work was good or bad. I believe in having students respond to each other's work, but there are times, rarely, when I have to disagree with them. You know I told you about that woman who cried in her scene and was applauded. Everybody said, "I saw this powerful raw emotion." But I had to say what I thought. I trust that they knew I have this experience behind me and this training, so that I had a different perspective from theirs. I trust they knew I would bring to bear on that opinion all the training and experience I've had. They're free to reject that. But if an actor wants to believe that that was good acting, then I won't fight it. But she will keep hearing the same thing from me. It's painful. We have to be honest with ourselves as teachers. It's a bumping up against another set of standards than our own. And the students are in a continuous process of reevaluating their standards. Eventually this woman came up to me and said, "I understand what you're saying." And she wrote about it in her journal. She thought that that was the same problem she was having with her teaching—doing it all herself, not sharing it with her students. I'm always refining my standards. They're certainly not fixed. Every student in that class comes in with an understanding of what they think acting is. And then that understanding is reflected off me. The student can change his view or not change it, or accept and absorb some of what I say. Or refute it all. There have been some who just resisted.

I think that's one of the main functions of being a teacher—to offer to other people a perspective on themselves. You have to trust in me, and that takes a while. It doesn't happen the first day. You have to trust that I will say back to you what I saw. When that woman did that scene in class where she was crying and being very moved herself but not acting with the other person in the scene, I asked the class, "What did you see?" and they all said, "I just saw this woman all torn apart." They had applauded. They don't usually applaud after a scene. And they asked me whether that was right to do, and I said, "If it's spontaneous, then by God, do it, but if not, don't do it." It's scary as hell when you've never acted. I think it's up to the acting teacher to kindle the flame, but we've got bastards out there who just look at the flame and go "Phwwww! We'll take care of that right now!" I'm sure that there have been times when I've done that unwittingly.

One of the things that I've learned from my husband Alan Mokler, who's head of the theater program at Princeton, is to try to be fair. I think that means sometimes saying a hard truth, but with caring. If someone brings a scene to class that they haven't worked on, I say, "Don't waste my time. Just tell me straight, 'I didn't prepare. I'll have it ready next week and it'll be terrific.' "

In the last set of journal entries, one of the kids said, "God, how I admire the work of my classmates. They had so much courage, and it was so good." I've had Princeton students say to me, "Couldn't we do some more exercises that would make the class closer and warmer?" I really don't believe in that approach. I believe that the audience, that group of people for whom they're performing, is potentially a hostile animal. There are tensions between a performer and an audience. If you eliminate all of those so the people are just acting in front of their friends and they're not going to get any criticism and everything is going to be positive, that's an unrealistic situation in which to train actors. But the other extreme is to be avoided, too, where all the students do is criticize each other. When you perform in front of any audience there are going to be people out there who don't like you. They don't know you, but they don't like you. And that creates a certain set of tensions that I think is good to have in the classroom. If you start out thinking, "They're all going to love me," how can you be vulnerable?

Students need to hear the truth. They need a perspective. That's what it is. Otherwise you can read it in a book, can't you? Well, I want to learn about acting or woodworking or physics—I'll go read a book.

Why do I need a teacher? I think a teacher gives you a perspective which a book can't, a perspective on yourself.

We did Chekhov's *The Seagull* at Princeton a couple of years ago, and I can tell you as an artist, and every actor in it can tell you, that it didn't succeed. But we learned so much, and we all felt great about that production. Everyone of those kids could tell you, "I just didn't understand experientially what that scene was about." I directed it. What Chekhov is talking about in that play is all these characters, most of whom have started to turn back to look at their lives. These kids who are nineteen years old are looking ahead, and that's the way it should be. That was very difficult for them. There's got to be that room for failure, and even though we all felt bad about it, it was a critical success and we sold out to packed houses. But we had our own standards. I think the actor has to be gracious and say "Thank you" to the audience and mean it, not pretend. But you have your own standards and you want to hang on to them. Otherwise you get neurotic, and don't know whom to believe. And that's what I do in the acting classes—try to give students a sense of what they're doing. "Boy, Carol, that was terrible. Oh, I just didn't get that. It worked so well in rehearsal, but I don't know what happened in performance." And I want for *them* to say that rather than someone else. Now they may not know how to fix it, and we hope that we can work that out. You don't always have the answer. But that sense must be nurtured—of having their own set of standards so that when they leave the class they don't need me.

Letting go. It's difficult in the theater, as in life. It's trusting that the actors at some point own that script and that they can't be looking over their shoulders at the director. It's a sense of ownership which you have to transfer. At the beginning, the actors are tentative, and it's the director who owns a lot of secrets. Rehearsals are a process of transferring the ownership in the understanding of that play. So the actors have to feel that. It's trusting somebody, and you know when someone is trusting you, when trust is not held back. The director has to allow the actors that faith, and faith to fail, if you will. A sense that the director is not behind them propping them up. They're on their own.

It's O.K. to fail. Hal Prince, one of the foremost producers in the New York theater, who did *Sweeney Todd* on Broadway, said at a seminar that he had failed a great deal. "I see actors," he said, "and I see directors—who are despondent over failure. I say to my actors, 'It's just a play!'" And that's it. I've told this to my students in classes so often. "It's always a work in progress. Don't do that to yourself—'I've got it. I've got it now.'" In the theater we get a chance to try it again. We're luckier than most artists. A reader reads your novel, and that's it. You can be thinking about it two minutes later and say, "Aw, gee, why didn't I do that?" Whereas in the theater we get the chances night after night. We can do it in the next performance.

Actors have to own the parts. By the time we get to the beginning performance, I know that the actor knows much more about that part than I do. And she should. That's where her pride—for the lack of a better word—will be, or her investment in it.

In my classes at Bread Loaf and Princeton I'm not necessarily preparing people for professional careers. But I believe we can teach any person what acting is about. The basic principles can be learned. And then it's talent that carries you further into the craft. In the class here at Bread Loaf right now the students have all grasped the principles of speaking in your own voice, understanding what you're doing, being honest in what you say and do on stage. Don't lie. Do *not* lie. Don't let one word out of your mouth unless you know what it means. If words, or a speech, are difficult, you have to find a place for them to come from. There's one student who's working on a Chekhov monologue— and true, this is translation, and that may make a difference—but the first line is "Oh, how I long to be free." How that student belabored the word *oh!* She just couldn't get it out of her mouth. So the way to solve a problem like that is to go through the word rather than around it. You get to a block, and you say, "This word is coming. There's no way that that word or phrase will make it out of my mouth." You must have them possess that word. Take it to an extreme so that rather than minimizing the word, they push it to make it the most important word in the sentence. Extend it so that they own it in the end, and they can own any part of it. A student will say, "How shall I stress this word?" and I say, "That's just cosmetics. I can tell you how to say the line, but you have to internalize it. It must mean something to you."

The acid test is when you get up in front of a bunch of people and bare yourself, not just with words but with your whole physical being, the instrument that is there. In the live theater you've got one chance. And that whole idea of spontaneity—that anything can happen—did you ever stop to think that that's why we watch kids and dogs on stage so intently? They can upstage any adult human being, because we expect spontaneous action from them. They have that potentiality, of anything happening at any given moment. But with an adult human being you know there's less chance of that. Unless you're a great actor—if you're Marlon Brando, who is a kind of animal. He has spontaneity. You know that he has limitations, but you never know what he's going to do next. And so you watch him. And Richard Burton—he may have been staid in the movie *Equus,* but have you heard the record he did of *Hamlet?* I used it in class this year. When he gives all the familiar speeches, it's as if you've never heard them before. Richard Burton has it. Rod Steiger. Meryl Streep. I saw her in a production of Chekhov's *The Cherry Orchard.* You didn't know what she was going to do next. For me, *The Cherry Orchard* was a play about the maid! Which was wrong for the production because you can't have, especially in Chekhov, that play be about one person. It's about that whole experience of the upper and lower classes. It's that quality. You're not sure what they're going to do next, so you have to attend to them. I saw Geraldine Page in *The Little Foxes* and I didn't know what she was going to do next. Her husband, Rip Torn, is another one. He played Richard Nixon in the Watergate Series. Actors like that are not being merely neurotic in those parts. You can get these neurotic types who are powerful on the stage, but they're not in control of the character and situation. But the great actor has a balance. He's spontaneous and unpredictable, and yet he's doing what he's supposed to do on cue, staying with the demands of the scene.

My students here at Bread Loaf are learning to be honest and real, but the big leap, which is a quantum leap, is getting theatrical energy. Because all of their choices, all of the scenes we've done in class, now are at the same level of energy, and I'd say that level borders a little on manic depressive. [*Here, Carol laughs.*] "How are you today?" "Good." They listen actively, and they speak. What they need to do now is loosen up and let go. It's like any art form, you know. You learn the technique and then just go out there and use it. You can't be thinking of the right pitch. It's just doing it and trusting that it will be there. That's more difficult for students. The challenge is greater.

More and more I'm enjoying teaching rather than acting or directing, but I can't improve as a teacher unless I keep directing and acting. I have to take the same risks the students are taking, so I can say to them as I did at the end of the run of *The Cherry Orchard* last year at Bread Loaf, in which I acted, "I'm never acting again! That was terrible. There were so many things I couldn't get, so much that I didn't understand. I was just beginning to understand it when we got to the fourth performance." I can empathize with their frustration.

I like to hear someone say, "I think I'm ready to take an acting course." Because that's the first step—to recognize that there's something else to know about the way we behave and the way we perceive. And maybe one way to know that is through acting, which makes you tremendously vulnerable. All the focus is on you. Everything you do is under scrutiny. It's saying, "I'm ready to jump in the pool. I'm ready to swim. I've been walking along the edge, and now I want to take it."

That's the first step, but there are others. You can ask any student in my class what Carol Elliott thinks about passion. I talk about the differences between sentimentality, emotion, and passion. When they came into class they were able to strip the sentimentality away and get to the emotion. But when they left the class, they realized they had a big step left. They looked at the plays of Chekhov and found that everyone of those characters had at his or her center powder kegs of passion. If the fuse were lit, they would explode. The potential was there and the

actors had to find it. It was based on something much bigger—sentimentality was left by the wayside. And I became passionate about what
the students were doing. After class one of them said to me, "You
really scared me," and I said, "You have to understand—that wasn't
anger. It was because I care about those characters and what is happening to them, and you have to come up to them in that way." No wonder
Chekhov is often boring, lifeless. You have to ask, "What is at the
core?" Because that was the impulse, the energy level, at which the
playwright created that world.

This passion I'm talking about must have a base. It can't be pasted on
to a character. I'm reminded of what Mike Kerin, who's interested in
becoming a writer, entered in his acting journal this summer:

> Another connection I made between writing and acting is both must be
> hinged upon some real experience. In acting a particular emotion, I must
> latch onto a memory strong enough to rekindle a similar emotion in my
> performance. That raw emotion will be shaped to the circumstances in the
> scene. I must channel this experience from the rushing river of experi-
> ence in my memory. The emotion I project may not be as intense as the
> original, but it will come from a real source. It will not be "acted."
>
> Similarly, my best fiction is the result of reshaping some real experi-
> ence. It is that experience that carries the charge to initiate that writing
> process. It's something you've lived through, and therefore, something
> you care enough about to write it well. The details of the experience will
> change to fit certain literary conventions, but the final piece will have
> evolved out of something real.

Another student wrote in her journal:

> Acting teaches you to listen to that very special voice inside yourself, that
> voice that tells you when to be angry, when to be kind, the voice that
> makes you an individual, different from anyone else. The hardest thing is
> to listen to that voice amid the clamor of social demands.

These students have worked their way into the belief that theater is
something more than representing life by reciting lines on the stage. I
feel that what's behind all this is a concept I call "living in the present
tense." You respond to whatever impulse is coming to you, without
stopping to think, without living ten seconds in the past or ten seconds
ahead, or a day ahead or five minutes behind. On stage you must first
of all be alive. Not be an automaton, not recreate what went on in
rehearsal, but live in the present tense. When theater is at its best, that's
what's happening.

Jimmy Britton, the listener, sits at his customary station.

17

JAMES BRITTON
Teaching Teachers, Graduate School

Prodigious is the word that comes to mind as I think of James Britton. Born in 1908 in Scarborough, Yorkshire, England, he helped found the London Association for the Teaching of English in 1947 with Percy Gurrey, Nancy Martin, and others working at the University of London. Just another teachers' organization wouldn't be worth special notice, but this one consisted of teachers who decided that members of their profession didn't know what they were talking about and should do something about that. They formed interest groups. Instead of meeting over tea and cakes to say something "interesting" about these "interests," or to do book reports on a topic, they set out to observe and study children in action. They shaped and refined their findings, reported them to the larger association, and then published the results in books like Understanding Children Talking *and* Understanding Children Writing.

In 1970, Britton's classic statement Language and Learning *appeared and then, in 1975,* The Development of Writing Abilities (11–18), *researched and written by Britton, Tony Burgess, Nancy Martin, Alex McLeod, and Harold Rosen. Americans have only recently begun to read and be astonished by these books.*

Prodigious, and yet soft-spoken, gentle, so much a listener *rather than a* teacher, *is "Jimmy" Britton, as he is called by most people who know him. In the summer of 1982 I was fortunate to be teaching alongside him at the Bread Loaf Graduate School of English in Vermont in the Teaching Writing Program. One day I asked him why he had designed a course for English teachers called Story-Writing in School. He answered:*

I've been interested in story for a long time. I'm thinking basically of stories about the writers themselves. Telling them is a means of learning, a digestive kind of learning which is so often ignored in schools. It seems to me to be the field of operation of most of the arts. So I want my students to move toward an art-like selection of the elements of their personal experience. The more sharply the form resolves the content, so to speak, the more sharply is it a digestive process. I try to interest students in writing both autobiographical and fictional stories and to find their way between the two.

When I was teaching children I discovered that story writing was central to them. They all loved stories at an early age and they liked to write them when they got over the hump, the difficulty, of shaping letters and words in writing. They get over that hump better, I find, by writing stories than by reading them. I think that's most applicable at a very young age, but it still worked when I was teaching eleven-year-olds. Barbara Hardy—who's the head of the English Department at Birkbeck College at the University of London—came down to talk to our teachers once at the London Association for the Teaching of English. She said that telling stories is not a way an artist has of manipulating an audience, but something that is transferred from life to art. She says that *narrative is a primary act of mind.* Her article, with those words as title, was printed in *Novel: A Forum on Fiction.* She wrote:

> We dream in narrative, daydream in narrative, remember, anticipate, hope, despair, believe, doubt, plan, revise, criticize, construct, gossip, learn, hate, and love by narrative. In order really to live, we make up stories about ourselves and others, about the personal as well as the social past and future.

She goes on to make the point that "Educationalists still suggest that the process of maturation involves a movement out of the fantasy-life into a vision of life 'as it is.' when in fact mature people are constantly moving between fantasy and reality usefully."

I said to Jimmy, "I've heard some of your students here at Bread Loaf talk about these story assignments of yours. Since I've learned that you're not very forthcoming with anecdotes that show how good a teacher you are, I guess I'll have to go to them for more."

"You might learn more from doing that than from talking to me," he said.

So I did just that. One of his students, Madeleine McElveen of Northway School in Northway, Alaska, talked to me at length. She said:

When I think of Jimmy's class, I remember feeling very warm. He talked about taking walks with his granddaughter. He gets really animated when he talks about being with her—that's the way he's spent so much of his life, studying language in the company of children. What we learned was a way to feel. Even knowing who Jimmy is, you are comfortable with him right from the start. He has a feeling for kids and people who are trying for truth.

One day he read a poem by a boy of eighteen in Illinois who committed suicide two weeks after writing it. The boy talks about going to school and making a picture he thought was really neat—of a rocket ship, and then going home and wanting to share something, and gets,

"Oh, that's wonderful. Now why don't you get ready for dinner?" He talks about his little brown room and his little brown house and how he sees rainbows. The way Jimmy read it was just wonderful because you felt like "That's a kid I'd really like to know." Jimmy had a sense of what was going on with that kid, while the things were happening, and you know, what possibly could be done. He doesn't have any illusions that a teacher can do a great deal in forty minutes a day. It's more what you give students for themselves than what you're doing that will change them. I'm not saying that he doesn't have a sense of mission about teaching, but he doesn't put you in a corner and say, "You must do this as a teacher," because that's unrealistic. But you can see from what he does that you have to let students express who they are without making a judgment if they are to write comfortably.

As you listen to Jimmy, you think this is a nice, good man. But his knowledge is intimidating. If you're sitting there and talking about theories of writing, he not only knows them, he wrote some of them. He wants you to understand what it is that informs your writing and the writing of children, but not because this is something you need to go and write down some day in a two-hour exam, but because if you understand why it is that you're doing it, or why you do it in this pattern, then you'll understand better how to get that story out of yourself or your student. When you think of it that way, theory is a lot more exciting.

On the first day, Jimmy said he wanted us to have some sense of who we were, so he asked us to write papers beginning, "I am the one who—" We did that in fifteen minutes. I wrote:

> I am the one who would like to become less frightened of this place here on the mountain. It would help in my teaching if I could discover some technique that would take the terror and anxiety out of the writing produced for school classes. My students enjoy talking to me or the people in our community and transcribing their interviews. And they seem to enjoy doing this quite a bit.

I was scared of this high-powered place, Bread Loaf. My fellow students were teachers—many from Eastern prep schools, and they knew so much and had traveled so much. And the literature professors were mostly from Yale, Princeton, and Harvard.

Then Jimmy told us, "O.K., why don't you take a childhood incident that meant something to you and write it up. Go away from this classroom for forty-five minutes and come back with what you wrote." And that was it. I was having a hay fever attack, felt utterly miserable, so I got up and went to the infirmary and got a pill. When we came back at 4:15, he said, "How well did you think it went?" He just accepted our responses. If the writing had gone well, fine. If it hadn't, fine. Mine went badly. I couldn't get into it.

At the second class, he said, "Here are your papers. I'll put them on the floor." I said to Karen, "Oh, would you pick up mine?" and she said, "Hunnh?" and I couldn't understand what was so difficult because she was already down on the floor looking. So I got down and picked mine up. I had missed the instruction that would have reduced much of the anxiety. Jimmy had said use a pseudonym on your writing, so Karen didn't know how to pick mine up. He had responded to each one of our writings on his own piece of paper. He didn't write on our papers.

When Jimmy discussed our writings, he said, "O.K., the Little General wrote—" and he talked about that one. He said something positive about every paper, mentioned something that struck him, that he understood. And when he got to mine he said, "And the person who didn't use a pseudonym—" [*Madeleine laughs.*] kind of narrowing it down. And he was so nice about it.

It was obvious from the snippets from our writing that he was sharing with us that some people were very talented writers. They had been writing, and some of us were new to it. I've always been afraid of writing and have written very little in my life. But I felt, "Well, that's just the way those people are, and I'm fine, too."

For my autobiographical paper, I wrote about my dog Shana, who looks a lot like a wolf, a Husky of the St. Bernard strain from the McKinley Kennels at McKinley Park. He was huge. Some adults were terrified of him but my four-year-old neighbor Chris would come right up to him and hug him. I wasn't feeling good, as I told you, and I didn't write much. I wasn't used to writing for others.

One day at the break, Jimmy said, "When are you guys going to buy me a couple of ales down at the Chipman Inn?" On Tuesday I got a ride down there with Roger Mork, and Jimmy was in the car. He found out more about Vermont in those three weeks he was here than I can imagine anyone doing, because he was so intrigued. He wanted to know the age of this, of that, what's in the cemetery there on the left of the road?

Jimmy said to me, "Then you're going to be returning to Alaska at the end of school here?"

"No, not exactly," I said. "I'll be in law school next year."

"Oh!" he said, "What's that? What are you going to do with it?"

"I thought about working in social studies," I said. "You know the kids are really intrigued by law. 'Aw, that's what the law is,' they say. They're involved with the law for a lot of reasons that you would probably understand if you were up there. I got permission to go to law school and maybe come back and develop a curriculum within the high school for social studies. I have a year's leave of absence and can take up to two. With summer work beyond that, I might be able to get my law degree."

At the Inn I mentioned Robert Frost, and Jimmy said kind of jokingly, "There's an excellent poem that I've used with younger children—'The Runaway.'" The reason he mentioned it was that we were talking about how Bread Loaf was the original site of a Morgan horse farm and Frost was writing about one of the Morgan colts. Jimmy said his students loved the poem. "Well," he said, "If I have a couple ales, I might say the poem."

Then Jimmy told us that he had had T. S. Eliot come into one of his classes [*Madeleine laughs.*] and he had read some of his poems. You know how disrespectful people at Bread Loaf are, and the first question was, "How did T. S. Eliot do?" and Jimmy said, "Not very well." I was in shock—"not very well"—didn't do very well reading his own poems! I guess Roger Mork from Wyoming has been here before, and Archibald MacLeish had been here one summer and done a poetry reading, the last one before he died, and Roger said it was wonderful. Jimmy said, "I just love his poetry." He was thrilled. Roger said, "You should have been there that summer," and Jimmy was really into it.

He was so excited about us. "You're from Wyoming, and John, you're from Michigan and run dog teams!" John would start talking about dog teams, and I—being from Alaska—started saying what I knew about that, and Jimmy wanted to know everything, how many dogs, how you get them together, and what kind of sled. I told him what I knew because I had worked at different dog races and live in a small town where you all help out with them. It was so easy to talk with him. He did that for the entire evening. With Eileen, it was about her teaching experiences because that's what really comes to her, and with Roger it was Wyoming. And Bill Noll—Jimmy talked to him about Vygotsky the psychologist because he knew that Bill was interested in him and the structure of the language. It was incredible.

But back to the colt. I was at the end of the table and Jimmy was one over. A fellow returned to the table and said, "We've got good news. We've found a copy of the poem. Now will you read it?" Jimmy said, "Yes, of course," and sat down and read us the poem "The Runaway." I mean at that tavern! That's something to write down. That was all right. He just read it to us and talked about how effective it was with kids. I was thinking it's pretty effective with a bunch of adults as well.

For the third assignment he asked us to describe a youthful person. The only one I could think about happened to be a four-year-old number, a kid I really like. First little kid I've ever known very well. So it worked out for me. But we had a bachelor in class who thought he had to write about a small child, so he made up a ten-year-old because he didn't have any children in his experience. Jimmy said later, "You didn't really have to do that." I wrote about my friend Chris.

CHRIS

Loud persistent tapping only about a third of the way up the cabin door let me out of an early morning reverie. Before I could shout, "Come in!" Christopher had sort of shuffled in, a four-year-old who had just watched the school bus leave without him.

The sight of my feet still in moccasins momentarily deflected him from the purpose of his visit. "Aren't you going to put shoes and socks on for school, Madeleine?"

"Yeah, Chris, but I'm running a little late."

"Me, too. Mom said to ask if it was all right if I could go to school with you. The bus left me."

"Sure, Chris, but I still've got to gather up my stuff."

"OK, I'll just turn on TV. It's all fuzzy. we goin' to go in your red car? Where are your keys? John Michael can't go to school yet. He's too little."

"Chris, if you pull the tablecloth, the lamp will fall. Be careful of the chair."

"Are you taking all those books to school in the red car? Are we ready to go yet? Those red socks you're going to wear? I like red cars. I like those shoes over there. Madeleine, how come you don't wear those?"

"There's still mud outside, Chris. That's why your mom put out your break-out boots. Maybe next week."

"You think we'll get stuck in the mud, Madeleine? Yesterday a *biiig* truck did, going out."

"Chris, we're already behind. Don't think such things."

Such satisfied roars of laughter. He's gotten to me. I really like that kid. I just really think he's a nifty little kid.

I've known Chris since he was two. It was easy to write. I was going to send it to his mom because she knows we're pretty close.

After we had discussed those writings, Jimmy said, "Now that you've written a portrait of a young person I want you to write a story that you think that person would like." That was Jimmy's fourth assignment. I had a very difficult time. It had to be fictional. We had about an hour and five minutes. We could go back to our room or the Barn, or anywhere. When we finished, we went back into the class and some people read what they had written, some didn't.

Chris was interested in my Volkswagen Rabbit, so this is the story I wrote for him:

The white rabbit made it all the way to California. We hooked the wrecked car to the belly of a big ship so that we could travel by water for a while. A strange thing happened on board that big ship. There were some people traveling with a big, growling black dog. I met them when I put my car next to their big gray van inside the ship. Their dog wasn't friendly like Puppy, at all. The dog never seemed to be happy. Whenever someone said, "Hi, Boy" or gave him a treat, it just sat there lumpily as if he wished the world would go away and leave him alone. It was pretty sad. I felt like I should do something. So one night I went down the long dark steps into the belly of the ship and found my car. I picked up some Dog Treats for the dog and started toward the big gray van with the big growly black dog inside.

When I pulled open the door, however, there sat a small, growly black haired *boy*. He looked as if he were about four years old. I asked him what he was doing down there in the dark belly of the ship at 3 A.M. He wanted to know what I was doing there. That seemed like a fair question, so I told him I had come to make friends with the big growly black dog.

I asked him again what he was doing there. He said he *was* the big black growly dog. I told him he didn't look much like a dog to me. But he looked just more like a boy who wanted to look around the boat while his parents were fast asleep. But then he started to grow, like a real dog. And then his hands became furry paws. I told him I believed him and he went back to being a boy again. I felt better when his fingernails took the place of his paws. He was acting pretty friendly, though, so I really didn't get too scared.

Then I realized, as much as Chris liked scary things, this would scare him too much and I didn't know how to change it. I'd gotten myself into something scary while I was trying to talk about a big black growly dog. [*She laughs.*] I had a real hard time with it, and it wasn't something I would revise. We got in groups later on and read our stories. I found I kinda like mine. I wish I could get an ending for it. I'd like to send it to Chris. If only I could get a friendly ending, something that would explain this big black growly dog that this boy is.

At the next class meeting, Jimmy said he wanted us to take either the story or the autobiographical account and shape it. I just added to the story about my dog Shana. I don't have it with me now. Jimmy's got it. He asked us to try—and I didn't get to this—to put some distance between that incident and us, for instance, have another character in it telling the story. But I'll tell you what happened.

Around Christmas time I left Shana in the care of Chris's older brother, next to my cabin. I had come back and it was like 40 below and my cabin was frozen. I unloaded my stuff—I'm telling you this because it's all written on the other paper that Jimmy has—and ran over to the lodge because for some reason my stove wasn't working. I walked in. The innkeeper is also a trooper and he's a friend of mine. He said, and this is in dialogue 'cause it was easier for me to write that way:

He said, "I'd like to beat up that SOB Cranmer, Madeleine."

"What'd he do this time, David?"

"You know he wasn't shot cleanly but he couldn't have made it anyway."

"What are you talking about, David?"

"When Cranmer shot Shana."

"I don't think that's very funny, David," I said. He has a weird sense of humor, although it's delightful, and I thought it was showing.

"You know what? I talked to Ruth just last night."

"What'd you talk to her about?"

"About Cranmer shot Shana."

"Well, where is he? Did you take him to the vet? Do I need to go to Fairbanks?"

"He said he ran home with a trail of blood after him. That's how he found out he was back."

"I don't understand."

"Shana broke his chain and took off. I think he was looking for you."

And then the story goes on. And I realized that if I were Mr. Britton, I wouldn't be able to make out what was happening. So I just ended it by saying, "My dog was dead, and I didn't see him, and my friends had buried him."

And then I tried to distance myself by comparing the ice and the tiredness and the silver dark of the day, and none of it was enough to numb me. I was trying to get through that some things can't be numbed, you know. It's six months now, and it's o.k. I think what struck me was that before Jimmy's class I hadn't been able even to talk about this, and yet that very first day I could write it. He could make you do that. I'm not sure I could have given the writing even to my best friend. I knew Jimmy would take it the way it is. So that was a good feeling.

Trying to think back on Shana's death to shape that story, I discovered [*She laughs.*] that people then took care of me. David truly didn't know. He thought I knew about Shana's death. I was going to try to rewrite the experience from his perspective because I found out that he went right down the next day to a friend of mine who worked at the lodge and kept saying, "Oh my God, I didn't know!" And I guess the reason that he opened with that to my friend—he's calm and collected usually—is that it's an Athabascan premise of thought. If you hear of trouble you kinda get tough, and he said, "We're going to beat him up." And I think I could work with that part of the story.

I don't think I realized until I got out of that class and am talking to you here about it that I can't imagine even trying to write that story before. I would have waited a long time before I even thought about doing it.

I'm beginning to understand what Jimmy told us that Barbara Hardy said on the poetics of fiction—that we write and live on different levels and sometimes it's fairy tale and sometimes real life. She says that educators think that students need to move from fairy tale to real life. And when they start reporting real life and you work with them, then you've done your job. You've pulled them from that make-believe world into the real world so they can function adequately. Hardy doesn't think that's the way it happens. We live on many different levels at all times, she says.

In class I brought up the fact that *Silas Marner*, which my students had just read, seems to be a very real novel until you realize at the end it's turning out to be what Hardy called a "wish fulfillment." The novel ends just the way you want it to end. Even George Eliot, who wanted to live in the real world and have her novels portray it, wanted a happy ending. Novelists use their everyday experiences, their planning, and their reorganizing of life in the story to inform what they write. We couldn't really live, even as adults, if we lived only in the real world. We have to be creating our own story as we go and kind of making and remaking something that happened.

"Memory is what *must* have happened, not *necessarily* what actually happened," Jimmy said on the first day. That's how you justify yourself to yourself. Sometimes there are things there you can't accept. When we were discussing Hardy in class I remembered and told about how two boys had written papers in my first year as a teacher. Lots of kids were out of school during spring muskrat season. They came back. I hadn't known that hunting season was going to affect the entire school. I had two or three sets of brothers in different classes and it was a lost cause—what they had missed in those days absent from school. So I said, "Tell me, write what you did." I didn't understand what a muskrat was. Actually that was the best writing I got from the two brothers all year. [*She laughs.*]

I knew for a fact that they had been on the same hunt because I had passed them on the road when I was coming to school, with their rifles slung across. And they each showed up in the other one's narrative. But the stories weren't alike at all, even to the extent of how many muskrats were caught. The differences weren't big. The stories seemed real to me. I enjoyed them. The boys were seeing the hunt. Who got what muskrat was important to them.

I told that to my Bread Loaf class and Jimmy was going, "Uh-huh, that's what we do." When I first thought about this, I thought that's what we all do, but it wasn't until Hardy put it in the context of "Look at these stories we tell to make sense of our lives" that I realized we do it, and all novelists do it. And even when novelists say they're trying to make a realistic tale, they're still changing it even when they're doing dialogue. The stories we tell each other eventually become our lives because they go on. That tends to become the reality. What happened or what I told you happened *is* what happened, whether or not that's true. I think it's important when you're dealing with students' stories to remember that. But sometimes those fairy stories about grandparents not being there are very real even though they're supposedly happening a hundred and fifty years ago and not in Alaska. It's still what happened last year with the grandparents. The telling makes the wish fulfillment part of the kids' lives.

Jimmy said that we all put into this pool we call *culture* what later we need to draw out of it, and whatever is in there you can draw on provided you have made a place in yourself for it. And you do that by participating in many different experiences. One of the ways of entering the pool is by reading. You can learn about who you are by reading and by knowing other kids you read about. That made a lot of sense to me.

18

FRED BARTMAN
Aerospace Engineering, University

In the fall of 1982, an undergraduate in Aerospace Engineering at the University of Michigan wrote me that he was excited to be taking a course in which students were designing and building an apparatus for carrying an experiment into space. He said, "It's so great to be working on something real—the students work as teams, do the planning and the work, and when we get stuck, the teacher makes suggestions."

I called up his teacher, Fred Bartman, in Ann Arbor, a professor in both the Aerospace Engineering and the Atmospheric and Ocean Science departments and asked if I could interview him. He wasn't sure he belonged with the teachers in this book. Twice in the conversation he said, "But I'm not a great teacher." I had my suspicions and went to Michigan to check them out. One Thursday evening in March of 1983 we sat at his dining room table and Fred Bartman talked. Here's what he had to say:

Actually, the project got started before I got involved. The history is something like this—after it began the Space Shuttle program, NASA began to sell payload space for various flights. One experimenter might spend a million dollars on a flight. NASA felt they wouldn't sell all the space for major experiments and so decided to offer the leftover space to individuals, to universities, to people in industries who might want to try to do something useful in space but didn't have that kind of money. So they came up with the Getaway Special Program.

We found we could spend $5,000 and get two-and-a-half cubic feet of space and 100 pounds, or $10,000 and get five cubic feet and 200 pounds. The Aerospace Engineering Department chose the cheaper and agreed to pay the money out of department funds. Later, the Pullman Company gave us that sum for a second Getaway Special payload. That's only part of the cost, of course. The expenses of designing and making the apparatus are additional.

I was one of the original group that participated in the first consideration of the project in 1977, but wasn't the teacher of the class. Professor Leslie Jones taught a course based on our upper-air research

Fred Bartman looks and listens as a learner explains.

using rockets and balloons, which became the Getaway Special Project in 1979. At that time, unbeknownst to the rest of us, he had become ill with leukemia, and he needed the help of Professor Harm Buning in order to help him finish the semester. Soon after that Leslie Jones died.

In 1981, I took over the course in the winter semester. I'm working out of a tradition established by Professor Buning, but I think I've gone a little bit further. One of the first things I did was to go to a symposium on Getaway Special programs at the Air Force Academy at Colorado Springs. The Academy is very much interested in having students build some of these things. In presentations the students talked about what they were doing, which was essentially what we're doing now in our course. They showed us the apparatus they were building. My first reaction was that it was not highly polished work. But then I realized it was a good thing for them to be doing. It was obvious that they had done this work themselves. They had not been guided into doing it. They had enjoyed doing these things and they enjoyed telling us about them. I decided it was the kind of approach we should be taking in our course.

Early in February 1981, we had not really gotten very far, and the class of nine students was surveying experiments that could be done. I thought students should do that, however difficult the task is. It's never possible that students can do something like this all on their own. They're going to interact with people, and when they do that, people are going to make suggestions. Some people are going to be quite forceful about those suggestions, and so at times a student may move in the direction of doing exactly what somebody has suggested. I've tried not to be one of those people myself, but on a number of occasions I haven't succeeded. We've had students who've gone to consult with people come back and say, "You know this person is willing to guide me and help me through the design of this part of the project. Should I let him do it?" And I said, "Do you want to?" And the student has said, "No, I'd rather try to do it myself." And then he's done a wonderful job.

What we did at this time was to say, "We'll read as much as we can." It turned out that students don't really like to go to the library too much. [*He laughs.*] They don't mind if you tell them what to read in order to find this or that, but they don't like to search on their own. I think that's the fault of our educational system. But the students did look into some of the literature.

We decided to send letters to professors around the university, asking for suggestions for an experiment. We got three. The first one came from the Department of Atmospheric and Oceanographic Science. A professor suggested the flocculation experiment we eventually decided upon, where small particles moving around in a liquid flock to each other and stick to each other—the aggregation of small particles.

This professor and a postdoctoral fellow were interested in the process that occurs in rivers and streams. Small particles of clay, for example, will eventually come together and form large particles. In fresh water, there are electrical forces that prevent this from happening. When they get close enough together, the electrical forces cause them to repel one another and they don't aggregate very much. But when they approach the ocean, and the water begins to mix with salt water, then the salt causes the conductivity of the water to be greater and the electrical forces are no longer operative.

Now in the laboratory and the rivers and streams, the first force involved is Brownian motion, which is just the random motion of molecules in the fluid. The molecules of water are moving around and bumping into each other and bumping into the particles of clay and causing them to bump into one another. The second thing is that you have currents flowing in these rivers, and they produce shear currents. Particles are moved by one part of that flow at one speed and by the other part of that flow at another speed, and so eventually they bump into each other and aggregate. The third thing involved is the acceleration of gravity. In the laboratory gravity overwhelms both of the other forces. If you put the experiment on a satellite in orbit around the earth, the centrifugal force of the satellite's circular motion is exactly compensating the gravitational force. That's also why the satellite stays in orbit, and therefore you get rid of that gravity force and can study the other forces better.

A professor in pathology came up with another interesting proposal. If doctors discover a person has cancer, they can treat it with chemotherapy, or radiation therapy, or they can go in and cut it out. Now the problem with that final cutting is that cancer cells escape the area. They move in the bloodstream toward other areas, and quite often the cancer starts in another area. This professor told us that certain chemicals you inject in the bloodstream in the body have the characteristic of attracting a certain kind of cancer cell.

Apparently one of the forces that's operating in this process is gravity. The professor of pathology said, "I can study it in the laboratory but I can't study it as well as I could in a gravity-less environment." Upon further discussion, it turned out that to carry out this experiment in the Getaway Special Program we would have to use the cancer cells in an animal, or part of an animal. NASA requires that we give them the payload three months before the flight date and not have access to it after that. They would put it in the shuttle long before the actual launch time. They can't spend a lot of time on the Getaway Special Program because it's not paying them a lot of money. And we didn't think—rather, we knew, that the cancer cells wouldn't live that long. So we couldn't do the experiment.

The third experiment we considered was suggested by a professor in the Mechanical Engineering Department. It was to study the thermal, or heat, conductivity of fluids. If you're working in a laboratory you have to try to separate the effects of convection from the effects of conduction. If you get rid of gravity, you get rid of the convection processes, and you can then study the conductivity. The professor had worked extensively on this kind of research and knew how difficult it would be to design and carry out such an experiment, and he communicated this feeling to the students, who came to believe it would not be the best choice for them.

Then the students made their decision: they would design an apparatus to carry out the flocculation experiment. I tried not to reveal that that was my choice also, but I fear they may have sensed that.

In Book Two of the Design Report for April 1982, the students listed the "broad range of applications" of this experiment in this way:

> a. Chemical firms—better understanding of the coagulation process in solutions.
> b. Natural Resources companies—sedimenting unwanted materials from lakes and rivers.
> c. Oil companies—prediction of the behavior of coal particles in slurries.

In the first semester of my teaching the course, all the students were seniors except for one graduate student. At the end of that semester, some of them continued working in the summer time just because they wanted to participate. Some went away for a holiday and then came back. One person was going to join the Air Force in August. He paid his room rent here and then said, "I might as well stay here and continue working on the project rather than go back home to Maryland." And so he did.

The students named the project SCORE, which was an acronym for Self-Contained Orbital Research Experiment. NASA had decreed that you have to put this experiment in a canister that they provide. They won't provide any power. It has to operate completely on its own, except that the astronaut will turn it on for you and turn it off. And he reserves the right to bring it to an end in case of emergency.

When new students came in to the course in subsequent semesters, they didn't necessarily continue the project along the lines laid out by the previous class. They wanted to change things or maybe start over. I felt we would lose a lot of time that way, although I understood this desire to consider how things might be done differently and therefore better. I decided that a second time we should have some sophomores and juniors in the project to provide continuity. We told them, "We'll give you a special directed-study course, so you'll work with the seniors this semester, but then when you're a senior, we'd like you to consider taking this design course rather than others." Some of them have done that, but not everyone. By the winter of 1982 we had in the project thirty-eight students, including seven women—nineteen seniors, two graduate students, and seventeen people who were either sophomores or juniors—for the project, which is at present scheduled to go into space in 1984.

The course is set up as a student organization, with a student Project Manager, who's elected by the class. We divide students up into various groups, with group managers and people working in the groups. The students make decisions. The Project Manager talks to me, along with some of the other group leaders, during the week. Often we have meetings on Saturdays, and sometimes go out to lunch. We meet maybe two or three hours weekly in addition to the class meetings, which are 1:30 to 4:30 on Tuesdays and Thursdays.

These rooms where we're working are ours. We have the apparatus there and students have keys to the building. Quite often when I come in at 10:00 at night students are working there. Our apparatus can be locked up when they leave, and they're free to come in to work as much as they want. We don't keep hours. Although we have these three-hour classes twice a week, students don't have to be there for all of those hours if they have things to do. They might go down to the store and buy something, or they might go to some other part of the university and try to borrow a piece of apparatus. One group working on the micro-processor likes to go upstairs and sit at a table in the library by themselves and talk about what they're doing and then actually work on it up there.

Initially we had the rule, that if students wanted to buy anything for the project they would have to get my approval. Sometimes they departed from that. I haven't objected, and as a result I think they're doing a little bit more of it all the time. But they're doing it well. I haven't seen them spending on anything I'd object to.

The project was expected to require $30,000 to $50,000 for expenses, principally contributed by engineering and manufacturing companies in the field. We make mistakes and waste some money, but not large amounts. And that's true in projects run by professionals. The university has a policy that if anything is ordered above a hundred dollars, then I have to approve it. If students went out and bought some $200 item and came back and said, "I'd like to get my money back," they would be concerned that maybe they would be turned down. Chances are, I suspect, that they would have a good reason for exceeding the limit, but I'd have to look at that pretty closely.

I should tell you about the apparatus that the students are designing and constructing. It consists primarily of an arrangement of two concentric cylinders, which is called a Couette cell. The fluid is in the cylindrical space between the two cylinders, which are about a quarter of an inch apart. That is where the clay particles would be placed so that their flocculation could be studied. The students saw such a cell arrangement in the laboratory of Nathan Hawley, a postdoctoral fellow. When they saw it, they asked themselves whether it would suit their purposes, and some of them went to the library and studied the original work done on such devices by G. I. Taylor back in 1936. This was a good experience for them. They determined that such a concept would fit the SCORE project. The Couette cell they saw in Professor Meadows' laboratory was made of high quality optical glass, very expensive. So one student, Brad Maker, decided to investigate the possibility of making the cylinders out of plastic. He contacted many different companies, including people who made glass not of optical glass quality. One Friday he drove down to Cleveland and talked to people. After surveying the possibilities, he suggested to the group that we buy some plastic cylinders that were standard production items reasonable in price, and that we work with these initially. Then if we decided we needed expensive ones, we could buy those later. We still haven't bought the expensive ones. Since then a number of other students have redone the looking into the quality of plastic cylinders and come up with new sources. That's been done several times now. In the final version of our design, the outside cylinder will be about 5⅜ inches in diameter and 11⅛ inches long.

You remember that the fluid will be in the cylindrical space between two concentric cylinders when the experiment is about to begin. We then have to take the clay, which is in a small container with a piston on the end, and produce a mixture of the clay particles in the fluid. That will be done after the Space Shuttle is in orbit, without gravity. We'll do that with an ultrasonic device that breaks up the clay into small particles. *Ultrasonic* means "higher than audible sound." In this case, the ultimate device will work at 40,000 cycles per second. The rest of the system we call a "mixer-feeder" system. It mixes the clay particles in the fluid and then pumps this mixture into the fluid between the cylinders. It makes a nice uniform distribution of the mixture. A micro-processor, which is a tiny but powerful computer, will be programmed to initiate the commands for the sequence of operations and to record whatever has to be recorded in the memory.

Many of our students have talked a number of times to the design and development engineers at a company that makes the ultrasonic device. They've discussed what they wanted and how it's unique, and the engineers have come up with suggestions. People at the company have told them that those engineers have taken the problem home and worked on it at nights and come back and made suggestions, and then called them back and said, "Look, I've been thinking about this—why don't you consider it?" When Bret Chambers wrote Professor John D. Boadway at Queen's University in Kingston, Canada, about photographing the particles in water, he received a highly detailed letter from him telling how had used a camera in a somewhat similar experiment. He said that one of his greatest problems in building his Couette apparatus

> was to obtain sufficient concentricity in the cylindrical surfaces so that the gap between them stayed fairly constant. I can foresee two possible problems with your scaled down version, namely that of obtaining the required accuracy and the greater curvature of the field being viewed by your camera.

The tone of that letter implies that Professor Boadway was corresponding with a distinguished colleague.

All these interactions of students with outsiders are different. Every student has had different experiences. Unless engineering students become research assistants—and usually graduate students get those assistantships—they don't have experiences like these. Most undergraduates don't get on the phone and talk to engineers about a new design project. You know what our phone bill was for January and February?—$590. Many students have made a lot of calls. The department chairman is a little worried, I think. I've got a record of all the calls. There's some duplication. The students were perhaps not real efficient in getting all the information every time they called, but I see them doing better all the time.

Now another thing we have to do is measure temperatures at a number of different locations inside the canister. The pressure and the temperature. If the temperatures are not in the right range, then the micro-processor will sense this and turn on either heating or cooling to bring the apparatus into the right temperature range. When the Shuttle is in orbit, the big doors will be opened, and depending on which way the shuttle bay is pointed, cooling or heating will occur. We're trying to achieve an earth temperature. The students have decided that 25 degrees centigrade would be about the right temperature, but I think we realize that to achieve that exactly would be difficult, so I think they will end up with a range between 40 and 10 degrees centigrade. Keep it from freezing. And keep things from getting too hot. And so if it would go out of those limits, they would have set up apparatus to bring it back.

The camera that's going to record the flocculation can't have a shutter because the whole apparatus will be enclosed in a canister that doesn't allow light in. The lens will be open all the time and the pictures will be taken when a stroboscopic light is flashed. One student last year put together a lens system out of a lens he took from a microscope he had at home and another lens he came up with. He had gone to the library and gotten some books on lens systems. He had used cameras a number of times himself. He succeeded in getting almost the quality we felt we wanted, but it was somewhat short of that. When the new students took over, one said, "Well, what can we do differently?" And he called the Nikon Company and succeeded in talking to some of their engineers. They said, "We think we've got standard lenses we could put together that would do the job for you." They loaned the student some lenses and a bellows system, and he's been working on that. Some others students are trying to perfect the previous system that the former student had worked out. The two groups are working in tandem, each trying to improve their system which they will submit to the SCORE group for a decision. I think they're both making progress.

The young man that used a lens from his microscope may feel, "That's my idea. It's original and I'm in love with it," and these other people come along and do something that doesn't seem as difficult but may turn out better. He has to deal with his feelings about that as well as the fact of the operations. This is teaching students things far beyond what a textbook can do. In other aspects of the project students are also showing initiative. For example, when we first started, the students interested in photography had a darkroom in another building. There some experimental research was going on in which systems of very finely powdered material in air are detonated. One of the problems our students encountered was that they couldn't get the extremely clean photographs that we need. We have a darkroom in our building that I hadn't been using for several years, except for storage. The students went in, took all the stuff out of it—after getting permission—brought some equipment over to our building, and now we have a working dark room that was formerly a storage space.

I believe I departed from the customary method of teaching by lectures and tests because I was influenced by Professor Buning's method with the class before I took over. It happened to agree with some things that I thought. Then long ago, there was George Rainich, who was a mathematics professor I had here at the University of Michigan. He was one of the finest professors I ever had. I took many courses from him. Normally in a higher math course you define terms, and state the underlying axioms. You come up with these. They're quite reasonable, and you set up a few theorems. Then on the basis of the definitions, axioms, and the few basic theorems, you logically develop all of the consequences of these assumptions and definitions. What Rainich liked to do was to give you one or two of the definitions and axioms and say, "Now I'm going to stop here. And I want you to think about it. And don't read any books." And then he would say, "Write me an essay about what you thought about. Be logical, and see what kind of consequences you find." And then the students would hand in their papers and he would read them over and show you how Student Number 5 almost came up with so and so's theorem—which is now named after some famous person.

I was impressed by that. It seems to me it has to do with—I'm not sure how to describe it—perhaps the difference between what's involved in learning as compared to being taught. We teachers pretty much—perhaps not all the time—tell the students what to do and how to do it. We demonstrate how it's done and they learn it this way. On the other hand, they could learn by themselves as students in Rainich's class did. In order to solve and understand many of the problems they face in the SCORE project, the students have to employ mathematical formulas, to think mathematically. For example, they have to state the velocity gradient produced by the concentric cylinders for the shear flow portion of our flocculation experiment by the relation:

$$G = \frac{2\pi N}{60}\left(\frac{2r_1 r_2}{r_1^2 - r_1^2}\right)$$

They learn to handle things like that because they need to.

I think I was also influenced by an experience I had in 1960 with a man working on his dissertation. We had a research project going where we were recording sounds arriving at the ground from aircraft, and were interested in determining whether we could use that propagation of sound through the atmosphere to determine temperature, pressure, and wind velocity in the air between the ground and the aircraft. There was research promise for that. So we asked this student to come up with an idea for an experiment. After a month or so, he came to me and said, "Look, I'm not really interested in this. I don't like this. I would like to be doing some reading and decide what my dissertation should be." I said, "In that case, if it's experimental, we're going to have to come up with funding, money to pay your salary and pay for the work." Well, he came up with a problem and together we wrote a research proposal and sent it to NASA. Your chances of getting funding for a proposal are poor unless you know someone there who might possibly be interested. I did, and we were funded. The student simply took off in that work and basically what I did for that dissertation was just keep up with him.

As I pointed out earlier, during the week I talk with the Project Manager and some of the group leaders. Before the class starts, I'm sitting at the back of the room in the center, where the aisle is, and the

Project Manager is putting a number of things on the board he wants to talk about. He'll write due dates for reports, reminders, and other things like that. Students will be sitting there talking and there'll be a lot of noise and he'll have to speak loud and shout, "All right, all right. Now it's time to start!" Then he'll go through the items he wants to talk about, asking for comments and suggestions as he goes. When he gets through and has decided we've had enough discussion, he'll say, "All right, every one go to work now." And people will start working on testing, making measurements, or other things.

Here's how these responsibilities were described in the organization Handbook for winter 1982, issued by Dan Bigelow, Project Manager at the time:

> The Project Manager is responsible for coordinating all phases of Project SCORE. He must ensure that *all* aspects—time, cost, safety, weight, volume, etc. . . . are taken into account in each and every design decision. He must set long and short range goals for the design team, and then see that work proceeds smoothly. He must be an impartial judge in matters requiring a management decision, he must listen to both sides in any argument, and show no favoritism. Procrastination is the enemy of any manager, and it should be avoided. Patience and level-headed thinking will be rewarded in the long run. The project manager must be prepared to devote large amounts of time to this project, and it is worth his best effort. The above principles are also valid on a smaller scale, for all group managers.

The Project Manager doesn't parcel out all the work. The students are working with their particular group leader on whatever phase their work is in. The Project Manager doesn't know all the details of that work, so he can't do that. Then each group has to interact with the other groups so everyone has the measurements required to match things up. They have to mesh with the other groups' time schedules, so they can know when to have their apparatus set up. The Project Manager suggests deadlines for students to do reporting at regular intervals during the semester, to make sure they write down what they've been doing and what they've accomplished during the last two months. Then if they go away at the end of the semester we have a record of what they've done, and what they were planning to do in the future.

Once the Project Manager came up to me and said, "Things seem to be going slowly. We think it would be a good idea if you assigned a mid-semester grade to each of the students." And I did, and I think it had a beneficial effect upon the work. For one thing, the written reports that came in right after that were better than they had been before. I see changes in the Project Managers as the semester goes along. The present one, for example, is developing a lot more confidence. At first he was quite hesitant. They haven't all been that way.

One, who was going into the Marines, and had spent a summer with them, had a great deal of confidence and ability to direct things, and felt he should be doing that. He had no doubts at all. But this semester's manager was a little hesitant at the beginning. The time he spent at the start of each class period was then a lot shorter than it is now. He sees now that there are many more things he should bring to the attention of the class. He's spending a lot of time, however, and this is something I worry about. Students are enthusiastic. They have a full load of classes, but many are spending tremendous amounts of time on SCORE. In some cases I fear it's going to be the detriment of their grades in other classes.

I realize that if I were to plan the course details myself and design the experiment and present this in lectures, I would probably proceed more rapidly and we could incorporate the knowledge of many experts from books and journals. I could consult the engineers in the aerospace industry and perhaps get systems engineers from, say, Lockheed, or other companies. I have contacts and could gather it all together and we could do it much more quickly, organize it, and present it to the students. But the students wouldn't be doing it.

Another thing that worries me is that sometimes I have difficulty comparing for the purpose of grading how one student is doing with how another is doing. Different students are working on different phases of the problem. And I know that each one doesn't get the same experience. Some get a better experience than others do. It depends on what they're working on, how difficult it is, how inspiring that part of it might be.

You might think that some students just don't take to this kind of method at all, and don't know how to cooperate with their peers, but that's not true generally. But one person dropped out of the course last semester. He couldn't come up with a working arrangement with other students. Now I feel that I failed that student because I let the difficulty get to the point where he could take such an action. He didn't come to me, but I believe he felt I should take a strong action as an arbitrator, which I didn't do. But I should have been aware of what was going on and have helped the students reconcile their differences.

The students do a great deal of writing. For example, each group must keep a log of its work. Here's an excerpt from a log summary for February 4, 1982, published in the Project Manager's Organization Handbook as an example for new students:

WHAT IS NEEDED FROM OTHER GROUPS

1. Primary experiment group—need to know if the silicone material would be adequate for water-tight sealing. Talk to Margi.

CURRENTLY BEING WORKED ON

1. Brad is investigating sources of the aluminum for the dummy mounting plate and the channels. Suggested alloy #7075 has poor welding characteristics. #6063–T5 alloy may be substituted.
2. Margi and Risto will pull-test some 10–32 stainless steel screws as recommended in report 2. Bill, who is in charge of the AM 211 lab, has agreed to help with these tests.
3. Bill is trying to contact Andy Maclellan and Dr. Alan Whittman from Hughes to obtain honeycomb material for the shelving. The material was demonstrated at the Hughes seminar.
4. Brad is studying the user's guide to the NASTRAN program and material on dynamic analysis.

ACCOMPLISHMENTS

1. Margi received sample of silicone material from S.W.S. Silicone Corp. on 2-1. This material will be used in adjustable shock absorbers on the G.A.S. payload. The company may be a source for other silicone materials and for dollar donations.

At the end of the semester, the students have to submit summaries of the work of the entire semester, in fairly polished form, and those generally are better written than the routine reports. Those students who have taken the senior Humanities required course in writing usually do well.

I generally don't talk to students about my own research, but I have discussed it with some students in this class because they've asked me about it. I spoke of research I had done in the past in rocket sounding work at White Sands Proving Grounds and at Fort Churchill, Nevada, and some of the work I did with unmanned balloons. And I have pictures of these things around in my office—that's why they asked me about them. Right now I've been trying to put together a detailed model of the earth where I specify for each of the twelve months of the year the nature of the reflectivity of the earth, the scattering of radiation by the atmosphere, and the reflectivity by clouds, for every 10 by 10 degrees latitude and longitude of the earth—and make this model agree with experimental data. And I'm going to do the same thing for the manner in which the earth emits heat radiation. Over a period as long as a year or so the absorbed solar radiation should equal the emitted thermal radiation so that on the average the climate of the earth does not change.

Then in addition I have a proposal in with a professor from the School of Public Health. He has participated in a survey in Nepal of cataracts in older people and has found, as other people also have suspected—that there's a relationship between the total accumulated exposure to sunlight and the development of cataracts. I'm going to work out calculations of total exposure to sunlight for people in different villages in Nepal where the environment is different—cloud cover, the effect of mountains shielding people from the sun for a certain portion of the day, and so forth.

Students who do nothing but read textbooks and listen to lectures don't get an idea of what real research is. They know none of the mistakes and poor or partial results that preceded the discoveries of the authorities. They get the idea that all you do is go through this logical process and everything comes out perfect. One man, Samuel Glasstone, has done something about that by publishing what he calls "Source Books." He's done one in Atomic Physics and one in Space Physics. He puts together a sequence that really describes how discoveries were made, showing what a first person did, and then a second, and so on, demonstrating how one authority learned from another.

Students come into my office to use the phone to call engineers around the country about design or materials problems, and they say, "I have to use the phone," and I move out of my chair to another. I think they consider me then "one of the boys," but that doesn't take away any of my authority. I don't have a problem there. I can remember in my early teaching days here my students weren't much different in age from me. I had good social relations with them. The University used to have Air Force students here in the Air Force Guided Missile Program, and I got to know many of those people very well. I was invited to their parties. They were very skilled at shaking dice and taking my money away from me, and they loved to do it. I think in lecture classes I try to tell students what I would like them to do. I grade them and give them exams and assignments, but if a student comes back and objects to how I've treated him, I'm willing to let the class decide what to do, and I tell them that. And I've done that all along. Sometimes I feel they don't believe me—that they have options and can take advantage of them.

In the SCORE Project three times a semester we ask students to fill out evaluations of each other. "Is the student you're rating enthusiastic about the project? Does he or she do quality work? meet deadlines? approach assignments with the professionalism one would expect on an actual engineering job? Overall, do you feel the student is making a valuable contribution to Project SCORE?" Their ratings, on a continuum from 0 to 4, are kept confidential.

I think when students believe they have learned from submitting themselves to drills and lectures, they have actually been learning because they took along inside them something that made the difference between them and people who didn't learn much in school. When I was younger I found that I generally did better when I set myself a heavier load than a lighter one. Students retain things they are really working on, not just studying. They do this with things that they are thinking a lot about and ultimately making decisions on. In the SCORE project, students not only make decisions constantly but they plan for making decisions in an orderly and timely way by designing such things as decision trees. And when it came time for considering how to program the microcomputer that was to control the workings of the apparatus, students had to do that.

Working on SCORE, students are influenced above all by the fact that the apparatus they're designing will be ultimately flown. I think they realized that especially when Jack Lousma, one of the astronauts, visited our class. He's a graduate of our aerospace engineering department at the University of Michigan. He's been back twice. He didn't come here for that purpose, but while he was here, we were able to arrange to have him visit the class. In a free-form, interactive way, he asked students questions. He came here the first time, sat down in front, pulled out a pad of paper, and said, "Tell me about it." He took notes. Then he proceeded to ask them very good questions. He showed a great deal of interest and made suggestions. That was a terrific session. He was saying, "I'm going to treat this like a briefing that I would have as an astronaut with some company that comes down and wants to find out something." I didn't have Mr. Lousma as a student, but I appreciate what he's done for the Project.

In this work students are being exposed to the real thing. At the end of this semester I expect them to come up with a complete initial design. But that set of apparatus will probably not fit into the two and a half foot cubic space, and we'll have to modify and rearrange it. Then we're going to have to put it on some sort of shaking device to simulate the shaking it undergoes during the actual Shuttle launch. We're going to have to realistically run it through a sequence of temperature variations to see whether the control system works and whether all of our apparatus works under those conditions. At that point we'll have to modify some things. That's going to be a learning process for the students.

I thanked Fred for talking to me and he said, "I enjoyed having your sympathetic ear," and added, "I think you'd be interested to know of two things that have happened recently. One was that a former student in the course who is now a pilot flying the Lockheed P-3C Orion sent us a check for $100 as a contribution to Project SCORE. Another is that some of the students in the Project came to me and said, 'We'd like to change the words behind the acronym SCORE, from Self-Contained Orbital Research Experiment *to* Student Coordinated Orbital Research Experiment.' *But I'm not sure that* coordinated *is the right word there. Do you think* created *would be better?"* I said I thought the word created *sounded more accurate to me.*

Before I left Ann Arbor I talked with one of Fred's students in the SCORE Project. He said, "The other day the Project Manager got on us for not keeping up the work properly. He gave us hell fire and told us we had better get on with it. As we were going out the door, Professor Bartman called out, 'And have some fun while you're doing that.'"

19

TOM SMITH
Mathematics and Computers, Private School

In the late stages of putting together this book, I heard about Tom Smith, who teaches at the Park School in Brookline, Massachusetts. I was unable to visit him on the job, so I interviewed him by telephone. Like other enablers here, he wanted to tell me about another teacher whom he thought I should talk to, but I insisted upon interviewing him. Because I had never met him, he came to me only as a voice, not strident or insistent, yet carrying the subdued passion of someone committed to making exciting things clear and compelling to learners. I asked him how he taught mathematics.

At the Park School the projects we do sometimes look a lot like science, and sometimes they don't look so much like science, but just fun things to do. For example, kids in sixth grade are always writing secret things to one another. That's a big deal, you may remember. I asked my students to study codes by finding out the frequencies of letters in the alphabet as they are used in English literature. We went to the library and each person got out a book that looked typical to him or her. And in pairs the kids began to count letters. They'd just open up the page and start in. They kept track of how many *a*'s, *b*'s, and *c*'s, and so on. Fine. I didn't say how many they had to find. At the end of twenty minutes that collection of kids had counted up thousands and thousands of letters.

From that data, using calculators, of course, they could figure out what fraction or percentage of the total each letter took up. *E*'s occurred 21 percent of the time and *a*'s 15 percent of the time, or whatever. They found that some letters were used much more frequently than others. Based on that, I gave them a coded message where all the *a*'s were transcribed into another letter, maybe *n*. I didn't tell them what the mistermed letters were. I just gave them this coded message. So they counted up the letters in the coded message and found out that 21 or 22 percent of the time the letter *q* occurred, and so they said, "Oh I'll bet that's an *e!* Let's put an *e* for *q*." And that was the start. They

Tom Smith enters into the subject of snow with his learners.

began to filter out the letters that made sense. It was a treat for them to unlock the code. It was a simpleminded one, but it had its uses. From the teacher's point of view it was a way to study percent, but from the child's view it was using percent to unlock some codes. Then they made their own codes and wrote secret letters to their friends, who had to decode them, based on the percentages.

Most of my students have calculators at home. We use them at school, but not indiscriminately. In figuring the frequency of the letter e, for example, the kids found it didn't come out to be exactly 21.5, but perhaps 21.498763892. Well, what does that mean? About 21.5. Let's call it that because we're not interested in all the rest of those numbers for our present purposes.

At the Park School in sixth grade we combine math and science, so that the math comes naturally out of doing things. It's not just the study of addition, subtraction, and multiplication. Take our study of the science of sound. We make a lot of sounds and talk through garden hoses and other things. Hang a fork on the end of a string. Loop the string around the end of your finger and stick it in your ear. You know there's a kind of folding down flap in front of your ear. Fold it down so the string actually contacts that flap, and have somebody take a pencil and tap the fork and the most incredible Big Ben sound will come about. The sound goes through the string and up into your ear. The kids love it. They start hanging other things from strings and we have something of an orchestra going with refrigerator racks, pliers, and spoons and so forth hanging from the string. Some things work well, some terribly, that's part of the process. You find out what you can use to make your music.

That leads into studies of sound and vibrations, because all sounds have vibrations. The problem in studying useful vibrations, as in guitar strings, is that they happen so fast you just can't look at them. They just happen, and they're hard to study. So we look at other vibrations and wonder if they're indicative of what happens with music and other such sounds. We take the toy called Slinky, a coil of wire. If you stretch it out and tap it with your finger, it sets up different waves and vibrations that you can see. We can understand the vibrations of musical strings by looking at Slinky. If it is elongated by say fifteen feet or so, and a person wiggles it, certain kinds of waves are set up. In some cases it's a wave that looks like an S. You can look at it—the Slinky bends a foot or more either way. You can put it on the floor in a hallway and hold one end while another person takes the other end, and wiggle it back and forth at a regular pace so you set up a vibration. That's very close to what a vibrating string does. It goes back and forth at a regular pace. That's what we mean by frequency—back and forth, how many swings there are in a minute.

One of our favorite vibrations is a pendulum. It goes back and forth at a regular pace. The first question we ask the kids is, "How could we change how fast it goes back and forth?" That is, how many times it goes back and forth in a minute. We're asking them to change the frequency. We get all kinds of hypotheses. One kid says, "I know, put a heavier weight on it." Another says, "Put a lighter weight on it."

We say, "Well, what would a heavier weight do?" Somebody says, "No, it'll make it slower because heavier weights are harder to move." And both seem reasonable, don't they? We run an experiment. We keep everything the same except for altering the weights at the end. Much to everyone's surprise, it makes no difference. Then we can bring up Galileo and his experiment dropping things off the Leaning Tower of Pisa and other such experiments.

"What else might change how fast it goes back and forth?" we say. "How long the string is." "O.K., we'll make it shorter and longer but leave everything else the same." And that doesn't change the frequency. We take data on that, and make graphs and charts. And we try other things—how far back you pull it, for example. It turns out the most interesting one is the changing of the length. Once they do that and start making charts, they make predictions. "Well, we don't have one that is three meters long, but if we did, how many times would it go back and forth?—based on our graph here." We chose to use the metric system in this particular class.

The culmination of this sequence was that in a three-floor stairwell we built this giant pendulum 7 meters long, which is like 25 feet. We just hung the pendulum over the stairwell. It moves incredibly slowly, takes about six or seven seconds to go back and forth once. We usually put on the end a weight of a kilogram, about two pounds. Kids love it. And all that knowledge—it makes vibrations that you can actually see. And the fact that an A note on the piano is 440 cycles per second, instead of 7, now has a lot more meaning for the kids.

Usually the last thing we do with sound is figure out how fast it travels. Because it does take sound time to go from one place to another. The kids say, "Oh yes, I know about echoes. My dad taught me that when lightning flashes you count the seconds and you'll hear the thunder and then know how far away the storm is." And somebody else will say, "Oh yeah, when I went to the baseball game I saw a player hit the ball and a split second later I heard the hit." So then we ask, "How fast is that sound traveling from the bat to your ear? How can we measure it?"

At school we have a huge field. We go to one end of it and at the other end we set up a pendulum that goes back and forth once every second. We commandeer a teacher from the faculty room to bang on a metal pipe to match the frequency of the pendulum swing, so that there's one bang every second. Then we keep on walking farther and farther away, and eventually get to the point where we see the teacher bang on the metal pipe and a split second later we hear it. We keep walking farther until we hear the bang by the time his hammer is at the top part of the swing—so that we're exactly out of phase, as engineers would say. When he lifts the hammer up, we hear him hit. We see him hit again, and then when he lifts the hammer up, we hear him hit, exactly the opposite of one another. We can measure the distance between us and the man and find out how far sound travels in one-half second. In that way the kids measure the speed of sound and then compare it with what scientists have found. We're usually within 10 percent of their measurement.

In the pendulum experiments you can see how we put math and science together. The question was "What can change the frequency of the pendulum's swing?" The kids have decided to change the mass, or weight, at the end of the string. So they take the constant length of string, put a variety of masses on it, count the number of swings back and forth, and make a data table. If you have 100 grams on the end, it goes this fast. If you have 200 grams, it goes that fast. If 300, another speed, and so on. Then they make a graph and see how it varies in that way. Then we'll make some generalizations or predictions. Well, we didn't have a pendulum that's 3 meters long, but according to your graph, what do you think the frequency of such a pendulum would be? Then they actually built it and tested it. We have a stairwell that goes three flights. So we built a pendulum that was 7½ meters long. That's quite long, about 30 feet or so. They projected what that would be, using their graph. And then they went down and tested out their prediction. That's a lot of math. They're graphing, they're doing metrics, and they're doing multiplications and divisions, finding what's the average per second, and so on.

In a more abstract way we discuss the speed of light. We talk about the fact that the closest star is four and a half light years away, meaning the light from it takes four and a half years to get to our eyes. Kids get incredibly philosophical when we talk about such things as infinity and the fact that parallel lines never meet. "Never meet? Aw, come on, really?" They wind up being philosophic in their own way, but their philosophy is not terribly rigorous. One of the things I can do as a teacher is provide kids with a rich set of experiences that later on they can sort out.

But I don't want to imply that all of this kind of knowledge can be touched and felt in the kids' experience in a real way. Until I was much older I never really felt it myself. It's not that I want to teach advanced things to kids at a younger and younger age. I just want to help them, especially in sixth grade, to experience all they can experience, and not to make them wait for it until they are juniors in high school and take physics.

This is exciting for me. I have a three-year-old at home and I get such a thrill out of showing her something commonplace when she is seeing it for the first time. I get that kind of kick teaching as well.

I think a lot of us have that same kind of response to not learning in school. We say, "Boy, I really could have used that," or "That would have made a lot of sense to me." I see it all the time when I work with teachers who aren't really mathematicians but are in a position to be teaching math. They say, "Why do I move the decimal over when I'm dividing?" And I say, "Let's take the chips out here," and I show them a little chip trading game. All of a sudden lights go on in their heads. "Why wasn't I told this?" At first they feel school cheated or deceived them, and they become angry. Then they become missionaries, and they bring the chip trading games to their own students.

It's important for teachers not to oppress kids in math and create a lot of stress over the rightness of the answer. Instead they should be encouraging kids to throw things around. Every answer is an answer. Let's see how reasonable it is and not condemn a "wrong" answer for being wrong as if there's only one right answer. There are a lot of right answers. And some are more beautiful than others. There's beauty in patterns, so it's more than just numbers.

We have a coed school, pretty much split down the middle. I've had the sensation that the more we've gotten away from the textbook-work-book approach, the more comfortable the girls have become. The tendencies are still there for girls to shy away, and that's where the talent of the teacher comes in—to bring them out of that. The fact that a boy is aggressive ordinarily will get him more attention from teachers, especially math teachers. Teachers should not allow themselves to be seduced by that aggression. Take the quiet girl and give her a forum for all that she has to offer, and she may not be loud, but there's a forum for her somewhere. I've found that girls are easily the equal of boys in talent.

We have a math team now. I thought at first I didn't really want a math team, but I went to look at the district competition and saw the excitement in the kids. So I decided to give it a try. I was surprised to find that there were a lot of kids who otherwise wouldn't have anything like this to do competitively. So they came out of the woodwork. Those shy kids had a forum now. And quite a few of them were girls.

But I'm not out to make girls equal to boys. I don't believe boys should be the standard by which we measure girls—you know, "Let's bring them up to where boys are." Girls have wonderful differences from boys in a lot of ways, more than just biological differences. All kinds of upheavals happen in adolescence. Lord knows what's going on both chemically and environmentally that destroys all kinds of balances. Carol Gilligan of Harvard has written some wonderful articles—and I think a book—about them. Differences in the way they think and respond. She came and spoke with us at school several times. Very practical her work became for me in the classroom.

I went to school at Massachusetts Institute of Technology here in Cambridge. In 1967 I took one of those awkward computer courses. I passed it, barely. I took a second one and did so poorly that I was all set to fail. So I did the smart thing. You know, no one at M.I.T. fails a course. He just drops the course before the final exam, which is what I did. And so I didn't really touch computers back then, except to use one a little bit later when I was an engineer. Several years ago when I was teaching here at the Park School, one of the trustees said, "Oh Tom, there's a computer conference at Harvard. It's going to be for two days. I'll give you the money if you want to go." You know, *gratis*—this was out of her own pocket.

So it was kind of a fluke. I went to the conference and all of a sudden—it was one of those times in a person's life when things come together—I was hearing new ideas and seeing new things that were extremely exciting to me. I took them back to school, and we soon bought two computers, and I just started.

I began by making mistakes. I play guitar, and that's the way I play guitar. I play every single note possible on the guitar. I throw out the ones that don't sound well, and whatever is left over is music. That's the way I approached computers. On the computer I did every single thing I could dream of, and threw out the things that weren't working. What was left over was music. With the guitar I had pretty much taught myself. The learning process was intense and put me in the position of being a student again—very frustrating. I did a record about that for children. My guitar experience gave me an entry into learning and teaching computers.

The first thing I saw was that kids who had learning problems seemed to be especially attracted to these machines. "What's going on here?" I asked myself. "It doesn't make sense. Here we have this machine that's totally unhuman in its demands for proper syntax attracting kids who can hardly spell." From that point on I began to realize that the software written for educational purposes is incredibly awful. And so I started writing some things myself, and having fun with them. Now I'm getting to the point where I'm going to stop teaching at the Park School for a while and do that full time.

I've evolved a computer program called Turtle Tracks, which is put out by Scholastic, Inc. It's for second graders through adults, in which a kid gives commands to a turtle that makes pictures on the screen. For example, have him make a square. First instruction: "Draw forward five (DF 5)." Second instruction: "Turn Right (TR)." Third instruction: "DF 5." Fourth: "TR." Fifth, Sixth, Seventh, Eighth, in a sequence like that, until the turtle has a series of instructions—draw, turn; draw, turn; draw, turn—that creates a square on the screen. When I say "draw," I don't mean he's drawing a line, but a series of characters, asterisks or letters or whatever. And then the child says, "Well, wait a minute, the turtle's doing the same collection of things over and over again. He's drawing, turning; drawing, turning. Always turning." And so the child sees that the program could be shortened if he could just tell the turtle to Draw Forward 5 and Turn Right, and then do those things four times. And so all of a sudden he has a three-line program instead of a seven- or eight-line program to do the same picture. It's not just squares, but kids have a lot of fun drawing houses and sailboats, and so forth.

Oftentimes we say, "Draw whatever you'd like." But we ask that the kids say what they want to draw before they start out, so we know what their goal is, and how they approach getting there. That's telling. Some start on the outside and work in. Others start on the inside and work out. Some kids when they run into trouble end up erasing the whole thing and beginning all over again rather than reworking what they have. All of this is a very interesting exhibition of what they do in other places in their school lives. I have the hope that sometimes one could remediate the problem. Say for example, the child who is frustrated and always wants to break the whole thing and start all over again—whether it be in building a block tower or running a computer program, or doing a long division problem—throws the paper away and starts all over. What I would like to be able to do is say, "Well, let's figure out where you went wrong part way through and take it from there." My hope is that by seeing it on the screen and recognizing the relationship of following instructions to what the turtle does will carry over to other activities in the child's life, whether building something or solving a problem, or working with people. But I can't tell you right now that it's really going to work out that way.

Since the kids have been working on the Turtle Tracks program, we have a new word in the vocabulary of the school. There's a command called "New." You press the N key and the RETURN button and the action wipes out the screen, wipes out the memory. Everything's gone, everything. You're starting again from a blank memory. The kids have begun to use that word as a verb. They'll say, "I'm going to *new* this paper," or "I'm going to *new* this assignment." It's an interesting parallel. The kids see it's a way they can also work on non-computer things. Sometimes there comes a point when you're hopelessly lost, when that's what you have to do—start all over again. But there are other times when that's the worst thing to do.

Most computer software teaches poorly. I've tried to do something about that in designing programs. For example, suppose a child decides to play around a little bit and draw backward two steps, and thinks, "I wonder what the turtle will do." The computer may say "Syntax Error" and give a number for the error. Then the kid has to consult a book to find a description of the error, and often that's not clear. In my programs I try to make that a little more approachable. In Turtle Tracks if the child does that, the computer says, "Whoops! The computer doesn't understand." I was careful in choosing that phrasing. I didn't say, "You made a mistake," because you didn't make a mistake. You had something perfectly fine in mind. The computer doesn't understand what you wrote. I chose the words *the computer* carefully, rather than *I* don't understand. It's very important not to project a human quality into the computer, into all of those transistors in there. It's not a human being with a brain.

That reminds me of the most important short piece of advice I ever got about teaching. It was when I was just starting. You say—and this is a trivial example that can be generalized to more complex situations—"2 times 3," and the child responds, "5." What do you do? You could say, "Wrong. What's the *right* answer?" or "Does anybody know the right answer?" Or you could try to figure out what the child is doing that's correct. In this case, it's likely that she was thinking of 2 plus 3. So you say, "What is 2 plus 3?" and she says to herself, "Oh, that's 5. Six must be the answer." When you or the computer asks a question and the child comes up with an answer, chances are she is coming up with the correct answer to some question. So if you can figure out which question will be the right one for his answer, ask that question back.

Seymour Papert at M.I.T. invented a computer language called LOGO, which is the source and inspiration for this thing I call Turtle Tracks. The whole idea is that the kid should be placed in front of the computer and then build things with it, do things with it, manipulate it, and change it. I got a lot of ideas from Papert's work. The common way of using the computer to teach kids is to give them a drill-and-practice program on their multiplication tables. The computer says, "What table do you want?" and the kid says, "Sevens." Then the computer asks, "7 times 7?" and the child says, "49," and the computer puts on a little happy face and says, "That's right," and might even say his name—"Johnny." "Now 7 times 9," and the child says, "83" and the computer has a sad face and says, "That's wrong, Johnny. Try again." And the same problem comes up on the screen again. Now that's the computer controlling the child, training him. That approach has some uses, but for me it's much less interesting than the child controlling the computer.

A kid in my class had trouble learning Latin vocabulary, and so I said, "Well, suppose you write a computer program that will test you." The child did that. The physical act of writing the program helped him learn the words he was testing himself on. He wound up writing a program that presented certain Latin words on the screen that he would have to know the definition of. Then he took the test he had devised. If he was right, the computer said he was right. When finished, his program looked very much like the drill-and-practice program I've been criticizing, but writing it himself was very much different from having some teacher or publisher being the brain and the student being the vessel that is filled with all that knowledge. This boy had to decide, "Now what is it that I'm going to put in here?" He didn't have to include those things he had already mastered.

There's a great difference between rote learning and real learning. One can do the same things in different ways. One way you may be unsuccessful—well, it may be successful but also painful. Another way, turning it around, you can make it all of a sudden very meaningful. When I'm playing the guitar I don't really know where the end point is before I begin. I start out and kind of steer as I go. I let the guitar take me places where I didn't know I was really going to go. The medium dictated where I wanted to go—how my fingers actually fit that, what kind of music felt best coming out of my fingers and my throat. I wound up being steered in various directions. I found I learned in plateaus, not in one big lump. I would learn and then might go for a few months singing songs but not really working on the guitar with the fingering positions and so forth. I would work on the songs and then reach a plateau where I would have to taste those songs for a while without learning anything new. Then I'd reach a plateau and not learn new songs but try to do fingering styles for a while. I'd reach a saturation point where I couldn't go any further until I'd savored those. And I continue to need climbing sessions and plateaus in other parts of my life besides guitar or banjo. I try to translate that into my teaching to allow for that very important time for the kids to taste and savor. You just can't teach something and say, "Now they know all about vibrations because I did my unit on sound." They don't. They have to savor what they've learned and come back to it after a while. Then it becomes unconscious and conscious too. There are a number of times when I've done public performing of music. At those times I pray to God that my fingers will know the song because I can't remember any of it in my head. In that respect there's kind of an automatic pilot there, but one can often depend on it very consciously because he doesn't have to worry about the finger picking. What he has to concentrate on at that time is the intonation, the presentation. The two work in concert.

In my ten years of teaching, I've seen about three hundred kids. Granted, this program Turtle Tracks has now sold about 1500 copies.

If I multiply 1500 times thirty or forty kids that would be encountering each copy, I feel like my classroom is all of a sudden continental. I feel like I'm touching all those kids out there. I'm not physically present with them, but I get a big kick out of it—all these kids, all over the world, even though it's not a bestseller, are just starting Turtle Tracks. It's a tool. I like to think of it also as an environment, in which kids can be freed of all the complicated syntax of computers and meet a rather child-oriented language. Non-typists can sit down and write a program to get this turtle to do something in fairly short order, so that they're freed from all the complex computerese. They're in an environment where they can try to get this turtle to do something. They can test things out. They don't even have to say, "I want it to do this." They can just say, "What happens if I do this?" They can explore at a lot of different levels. One can be very academic about this or very playful. Sometimes kids who have no idea of what they're doing come up with the most interesting shapes and patterns on the screen. And everybody else gets excited and all of a sudden the kid who's the classroom dolt is the center of attention. He doesn't tell anybody he did it by accident, or maybe he does—it doesn't make any difference. Suddenly he's important. That's the kind of thing Turtle Tracks is designed for.

The child is writing a list of instructions that this turtle creature on the screen will carry out. That's all that computer programming is— writing a list of instructions for the computer to carry out. But in this case there's a concretized version of the computer in the turtle. The child writes a series of draw forward instructions and turning left and right and jumping. Just a collection of one-after-the-other instructions that say, "Turtle, go ahead and do them." Maybe the kid is surprised and maybe not, but usually what happens is that some sort of picture begins to emerge on the screen and often what happens is that the child will make the program longer and longer and the turtle will make more and more complex, pictures on the screen. Generally speaking, what happens next is that the child begins to perceive patterns and then says, "Oh yeah, I can do this shorter and easier," and by doing that she begins to learn to do elegant programming.

Soon I found myself describing several roles for the computer—in an effort to figure out what's important for me to do and what's not important. In schools we can treat the computer as an object, as we treated the pendulum. We can study it, massage it, change things and measure them, and poke it and see what happens. We can turn on the computer, program it, try this number and see how it responds, and so on. That's just treating it as an object and observing how it responds. Or we can use it as a tool. We don't care what's going on inside it as long as the word processor works and we get the damned thing done by tomorrow. That's the computer as a tool.

In some places, not too many, the computer is used to manage instruction, helping the teacher figure out grades or bring about individualized instruction. And there's the computer as teacher, a role rather misused and misunderstood today. It has several parts itself. Kids can play games on the computer and learn certain things. And there's drill-and-practice, the most common use. The computer flashes up a question—"What's the capital of Arkansas?" The kids write in an answer and the computer says "Right" or "Wrong."

In the role of the computer as teacher, there's a type of program called "Simulation." A child is placed in an environment generated by the computer which allows persons to test certain things out in a safe way. For example, there's a simulation of a nuclear power plant. A child is put in a position of managing the plant. What happens if you turn this valve or do that? Well, that temperature goes up and this thing goes down. Now what are you going to do? You start changing certain things, and perhaps there's a meltdown. Or perhaps you manage things well and there isn't a meltdown. A child couldn't possibly do something like that in real life because of the consequences, but the computer can simulate that in a safe way, which takes a lot less time, too. One can learn about the various things that go into the pluses and minuses, the balances of managing a nuclear power plant.

One can role-play in social science, too. There are some wonderful simulations. One is called Community Search. You're in a position in a new land. You start growing in this society and trading with other places. Various things happen that cause you to respond in certain ways. Maybe by the end, there's a revolution, or maybe peaceful coexistence between societies. The child role-plays three or four centuries of history in an hour or two on this computer program. There's always the danger of children believing that the world behaves as the computer behaves, but the responsible teacher points out the shortcomings of the computer.

And then there's the computer as toy—that's well known. And there's the computer as worker, *robotics*. The blanket overall question is the ethics or social responsibility of using computers. I found it useful to think about all those different roles the computer can play, so I don't wind up just thinking of it as something to use for learning the multiplication tables or the names of the capitals of the states.

I've seen computers in environments where kids could explore, where they have the opportunity to effect new ideas and test them. I'm excited to see that they don't just appeal to kids who are very bright, but also to kids who have learning problems. Computers also provide a social medium, which really surprised me when I first began to work with them. There are kids who have a lot of difficulty communicating and being involved socially, for whatever reasons, sometimes very complex. Often the computer breaks down those barriers. It's possible to stick a child in a closet before a computer. But the most exciting things happen when you stick children and computers out in the center of the room and see what goes on around them.

A computer is a machine that allows you to do something for yourself. I feel the same way to a great extent about the calculator. It freed me and my children in school to explore things we couldn't possibly have explored otherwise. But it's been a lot more difficult for me to go out and get a couple of hundred dollars for a couple dozen calculators than to get $10,000 for a couple of computers. People seem to think that calculators are a crutch but computers are the wave of the future. They're more exciting.

Because this whole thing is so new, all of a sudden I'm an expert. I've had to act as a consultant to a lot of schools around here. The administrators say, "What's all this about computers? I just spent $20,000 to buy these computers and my teachers don't know what to do with them. I want to hire you to go in and make all my teachers computer literate by December First." I'm pretty conservative about such things. Personally I'm excited about computers but I'm not going to club somebody over the head and say, "You will also be excited about computers." So what I try to get across to teachers and administrators is that I've seen some teachers get worse in teaching by using computers. Computers can destroy many good things about a person's teaching. One doesn't force that upon a teacher. You don't force a teacher to use Magic Markers or a blackboard. You certainly don't force them to use a certain videotape, or tape recorders, or anything like that. What you do is present these tools to people and show what they can do and can't do, and they make the choices that fit in with what they want to do. If it doesn't, that's fine. We present computers to the children and work with them. There's a certain amount of mandatory work that they do with computers in this school, but there's ample free-choice time when they can use the computers.

Let's take our Middle School, grades three through five, where frequently in the early part of the year a class consists of about fifteen to seventeen kids. The teacher is simultaneously student of computers and teacher of them. I'll do two or three sessions with something like kids' math games. It might be forty minutes in a week, but the kids through the day have certain amounts of time when they can do homework, or build a project, or whatever. Or they can also work on the computer. Now if everybody wants to work on the computer then we have to have a signup. And that's always been the case. The list goes up new every week. In our school everybody has some free time during the week. And there's recess time when they can be outdoors, in the gym, or in the lounge, or maybe with the computers. I'll only allow them to sign up for certain amounts of time so they won't monopolize the computers. I don't think it's good for them to be put onto computers all the time. Oftentimes the kids congregate at the machines to play games. I don't allow violent games and shoot-em-ups. I provide games that require kids to think and that are also very much fun. And then it usually progresses from that. They start playing games and all kinds of exciting things happen.

Doing some classwork and then playing freely with the computers—one thing inspires the other. At first the timid kids hold back and the aggressive ones get high. By showing the timid kids what's going on, I find they get excited, too. Now even the timid kids sign up for the free period, and once they've reserved it, the system says, "Thou shalt not be removed from the machine." An athletic boy can't come up to a third-grade girl and kick her off the computer just because he's bigger.

The computer is a bad calculator. If you want to add a list of numbers, it's a lot easier to do it with calculators than computers, which are waiting to be fed instructions rather than a bunch of numbers. You can write a computer program that will make the computer behave as a calculator, but it doesn't actually know it. There are a number of programs that translate your computer into a calculator, however. Visi-Calc, for example, will allow you to input a couple of formulas and figure out what's going to happen if the interest rates are this or that. But if you just turn on your computer and write on the screen 5 + 5 =, it'll probably give you nothing or tell you that there's a syntax error or something. It's not naturally a calculator. If you have the Visi-Calc program it can do a lot of things that the calculator can't do for you. But if you want to find the average of a column of figures, you'd do much better to grab a calculator on the desk and use it.

We use the computer as a pattern generator. I have a sixth and seventh grade challenge out to kids. Our computers also work in BASIC, which is a computer language that's pretty good for starting. The challenge is: Write a program that gives you a list of prime numbers. It challenges them to construct a program that will provide a list of prime numbers very efficiently. The prize goes to the program that can do that the fastest. If I have a number, I don't have to divide it by every number left in it to see if it comes out even. I can eliminate all the even numbers, for instance, because I know that all of them are not prime, except for 2. There are certain numbers you can eliminate because you know they're prime or not prime.

Computers can challenge every kid in a class one way or another. I'd like to tell you about a boy I'll call Benjy. He's one of those dyslexic kids you hear about, a real struggler. He cuts up in class. He's got a lot of energy. He's been considered as a pretty slow kid, although fortunately at the Park School we have a very professional bunch of teachers who don't allow that to dictate their work with him. Nobody's given up on Benjy, and he's progressed a lot, but he hasn't been anybody's budding academic star. One day I was walking through the computer project area and there was Benjy playing a game. That must have been about the fourth or fifth time I'd seen him playing this particular game, in which you have to mow a lawn in a certain amount of time. I said, "You're really interested in this game. What are you doing?" He said that after he had played the game for quite a while it had become boring, but he didn't just turn off the computer. He tried to figure out how the computer programmer had made the game do what it did. He listed the steps in the program and then changed them in various ways, one of which was so his lawnmower could go through houses and trees. So he racked up all kinds of points that none of the other kids could get on that game. Now here's a kid who felt confident enough that he could control the computer. It wasn't telling him to do this. That was a valuable lesson for me because it came from Benjy, who had difficulty in school but could go in there and move things around at his will. He did that during one of his free periods, at recess time. Benjy is tutored three times a week outside class by a special language teacher from the general hospital. I think Benjy has added a new dimension to his life in school here, where he has control. He has no control over spelling. Often he has no control over what he's going to say and do next. But ever since he reprogrammed that game, his eyes are lit up. He comes to school incredibly happy about doing things with the computer or without it.

20

JOHN SHEFFIELD
Soldiering, Army

The last profile in this book is a memory rather than an interview. It says a good deal about the learner, me, in order to reveal the achievement of the teacher, whose values and experience were so different from mine.

When I met John Sheffield, I was twenty-four, a college graduate who had volunteered to be drafted—after agonizingly considering conscientious objection—a man who had been raised till then mostly by his mother, drank absolutely no alcohol, and carried with him a little black memorandum book in which he made entries like this:

> Be not so angry that you cannot make others as you wish them to be, since you cannot make yourself as you wish to be.—Thomas à Kempis

When our truckload of recruits stopped in the small parking lot just outside the headquarters building of the Detached Enlisted Men's List at Fort Eustis, Virginia, during World War II, I saw Sheffield nonchalantly resting his elbow on the laid-down tailgate of another army truck. To me he looked an exotic, swarthy skin, dimpled chin, and long sideburns, back in the days when most Regular Army sergeants wore their hair butch style. In his gray-green fatigues, he was a mustachioed Spanish don. I was frightened. Not my kind. For the last two weeks of my new life I had been sensing that I was square, and he was obviously all rounded and loose.

We had to jump down from the truck. Calculating the distance to the ground, I wondered if with backpack and heavy duffle bag I would be able to land gracefully. I made it without stumbling, but the jolt to my spine unnerved me further. Sheffield didn't line us up and call us to attention as I expected, but simply said, "O.K., you guys, follow me to the barracks."

He took us to the first building in the row and said, "I'll be back in an hour to show you how to make your bunks. In the meantime, draw

your blankets and sheets at the supply room." In those first minutes at
a permanent post, every act and word struck me in the face as the
beginning of a series of actions that might end with my death in battle.
At the time, I had no idea that Sheffield understood that most of us
were feeling as awkward as we ever had in our lives. Not until months
later did I realize that without clock or written schedule, Sheffield was
timing our lives so we would learn at a pace we could handle. He had
absented himself so we would have time to examine our digs, use the
latrine, stretch out on our mattresses, and renew our courage. He was
not a proper non-commissioned officer trying to break our spirit so
that we would thoughtlessly obey all commands, including the one to
advance under fire.

But at that time I didn't know any of these things, and I feared
Sheffield. He looked to me like someone you would meet in a pool
room, and the only pool room I had ever been in was in a resort town
on Lake Michigan when at eighteen I was working as a bellhop in a
nearby hotel one summer. In a cool tavern on a hot afternoon I had
stood at a jukebox feeding nickels to Coleman Hawkins sliding up and
down the scale narcotically as he played "Body and Soul." Occasionally
I had looked up and across the empty dance floor to where two men
and a woman sat at a table near the cue rack and laughed and talked
loudly. As I put my fourth nickel in, I glanced up and saw one man put
his arm around the heavy woman and press her breast firmly. She
giggled. I didn't stay for the rest of "Body and Soul."

In approximately an hour Sheffield reappeared and said, "O.K., you
guys, I'll show you how to make up your bunks. I know you were
taught how to do it in the induction center, but here you're going to
learn to do it right. Draw everything tight. A quarter's got to bounce
off that blanket." We made up our bunks and Sheffield walked up to
one across the aisle from me. "This one's pretty good," he said, and
pulled out a quarter and slammed it down on the blanket. It sank into
the slumped cloth. He laughed and said, "But not good enough."

He whipped off the sheets and blanket and spread out the lower
sheet, smoothing it with his fingers as if petting a cat. "You must pull
everything tight." With the sheets, he made hospital folds of exactly 45
degrees, and inched the blanket, which was tucked in at the other side,
toward him, holding it with one hand at the edge of the bed while
pulling it down and under with the other. He covered the pillow with
the second blanket, folded in half, tucked under, tightly descending to
the sides from the pillow's height so that the head of the bed looked
like a sculpture by Brancusi. When he slammed the quarter down, it
jumped two feet high. I made up my bunk to his satisfaction, but I
could see from his face that it had just barely passed. When I looked
across the aisle at the bunk he had made up, mine looked rumpled.

Next day it was short order drill on the field across the company street from the office. "Detached Enlisted Men's List" meant the company was composed of men who took care of the post—worked in the Officers' Club, Post Headquarters, and the movie house. Bunch of servants and clerks. But Sheffield expected us to drill better than the combat troops on the post.

He was not in a hurry. First, we would learn to stand at attention. "I was in F.D.R.'s honor guard at the White House," he said. "We had to do all kinds of ceremonies. Stand there at attention for a half hour while somebody read something or the band played through a whole program. You know you can paralyze your body so you can't walk—if you get too tight at *Attention*. Now, get your head located so it feels like it's over your feet exactly. No, don't try to stand at *Attention* right now. I'm getting you into this thing. Head over the feet so you feel comfortable. Level. Look straight ahead. Weight on the balls of your feet, not the heels. Don't strain. Don't try to extend your arms right down straight. Just let 'em hang, natural." I was following all this religiously, but it wasn't like taking communion at church, where everything had felt unnatural. "Now move your hands back a couple inches until your thumbs are touching the seams on your pants." I did that and was amazed. My chest had moved forward and expanded but I felt no strain. "Now you're at *Attention*." said Sheffield, "and you can stand that way for hours as comfortable as a raccoon sleepin' in a tree."

My dislike for Sheffield, and what I now realized had been fear, were beginning to leave me. But I didn't give in to the new feeling completely. First impressions either way, I thought, can be wrong. Then Sheffield showed us how to pivot on the ball of the foot, how to take off, how to do an *About Face!* I enjoyed that swinging movement, and suddenly remembered that although I was a college graduate, a bookish man, I had once played a lot of basketball and golf. As this group of diverse individuals marched raggedly back and forth on the field, I began to feel proud of my control over my body. Some of the others were out of rhythm and getting worse, like motors off center. Marphal, the short kid from Pittsburgh with a shock of black hair, kept turning left on the command *To the Right, March!* On the second day of drilling, when we had to do *To the Rear, March!* while marching, and then quickly, *To the Rear, March!* again, so we returned to our original direction, Marphal walked off alone away from the company like Harold Lloyd in a movie. And he did it again. He would get four or six paces away from the rest before he realized he had lost us. Sheffield yelled, "Dammit, Marphal! Wake up and get with us!" but I could hear a chuckle under his words. *Company, Halt!* he would command, and Marphal would hurry back into line smiling sheepishly and say, "I'm sorry, but I can't help it."

"You better damn well help it," said Sheffield, and turned his head aside, smiling. The rest of us were smoothing into a unit. We had done short-order drill at the induction center, but something was different here. After about three days, everyone, except occasionally Marphal, was moving as one, and it was fun drilling. We had the rhythm. I felt when I turned or stopped, Sheffield's voice was touching me gently on the elbow and making it easy, automatic. And so did the rest of the men. We talked about it in the barracks.

Several months later, when I had been made corporal and Sheffield asked me to drill a dozen new recruits, he told me the secret. "Most drill sergeants," he said, "give the order *To the Right, March!* with the men's right foot hitting the ground as they say *Right,* and then the next time the right foot hits, they say, *March!* Then you pivot on your left foot and move off to the right. But that's just a little fast for the way people catch things, so I say *Right* and *March!* just a half beat earlier."

There was nothing gentle about the sound of Sheffield's commands, but they weren't bellowed. He and his buddies in the President's Honor Guard had worked on every detail, thought it out beyond the simplistic instructions in the Army Manual. What works and looks and sounds best in particular circumstances, with real, faulty human beings—that was the answer Sheffield looked for. He knew that you can't shout the word *Attention!* as an order that punctuates a ceremony while a band is playing, because the word ends with an *n* and won't be heard. *Ten-shun!* is a common translation, but has none of the cleanness and pop of Sheffield's *Ten-shut!*

When I first began marching a platoon, I was sick with fear that I would march the men into a building or a parked car, but following Sheffield's ways, I soon began to enjoy snapping orders and seeing the men move like a flight of migrating geese. I had learned to work with them and they with me. It was not an exercise in *machismo.*

After a few days on the post I was assigned to take over the job of the company clerk, who was shipping out. Sheffield said, "Your big job here will be the Morning Report. Russell will show you what it is." He looked at me steadily and said, "So you went to college." Before I could comment, he added, "I got kicked out of school in eighth grade for foolin' around with a girl on the fire escape." I didn't know what to do with that remark, so remained silent, thinking, "How disgusting. I'm working for an animal."

I was so happy being behind a typewriter rather than at the Officers' Club carrying out garbage that I learned my job quickly. Everything official that happened in the preceding day had to be noted at the time and then typed in prescribed form the next morning. I liked the abbreviations and saw the omission of periods as wisely functional: "Pvt Emil

Jones trfd Fort Meade 0800" and such. All my life I had been fascinated by words and the look of letters on a page.

Sheffield appreciated my skills as he began his first months as First
Sergeant of the company. "Geez, Mac, you can sure type fast," he said.
With his approval I determined to be the best damned company clerk
on the giant post. My first step was to learn to type numbers without
looking at them, fast and accurately. To move the fingers from row two
to row four confidently in that long leap was something I wouldn't
have been able to take on a week earlier, but the influence of Sheffield
was beginning to work on me. And I was a good speller, a fact that
filled Sheffield with awe.

Since "Shef," as I soon came to call him, was not in charge of a
combat troop, but a headquarters company, he was seldom in the field
with the men. We sat together in that tiny office, he about eight feet
away from me at his desk, and I listened to him take innumerable
phone calls from the offices his men worked in around the post. When
he talked to enlisted people, noncoms or privates, he began each call
with a buoyant greeting, usually followed by a jocular remark. "Hello
dah!" he would say with mock enthusiasm, "How you feelin' after
chasin' Rosie [the general's secretary] through the woods last night?"
He played different parts in phone conversations, like a little boy, but
with the sophistication of an army veteran. Underneath the playacting
was an effervescent humor, a joy in being alive even when he was
describing a hangover of profound extent. After a week or so of struggling to learn the niceties of the Morning Report, I found myself eager
to enter the front door of that little office every morning. People were
in and out constantly, the phone was ringing, and almost everyone who
talked to us made the moment an occasion because Shef's good humor
elevated the tone of the place. A problem—and there were many because he was essentially an administrator—was not a matter for solemn
frowns and frustration, but a chance to imagine a new way of proceed-
ing. My mother had been a Puritan; Shef was from a different church.

Like most soldiers I met from Virginia, or his friend Sparky from
West Virginia, Shef liked to tell stories, short and long. Of his time in
the Honor Guard at the White House he said, "We had to work funer-
als, of big guys like admirals and generals, at Arlington Cemetery. You
know when Taps was finished you had to fold the flag into a triangle
and walk over to the widow and present it to her. We could fold the
damned thing so tight and so small it wouldn't fall apart if you
dropped it.

"I remember one day we were burying a general. We were all hung
over, as usual for a funeral, 'cause we liked to take on somethin' like
that and see if we could do it just as perfect drunk as when we were
feelin' good. It had been rainin' that day and it was cloudy and dark,

and Jones, the bugler, was the worst off of any of us. When it came time for Taps, he took a couple steps to the edge of the grave and began to blow. I could see the earth was crumblin' at the edge where he stood. He couldn't see, but he was blowin' beautiful, and as he came to the long last note, the ground gave way under him and he fell into the grave. He kept on playin' as he went down. Finished that last note."

I'm just realizing now that the oldest soldier on the post, Sparky, grayhaired and in his forties, was Shef's friend because he was so kind, especially to the younger soldiers. He was an uncle or grandfather who put the recruits at ease by talking of their families and girlfriends. Shef and Sparky had known each other before coming to Fort Eustis. Because Spark drank too many beers of an evening, he came across to some as a bumbler, a man on the skids, to be ridiculed, although in his job as post projectionist he seldom missed a cue during a film and rendered the screen dark. He was a Wizard of Oz scarecrow with soft eyes and the gentlest voice of all the men I had met in the Army. Every Friday and Saturday, Sparky carried his six-pack to the projection booth and finished rolling the movie with a high buzz on.

One night our barracks were inundated by a group of Air Force recruits, whose plane connections had been disrupted on their way to Texas. When Sparky got back from the movie, he was told of their presence. Opening the door to the blindingly bright latrine—the sleeping quarters had already been darkened—he stepped in and down on the one riser before him and said in an avuncular, drunken voice, "So yer gonna be flyboys, eh? Well, I want you to do somethin' for me. When you get over to Germany, I want you to bomb the schools."

He took a breath and burped. "I want you to bomb the churches."

He paused again, and with professional timing, said, "And bomb the hospitals!"

I stood there wondering if he had at last gone crazy with alcohol. And then he staggered to his knees, into praying position, and said, "But save the breweries!"

There was Major Bledren, who in civilian life was the president of a bank. He stood straight, had had some previous military service behind a desk. He thought of himself as a kind of Mormon conscience and model of a soldier—although he was not a Mormon—to the "troops" under his command at this ridiculous rag-tag of a headquarters company that brought together a few college graduates, many men who had known nothing but manual labor in their lives, an Irish poet, and a former swimmer in Billy Rose's Aquacades show. On the major's first day on duty, Sheffield approached him with extra respect, I think because he sensed that Bledren was trying to make something of his laughable position, however much he acted like a Boy Scout leader who wanted to carry out his job with Gary Cooperish integrity. He was fair and he was terribly square as well, without any awareness of what the enlisted men were thinking or feeling. And he was older, in his early fifties. Every once in a while he showed he would like to be paternal as well as military. At the first meeting with this supremely soldierly first sergeant he had been given, who approached him with all that snap and army savvy, I think he was overwhelmed, and slid into Walter Mitty dreams of glory as commander of a battle unit led by this professional who knew more about the army than any other soldier on the post, and a hundred times more than Bledren, who had spent many of his years sitting in an oak paneled bank office back in Pennsylvania.

On Saturday morning inspections of the personnel and barracks, the first sergeant's job was to lead the commander through the company and help him decide what level of performance had been achieved in scrubbing floors, washing windows, cleaning latrines, and presenting beds and open foot lockers in perfectly folded array. One Saturday after a number of the men had taken part in an unusually heavy binge instead of devoting two hours to Friday night cleaning, Shef led the major more rapidly than usual through the inspection tour, hoping to hide the blemishes. At the last of the three barracks, the major began to sense something was different, and said, "Sergeant, let's slow down. I don't think I'm seeing things as fully as I should be. What about those windows? They're badly streaked."

Without a pause, Shef said, "Right, sir. They look awful, but that downpour last night—it was really early this morning, long after the men had gone to sleep. It lasted until 6:00. There was only time for the men to get dressed and eat breakfast before inspection, Sir. Do you see this streak here on this pane? That came from the rain."

"Oh yes," said the major as Shef hurried him on to inspect the non-coms' bedrooms. The major never thought to look outside for verifying puddles of water in the company yard. Later in the day, he came out of his office and said to Shef in the orderly room, "Sergeant! I don't remember any rain last night!"

"Oh it rained hard here last night, Sir. Maybe up at the officers' quarters—you know that's at the other end of the post—there wasn't much rain, but here we had a terrible storm." Sitting there next to Shef, I began myself to believe that it had rained the night before.

The major looked at him quizzically, but said nothing. He wasn't sure about the rain but he was sure he had the best first sergeant on the post and since Shef was keeping a straight face, he wasn't going to cross him. He was right. Shef would never have made an ass of him in front of others. As long as the major attempted to be fair with the men, Shef would protect him, as he protected everybody of good will in the unit, with as many lies as necessary.

Thinking back on those days, for the first time I realize that Shef said little to us men about getting the barracks ready each week for inspections, but even the meanest officer we ever had, Lieutenant Creven, with his white gloves, seldom could find anything to complain of—a soldier or two here and there whose footlocker or uniform wasn't up to scratch, but nothing formidable was ever wrong about the condition of the barracks.

Responsibility for the performance of Saturday inspections started with the individual soldier and went up to the ranking noncom living in each barracks, and then to the first sergeant, who was, in effect, defending himself as he walked the commanding officer through inspection. In other companies later in my army career, on Friday nights there was a lot of badgering of troops by noncoms, and occasionally an unexpected visit from a first sergeant who would take out his fears of being upbraided by the commander the next day by yelling at the soldiers. With Shef in charge, we had none of that. Men came into our company of post clerks and servants in small shipments and were trained for inspections and parades by Shef. We knew more about making things look good than combat troops did. We had all seen or heard of Shef shining his shoes on Friday nights—clean, apply liquid, polish once, shine with a soft rag until the elbows tire, apply polish again, shine, and once more apply polish and shine until you could see yourself in the toe. There was an extra ingredient in the mix of liquid polish Shef made. Maybe it was whiskey—I can't remember—but he laughed as he put it in, and we all talked of it as a kind of medicine man's secret.

So Shef didn't bother us on the night before inspections. Most of us were working to attain his standards, and if any laggard wasn't, we jumped on him. At 7:00 on Saturday morning we stood by our bunks—we would never sit, even lightly, on those olive drab blankets so smoothed they looked plastic—waiting. We were nervous, as much because we wanted Shef's approval as because we dreaded not passing our personal inspection and losing a weekend pass. And then the sound of the door opening and Shef's musket shot of *Ten-shut!* and we were into it, standing there by our footlockers at the easy *Attention* he had taught us, watching him lead the commander down the aisle to the latrine, where everything was spotless for the only moment during the week, and seeing him come back, pointing here and there like a *major domo,* resplendent in his newly laundered uniform, bright metalware, and mirroring shoes. It was a performance that the most jaded or unhappy soldier couldn't resist taking pride in. Now I realize how Shef pulled it off—showed us how down to the tiniest detail to fold and scrub and shine to a standard that could be attained only by persons who wanted so to exceed the average that they devised ingenious, original ways to reach a new excellence. His expectations and his model were such that he didn't have to visit us on Friday nights and nag or exhort us.

But what of all this effort being for such a piddling objective, shining up oneself and the barracks so that an officer could walk through the company for fifteen minutes and pronounce on that brief moment of spit and polish? Does excelling in such an inconsequential endeavor make Shef a great man or teacher?

He was Regular Army. As a youth he had decided upon that as a career, until retirement, or death in battle. In that world, before a three-star general from Washington visited Fort Eustis for a post inspection, an order was issued by the post commander and read to us at a special formation by Major Bledren: "Any man who fails to salute when the General's car passes by will be sent overseas to battle areas immediately." That threat was issued on Saturday, November 7, 1942—I found the entry in my little black notebook. And yet in prior lectures, officers had always implied that the goal of all training was to make soldiers combat efficient. I thought about that a while. The army was threatening to send the most careless boys to the spot where the most efficiency was demanded. It was this sort of organization that Shef had dedicated his life to.

But like all great persons working within institutions, Shef made his career a counterforce to the narrowness and idiocies of the system. When Second-Lieutenant Creven arrived to take command of DEML from the departing major, he was immediately promoted to first lieutenant, a rank befitting the position. He had been a Sears Roebuck salesman in Pittsburgh. He took to carrying a quirt, as if he were commanding a cavalry unit instead of a bunch of clerks and busboys, and he strutted around the drill ground, a popinjay who had inherited a first sergeant who had hunted raccoons all his life and knew the field as he knew a whiskey bottle. One day, having read up on "natural features" in the Army Manual, the lieutenant took us a few yards into a nearby field, and pointing to a long straight ditch whose furrow created a berm that had grown up heavily in weeds, said, "Now that's a natural feature. You can tell by the vegetation." Standing behind Creven, Shef smiled broadly at me. He wasn't going to correct the lieutenant, because he knew that most of us could see we were looking at a man-made ditch.

A few weeks later an officer in higher headquarters decreed that DEML soldiers should carry out some mock war maneuvers in the field and told the lieutenant that from a designated point he should take one platoon out in the woods, and that his first sergeant, not ranging more than a mile afield, should hide himself and his men in the woods while the lieutenant's group tried to discover them in guerrilla fashion.

The lieutenant's platoon moved out. After giving his men some hints about hiding themselves, Shef climbed a high pine tree and sat in a comfortable crotch reading a comic book. Hours later, after rounding up all the men, the lieutenant was still fretting. At the foot of the tree, his frustration exploded, and he yelled, "Dammit, Sergeant Sheffield, where are you?" and Shef slowly climbed down the tree to stand behind him and speak a startling, "Here, Sir!" The point of the exercise was to teach men how to hide themselves in the field.

On the firing range, Shef was the best shot on the post. One day he drank half a bottle of whiskey and then shot bullseyes with every round except one. When I went out with him and a group of raw rookies, he said to me before they loaded their guns, "Now Mac, when you see one of these crazy sonsabitches with a loaded piece stand up from his sittin' or prone position, you hit the dirt. There's always one or two who go nuts with all that sound, and if they've got an M-1 in hand they're just as apt to shoot you as the target. When they start wavin' a gun around, get down, and then try to jump 'em when their back is turned. We're not out here to kill each other." Moments later when a boy rose up waving his rifle, Shef was the first to hit the ground and first to wrest the gun from the boy, who had just introduced me to what the word *berserk* means.

Shef had come from a boyhood of guns and dogs. When a black and white spotted puppy about five weeks old appeared one day waddling up the company street, Shef picked her up and began calling around the post to see whom she belonged to. He could find no owner, so adopted her, although housing a dog was against post regulations.

At the mess hall Shef found a cardboard box and kept the puppy in it. Often he would sneak away from the orderly room during the day to play with the dog and talk baby talk to her. By this time I had been promoted to corporal and Shef had made me his roommate in one of the two non-com rooms at the head of the barracks. One night when I came back late I found Shef, Sparky, and another soldier from down the street sitting on the beds drinking beer. I glanced at the dog in Shef's arms. Her eyes and nose were running, and she looked almost lifeless. "What's the matter with her?" I asked.

"Aw," said Shef, putting her on the floor and watching her stagger a few steps, "I think that damned dame has caught the clap."

The next day he took the pup to the veterinarian on the post, who ordinarily took care of horses. When Shef returned, he brought the dog to the orderly room, where he could keep an eye on her recovery. Several days later, when she had become more lively, Shef had to go on an errand, and Lieutenant Creven said, "Leave the dog with me. I'll watch her." Shef looked at me as if to say, "What's got into him?" We both expected he would be reporting us to someone for keeping a dog contrary to regulations.

After Shef left, I heard squeals from the office, and thought that the lieutenant must be having a good time playing with the puppy. But then another sound I couldn't identify. I was hearing that sound and then the puppy's squeal in succession, again and again. And I realized the squeal was registering pain. I entered the half open door to find the lieutenant dropping the puppy from a height of two or three feet onto the bare springs of an army cot that stood in the corner of his office. He looked at me and then said to the puppy, "Isn't this fun?" and dropped her again. I said, "I'd better take her out so you won't be bothered by her," grabbed her, and left the room. When Shef heard what had happened, he said, "I'll get that sonofabitch."

Among its motley crew, DEML had one young man who was mentally retarded and worked at the officers' mess. One day Lieutenant Creven called him off his job and commanded him to report to his office. Sean arrived, tall, blond, fair-faced, and wondering.

Shef said, "The lieutenant wants to see you."

"What's the matter?" said Sean.

"I don't know," said Shef, and opened the door to the commander's room. It was then closed from inside and we heard the lieutenant bark at Sean: "Do you think you're a soldier?"

"What do you mean?" said Sean, weakly.

"I said, 'Do you think you're a soldier!'"

"I don't know. I guess so."

"You guess so! You stand here in front of your commanding officer and say you guess you're a soldier?"

The upshot was that the lieutenant claimed he had seen Sean sweeping the stoop at the officers' club and failing to salute when a colonel had entered the building. He grilled the boy, asking him questions about his parents, his birthplace, his life in school—while sad Sean stumbled and stammered, not understanding what these questions had to do with anything.

Shef called up the sergeant major at post headquarters and told him to invent a reason for speaking to the lieutenant. When the sergeant major called again, Shef knocked on the office door and walked in, saying, "There's a call from post headquarters for you, Sir," and shepherded Sean out the door as the lieutenant reached for the phone.

Henceforth, Shef began to act as a nursemaid to Sean. When one of the other workers at the officers' club was reported to have yelled at Sean for not understanding something, Shef went over and told the man, "If you ever do that again to him, I'll kill you," and that was the end of that, because Shef had a reputation for meaning what he said when he talked to enlisted men.

Not long after that, Ben Sarone, the veteran cook of the outfit, cherished by the men for his attempts to vary the menu, was reported to our office after medical inspection as having venereal disease. Apparently the lieutenant had taken a dislike to Ben earlier because, although Ben always treated everyone with respect at the mess hall, he hadn't kowtowed enough to the lieutenant, who wanted not obedience, but obeisance, from his men. When the lieutenant saw the medical note about Ben's disease, he said to Shef, "I want Sergeant Sarone broken to private—immediately. Write it up, Macrorie."

Shef and I walked out to the orderly room and I said, "What do we do?"

"Wait a minute," he said. "I think I remember something about you can't bust a man for having a venereal disease. Look it up in the regulations." He was right.

"O.K.," said Shef. "Write up the order to bust Ben."

"What?" I said.

"We'll try to get this through before anyone at headquarters realizes what's happening."

The order was published, and Lieutenant Creven was shipped out much earlier than anyone had expected. Later, Ben's sergeant's stripes were restored to him.

At the time I didn't think of Shef as a teacher, but over the years I've realized that not only did his soldiers do good works under his direction and example, but many of them, like me, were moved to be more open in their judgment of other people with different backgrounds from theirs.

In my spare moments on the post, I would take a book to my room and lie in my bunk reading. Shef read little, and then nothing more than comics or newspapers. I was one of the few soldiers on the post who didn't drink, and Shef was famous for being able to hold his bourbon and perform difficult tasks meticulously. The thought of having sexual experience with the girls from the Women's Army Corps stationed on the post or other employees frightened me. In idle conversation Shef talked constantly about drinking and women—with Falstaffian exuberance. Two more unlikely friends could hardly be imagined, and yet Shef invited me to room with him and became my close friend.

One Saturday night I turned off the lights and went to bed as usual, about 11:30, after reading. At what I found was 3 A.M. when I looked at my alarm clock, I heard the soft closing of the door, and the rustle of clothes. In the beam from a light outside in the company yard, I saw a hand place two shoes under the bed, and I realized that Shef had taken off his shoes before entering the room so he wouldn't wake me. I heard a small thud: he was rolling into bed. Next morning from a conversation with Shef's buddies of the night before I found that he had been very drunk. He never would have admitted to those men that he was so thoughtful of me after a wild night.

When Shef was given orders to ship out to New Guinea and join a chemical warfare company, the branch of service he was trained in, I accompanied him to the little train station at nearby Upper Valley. I stood there on the platform with him, a man foreign to me in so many ways, whom I now couldn't bear to see leaving. He was quiet, partly because of a large shipping-out hangover and partly because he knew we might never see each other again. "Well, Mac," he said, forcing a smile, "we need to drink to this." As he reached for the bottle in his overcoat pocket, he suddenly looked discomfited. Then he led me to the Coke machine at the side of the station, got two Cokes, and handed one to me. I think it was probably the only time in his adult life that he had drunk to an occasion with soda water. I've never felt more honored.

WHAT ENABLERS DO

The teachers, or enablers, in this book work in startlingly similar ways and share many attitudes and principles. They all hold high expectations for learners. They arrange the learning place so that people draw fully on their present powers and begin to do good works. They support and encourage rather than punish. They ask learners to take chances that sometimes result in failure, and to use their mistakes productively. They nurture an environment of truthtelling that puts learners at ease while they are experiencing the excitement and unease of challenge.

It's a Moebian way, fusing polar opposites like subjectivity and objectivity, freedom and discipline, the individual and the group.

Meeting with these enablers, people learn, not by endless preparatory exercises, but by doing something worth doing. They learn from each other's responses and good works.

A reader might well be thinking, "These are remarkable teachers you've collected in this book, not just people who use certain effective methods. To do what these enablers do, individuals must be endowed with uncommon traits of personality or character." But think of most conventional teachers who manage to inhibit and paralyze their students' powers. That's an achievement. It's no less or more of an achievement to unloose those powers and help learners extend them. We can't say that teaching truly requires a rare breed of person, for we know thousands and thousands of well-intentioned bad teachers are at work every day in conventional schools. What they are doing takes remarkable skill in going at things wrongly, in demeaning human beings, in lock-stepping large groups of people, in drilling them out of their spontaneity and undermining their control over their own powers. I refuse to believe that all those teachers are by nature unfeeling and inept.

Human beings, including teachers, can learn and change. Certain methods and principles help learning more than other methods and principles. Some teachers will never be able to overcome their self-doubt and become open and trusting. But most will, for the Moebian approach produces good works, and good works move learners and teachers from success to success.

Readers of this book might also say, "You found teachers who are much alike because you were looking for them, and if you weren't doing that consciously, your predilections would have led you to them." To an extent, that's true. No human investigator can be absolutely objective. But there's a danger in trying to detach oneself as inquirer. What were my alternatives in this project? I could have selected three times as many teachers at random and attempted to determine which ones were good teachers. I could have examined two hundred teachers and devised a quantitative set of measurements for grading them. But it is this sort of unfocused, undirected activity in the social sciences and education that has so often given us meaningless results. I was looking for ways of enabling people to do good works that counted for them, their fellow learners, their teacher, and people beyond the classroom. From the first, I was concerned that this be not an examination of how poor or empty works are produced, but a useful investigation into the ways of teachers and students.

At one point in my study, I clearly let my prejudices influence which teacher I would interview. A friend had told me that he knew a swimming coach whose athletes frequently won state championships. I thought, "Surely such performance fits under my definition of good works." But when my friend added that this coach was an extreme disciplinarian who trained his swimmers ruthlessly and always put winning above enjoyment, I decided not to interview him. I'm sure that winning state championships constituted a good work for most of this coach's swimmers. But from the enablers who appear in this book I have learned that truly good works not only enhance the lives of the learners doing them but encourage others to grow in the same way. These good works are the products of collaboration as much as of competition. Winning and losing are not central in the minds of enablers.

I admit that I knew what I was searching for in this research, but I was surprised to find it. I don't *hope* that the list of doings, principles, beliefs, and attitudes I have brought together will be helpful to whoever wants to improve as an enabler. I *know* it will. And I know that people emulating the enablers in this book will help learners do good works.

Here is a checklist of what these enablers do. Not every one of them carries out all these actions or holds all these beliefs, but the commonality is astonishing.

At the First Meeting, Enablers—

1. Bring learners into a place containing good work done by past learners.

2. Explain why conventional school unwittingly interferes with, or prevents, learning.

3. Begin demonstrating the power that truthtelling can exert in learning.

4. Get people doing a good work that counts for them, their peers, the enabler, and people beyond the classroom.

5. Along with learners, start a good work of their own.

6. Begin to know learners as people rather than students.

7. Make plain that they have faith in learners to work at high levels of excellence.

Throughout the Term, Enablers—

8. Sit on the same physical level as learners when conversing with them, and speak and write to them in language alive and clear, expecting they do the same in return.

9. Eschew lectures. Don't conduct pseudo-discussions that ask for answers already in the leader's mind.

10. Set up dialogues between the experience and ideas of learners and the experience and ideas of "authorities."

11. Don't give conventional tests.

12. Help learners work out of experience into theory and vice versa.

13. Lead learners to surprise themselves and the enablers.

14. Move learners from success to success, yet prepare them to accept occasional failure.

15. Help learners see errors as opportunities.

16. Help learners exercise their imagination.

17. Capitalize on the power of storytelling.

18. Provide learners with opportunities for making choices—so they become producers and creators, and thus develop responsibility.

19. Avoid frightening learners out of their unconscious selves.

20. Help learners become finders as well as receivers.

21. Aid learners in making Moebian fusions between polar opposites like subjectivity and objectivity, emotion and reason, particulars and generals, playfulness and planning, dependence and independence, the power of the group and the power of the individual.

22. Lead learners into whole acts rather than bits and pieces.

23. Become vulnerable to learners by sharing feelings with them about doing good works alongside them.

24. Arrange that learners see, experience, and remember in con-

texts, so that the things they are learning inhere in and adhere to other things, some of them familiar to, or part of, the learners' conscious/unconscious selves. So that learners come alive and the thing to be learned takes on a "virtual life."

25. Help learners cultivate humor and spontaneity.

26. Set up the course so that none of the learning is useless.

27. Help learners come to own their knowledge.

28. Cultivate rigor and joy in the classroom.

29. Help learners refine their uses of emotion.

30. Make practice always an act with meaning.

31. Avoid badgering and cruelty.

32. Avoid excessive praise of learners' works.

33. Test the work of the classroom against work in the world outside.

34. Show learners how to profit from the responses of their peers rather than dispute or reject them out of hand.

35. Train learners to respond to the work of their peers in helpful rather than damaging ways.

36. Find ways of making public the good works of learners.

37. Show learners that working habits taken on in the classroom will prove valuable beyond it.

38. Grade learners' work, if at all, at a time when grades least interfere with learning.

39. Give learners ample time to complete their work.

40. Help learners polish and refine work as they bring it to completion.

41. Never deny the learners their lives.

42. Sense what are ripe moments for letting go of learners.

43. When the burden of dealing with so many lives becomes overwhelming, take a vacation or a leave of absence, or move to another profession.

One day long after I had made up the above list, I was thinking about how hard it is for all of us to live together—wives, husbands, parents, grandparents, children—and I thought, "How would I like to be treated by other people in my home if I had the power to determine that?" Immediately I began to hear myself repeating the list of points of what enablers do. I think that suggests the humanity and universality of those points. Designed for the classroom, they transfer almost in their entirety over to other human meeting places, like the office, the factory, the home. They speak in the same spirit Jimmy Britton did when I asked him why he was such a good listener to students, and he said, "Do you suppose it has something to do with being sociable?" *There* is one of our great blind spots in schooling: when we walk into classrooms we forget that we are still human beings.

OPEN LETTER ABOUT SCHOOLS

Most of us have only the least notion of what a ridiculous institution school is. It has always been part of our landscape, like rocks and trees. Because we live in school a good number of the years of our lives, we don't see it any more than we see the air we breathe. We give our obeisance to school, although as kids it bored and irritated us. And rendered us powerless.

We would all like school to be something better than that, but we take it as a given. The teachers teach the way they were taught. The students come to a place where they can socialize with their peers. The parents are relieved because someone else is looking after the children; and however much the kids complain about their lessons, parents can always say, "We had to go to school, too, you know." I don't mean to assert that conventional school is not useful in our society. It introduces students to peers with different experience from theirs, but it fails to nurture good work habits, rigor, self-discipline, curiosity, a sense of humor, the habit of telling stories, responsibility, and sustained thinking.

Every seven or ten years we read in the papers and hear on TV that education is in crisis. Our schools aren't turning out children competent in math and science. They can't write or read. We are falling behind other countries in high technology. We're hearing those complaints now. In the fifties we heard them about our failure to keep up with the Soviet Union's Sputnik. Now we're hearing about our failure to keep up with Japan in electronics. Old story. In 1893 a writer in the May issue of *The Atlantic Monthly* was discussing the "great outcry" about "the inability of the students admitted to Harvard College to write English clearly and correctly." He said the schools required frequent written exercises that were corrected and commented on by the teacher, and asked, "With all this practice in writing, why do we not obtain better results?"

Most of our schools have never found the answers to such a question, yet the interviews with teachers presented in this book suggest that human beings of all ages are learning creatures. That's their nature.

Rocks and dogs and plants may learn also, but they're dumb compared to *homo sapiens*. School isn't a place where that fact is usually built upon.

Most people think that teaching is throwing information at students and hoping they'll remember it. But people on the receiving end have to catch it and do something with it, or no learning takes place. True learning is rather an act that requires us to call upon our past experience and present powers, and to rise and meet new information and ideas—transforming them into something useful, taking away their sanctity, their pure authenticity, and transfusing them into our earthbound self so they develop a new authenticity and sanctity. It's a kind of alchemy, or fusion. In a true knowing place, teachers and students are surprising both each other and themselves.

It Couldn't Be This Bad

In conventional school, attendance is kept religiously, but not much except lectures, tests, and grades is treated with reverence. Scores in quizzes, finals, and proficiency tests are recorded, but few good works are done. It's a receptive climate for sadistic and perverted acts, like the one reported by my stepdaughter some years ago. One day, the touring music teacher for the district found the class boisterous and said, "If you kids back there don't quiet down, you'll have to come up in front of class and sing a song!" She was making the object of their lessons into a punishment.

"How could that be?" you might say. "If this is the way of schools in the United States, and I guess Europe, and maybe Asia, why hasn't something been done about it? Would decent people put up with such mind-deadening instruction for their children? You must be speaking of exceptional cases." No, I'm speaking of routine school. There are moments of exception and teachers of exception, but the standard thing there is cramping minds and bodies.

"But I sort of liked school," you may say. Yes, "sort of," because it wasn't the classroom that beguiled you, but the playground, the halls, the cafeteria, and the bathroom gossip. You may say, "But human beings just wouldn't permit such anti-learning environments to be perpetuated for centuries." Oh yes, they would. We build all sorts of things as stupid and totalitarian. We can indeed maintain monstrous or vapid self-defeating ideas and institutions. Once we get them going, we're better at continuing them than stopping them and reforming them.

Good Works

If the twenty classrooms of the teachers presented in this book were lifted out of their real settings and dreamlike gathered into one building, that learning place would be drastically unlike school as we know it. On the first day the learners would be expected to begin to know the place, to find where the rooms and the library are. The teachers would be expected to begin to know the learners, to inquire into the rooms of their minds and experience. Both would immediately begin doing things that build mutual respect.

In that learning place the accepted word and discoveries of the authorities—"the best that has been thought and said in the world," as Matthew Arnold put it—would count a great deal. But the experience and thought of the learners also would count a great deal. The two would meet every day and swap responses, not with the assumption that the learners knew as much as the authorities, but that they would meet them with strength, with some sense of power, so they would feel up to the challenge. In this place there would be no *teachers* in the conventional sense, only *enablers*.

To understand some of Shakespeare's profoundest insights, to build a chest of drawers as competently as a professional cabinetmaker, to work through proofs with one's classmates in higher mathematics without instructions from the professor, to learn to write fluently in a foreign language, to move from awkwardness to control over one's body—these are good works of a high order. Conventional teachers who decide to try the Moebian way must be aware of the quality of work and understanding accomplished by enablers. Their learners don't produce the crude, ugly, unimaginative footstool I made in "manual arts" back in junior high school, following exactly the model and "destructions" given me by a careless teacher. This is not the annual Youth Talent Show at the school or community building where hundreds of slipshod, sentimental creations of children are oohed and aahed at by adults who actually find many of them puerile, empty, or pretentious.

The twenty enablers presented here draw out learners and challenge them to produce works better than they have ever imagined possible in school or outside school. They get to know the learners, put them in propitious circumstances, and move them from success to success so they gain respect for themselves and for the authorities that conventional school often makes them hate. These enablers act as if the learners have powers. And the learners find they do. To use one of the many eloquent phrases of the sixties, the enablers encourage the learners to "tell them where they're coming from." The enablers value those places and help the learners go on to new ones.

In the Moebian classroom *good works* carry meaning. They redefine the term "useful," which for centuries has been maligned by school people. The university, which emerged from the church's notion that a special class of persons—priests and bishops and popes—were the keepers of the sacred word and the spreaders of it, understandably arrogated to itself the mysteries, the abstractions, the "higher" things of life. Out of that tradition these "masters" extended the notion of the usefulness of useless knowledge into a convenient and subtle rationale for universities as we know them today. Not consciously, but in effect, they were saying, "We have the word, will tell it to you, and examine you to see if you got it right. But if it is easy for you to get it right, if learning it seems a natural activity for you, then we might lose our authority, our special position as guardians of the mysteries."

When alchemy turned to science, and measurement replaced intuition, scientists sometimes found that apparently useless theorizing, "pure" science as it came to be called, in fact turned out to be useful. In our times, the higher mathematics and physics, played with as intellectual games, under pressure turned out to have a real application: one outcome was an atomic bomb that killed thousands of horrified Japanese, a people who excelled at physics, mathematics, and their applications.

Useful Knowledge

In the past hundred years when the emptiness of conventional education was attacked, professors often defended it with the doctrine of the usefulness of useless knowledge. Their position was much like that taken by priests in the Middle Ages: you can't criticize us because you don't know what we know, and we won't explain what that is in terms you can understand, because there are none. You're too ignorant.

Some professors let themselves believe that if students are continually tested on their remembering of theories or information they never use, they are engaged in the highest of intellectual pursuits. Sometimes that might be true in school, maybe once in a thousand instances. But most of the time the uselessness of school knowledge in students' lives is absolute and unarguable. The performance, the doings, of students are not exhibited, or evaluated by those outside the classroom because they aren't worth looking at. They're nothing more than an echoing or mirroring of what belongs to someone else, and are accordingly lifeless. Students need to make the knowledge of the past *their own* before they can become learners, and most of them don't.

And so—one more split between opposites that could become fruitful when considered Moebianly. Dr. Sidney Finkelstein, a psychiatrist doing research on students' responses to their medical education, says, "Medicine is taught as a left-brain, scientific, factual profession" without concern for feeling (*New York Times*, April 19, 1983). Conventional school embraces objectivity, and considers subjectivity the property of the unwashed. It embraces the conscious and dismisses the unconscious. The result is that when we leave school we behave like half-human beings and know not our powers.

This suppression of feeling occurs at all levels of schooling. Consider the community schools art exhibit. The drawings and paintings of children up until about eleven years of age are alive and imaginative; after that most of them look as if they were produced on a surveyor's table. They're almost totally lacking in art—that fusion of spontaneity and control brought about by the focusing, organizing drive of the conscious/unconscious. If we've been educated in conventional school, we're sure we can't paint pictures, make jewelry, carve wooden saints (as country folk do in my state of New Mexico), make music, write powerfully—unless we were born with the talent or majored in the craft in college. The list could go on. School has succeeded in making us forget the powers of the human species.

In the Moebian classroom many learners find their powers. There they don't use them with artifice, but with art. And they redefine the concept of useful knowledge. No longer do they see it as something base and "vocational." For some people in universities "useless" knowledge has always been attractive for two reasons: it was recondite, and therefore could be owned exclusively by the professors and researchers, the priestly class. And it was the opposite of "useful" knowledge that would appeal to the uneducated, the manual laborers. I don't believe the priests of higher education ever consciously worked out such a class division, but it was Aristotelian, and therefore comfortable.

In recent years, Moebian enablers have been led by their learners' work to see that knowledge of many kinds may be *useful*. For example, when teachers of literature ask students to respond freely to the works they're reading, they find that the learners' experience speaks to the experience of the characters in the literary work, so that what the critic David Daiches has said about the uses of literature comes true. In describing different levels of literature, he says:

> The first stage is where we recognize what we know. The second is where we recognize what we might have known, and there is a third—where, while we recognize what we have known or might have known, we at the same time see, and know to be authentic, what we should never have seen for ourselves. (*A Study of Literature*)

To read of Bloom in James Joyce's *Ulysses* worrying about his digestion or bowel movements is to know that our own secret concerns are universal, and not to be ashamed of. To understand how wavering is the line that separates sanity from insanity in Hamlet is to understand others and ourselves under duress. These sharings maintain us as thinking/feeling, conscious/unconscious creatures.

We all have powers as responders to art and makers of it. The urge to produce art that symbolizes and comprehends is in all of us, but conventional school introduces us to the masters in ways that separate us from them until the enterprise seems beyond us. And so with the urge to inquire into the way things are, which is science. It, too, resides in us.

Certain subjects, like metaphysics or aesthetics, have long been considered useless in the workaday world, and that has been part of their attraction for some persons. But now I read in the papers that philosophers are being hired by prisons and hospitals to help professionals make decisions about life and death, and a program in applied history is placing graduates in jobs where they are paid to bring their knowledge of history to bear on contemporary matters. But many school people, especially in the Humanities, avoid being tested in the world beyond their walls. People who study philosophy should *do* philosophy. They should construct statements that count in the world. Marx and Jefferson and John Stuart Mill put together words that became manifest in the world. Ideas have consequences, Max Lerner once said. If they didn't, we would have no notion of how good they are.

The Lecture-Test-Grade System

It was not easy for school to talk us out of our nature. Centuries of drawing back from the tendency of the species were required to carry out the job, and to evolve the structure that runs throughout our educational institutions like a spine. I call it the Lecture-Test-Grade System. It supports the weak, but central, nervous ganglion of conventional school. It doesn't support enabling.

No matter that tests don't help people learn. Tests are good for you. They reveal your ignorance, unless because of chance or remarkable memory you "miss" none of the questions. Most of the enablers in this book don't talk about tests, because they know they are seldom instruments for learning. When they do talk of them, they speak of devising unconventional ones that demand initiative from learners. In their classes, the daily work they assign students tests them more fully than any written examination ever can.

Proficiency tests given across cities, districts, states, or the nation, tell little about students' ability to do something with knowledge or a skill. And laymen have to take test-score numbers on faith because there are no genuine performances or good works of students to look at. Most of these measurements ask for "minimum competency," a goal which steadily scales down the expectations of teachers and students. In Moebian education, the expectations are solid and positive and high, and they include fumbling and making mistakes.

For most people school is first frightening, then boring. The books and teachers represent so much knowledge that they can only feel their ignorance. Lectures—"Of course, Percival II knew nothing of Ferdinand's intentions"—and tests—"What were the names of the hero's three girl cousins?"—and grades—"You get a D." Those three instruments of the inquisition produce fright and boredom, sometimes mixing them into a strange, foul-tasting soup. After students drink that soup day after day as their only food, they lose their discrimination, curiosity, and zest. Like prisoners in a concentration camp they begin to fantasize that this routine is o.k. because it's the way things are. If they don't do that they may lose their minds, which will simply disappear into the white walls. Seems right, because they have no use for them anyway.

Where there are no good works by learners, grades are necessary. They keep distance between teacher and students. Few people in or out of education know that a number of schools and colleges don't give grades. The University of California at Santa Cruz, for example, doesn't give grades, but written evaluations, which graduate schools and industries find more useful than A-B-C-D-F. A number of enablers in the country give no tests of any kind in their courses. And no lectures. They are enabling people to do good works. Along with learners, the enablers are doing good works themselves. Most lectures, tests, and grades are hindrances to such learning.

An Attack on the Mind

Many readers of this book, being successful professionals, may find its attack on conventional school exaggerated. They attended that school and turned out to be literate and knowledgeable individuals, their curiosity heightened rather than dulled. But with few exceptions, they became those superior people in spite of school rather than because of it. When I ask them to tell me of teachers they are indebted to, they customarily find only two or three in their long educational careers from kindergarten through graduate school. They don't realize how much they were influenced toward learning by people outside of school, usually their parents. In their earliest years, before school could affect them, they accomplished the most astounding learning feat of their lives—mastering their Mother Tongue, with the support, direction, and encouragement of no one but their mothers and fathers. Then school drilled them in grammar and math senselessly. Bored, they carried out the lab exercises in science or the essay assignments in English and later became scientists or writers who inferred a cause-and-effect that wasn't there.

Some of these professionals as children came to conventional school with such a passion for using words and inquiring into the ways of the natural world that they learned even from bad teachers—who, however wrongheaded in method, shared those passions and introduced students to the work of authorities in the field. Once the students met those authorities, they were captivated and began to converse with them—usually outside the classroom or apart from the ongoing routines of school. If these brilliant young people had been lucky enough to find enablers instead of teachers in their classrooms, they would have begun careers of inquiry and performance a dozen years earlier than they did. Mozart and William James were geniuses, but had their parents acted as teachers rather than enablers, Wolfgang and William would never have found themselves so early and produced so many good works.

Few novels or biographies present exciting learning moments in classrooms. They concentrate on extracurricular school experience. I know of only one person who has written a case history of a year in the classroom. I've even suggested the idea to undergraduates—"Keep a journal of your classroom hours in freshman and senior years"—but none has done it, I think because most of those hours were so dull that such an enterprise is unattractive. School's oppression is often subtle and hidden, and few students would think of keeping a log of prison days.

The stupefying practices of conventional school are all about us, if we begin to look at the place instead of romanticize it. Recently I attended an auction held in an elementary school. In the room where I ate supper, I saw a large placard lettered by the teacher, which read:

I AND MY WRITING

1. Do I have complete sentences?
2. Are my capitals in the right place?
3. Have I used the right punctuation?
4. Are all my words spelled correctly?
5. Is my writing well arranged on the paper?
6. Is every letter plain?
7. Do I have good spacing between my letters?
8. Is my writing large enough?
9. Is my slant even?
10. Do all my letters touch the line?

In that series of questions, it's not that form is emphasized over content, but that *meaning* isn't mentioned at all. The question "Have I said what the teacher wanted me to say?" would be a possible addition to that teacher's list, but the question "Have I said anything that means anything to me and my classmates or people outside this room?" is beyond that teacher's comprehension. The attack of conventional schools on the mind can't be exaggerated. Most of them should have a Bill of Wrongs at the front door, cast in bronze, that lists the practices employed to impair students' minds.

An Off-Center Enterprise

The efforts of conventional school to correct or improve itself are endless, and usually off-center. In thirty-five years of close observation of schools from both within and without, I've seen again and again the same supposedly drastic or fundamental reforms of curriculums brought up as new ideas and dropped after a few years of disillusionment. When I began teaching in 1946, there was a movement in some universities toward what's called "General Education" in an effort to counteract the divisive, fragmenting effect of studying human knowledge in compartmentalized units called "fields." Knowledge was to come together for students as they saw relationships, for example, between John Brown's hanging, Dostoevsky's *Crime and Punishment,* Walt Whitman's *Leaves of Grass,* John Stuart Mill's *On Liberty,* and Darwin's *Origin of Species,* all of which reached public notice in the middle of the 19th century. A decade or two after that notion of General Education came to life and caused a comprehensive reorganization of university departments, it was dropped here and there because like other such major reforms it didn't change the Lecture-Test-Grade System, and thus failed to improve learning. The return to the departmental emphasis in undergraduate education was then hailed as a re-establishment of intellectual discipline and purity, and it then stimulated no more learning than it had before the General Education movement.

The *New York Times* of April 18, 1983, reported that New York State was considering abandoning the chronological approach in teaching social sciences for an issues approach. The plan proposed to "organize the study of the world in the ninth and tenth grades under six topics, or concepts—ecology, human needs, human rights, cultural interaction, the global system of economic interdependence, and the future."

General Education and the topical approach to social sciences make as good sense as any other concepts in conventional teaching, but they're not fundamental. Where things come together and stick, or lie jumbled and disconnected, is in individual human beings. If their experience and ideas and the experience and ideas of the authorities whose findings constitute our canonized "knowledge" don't meet and mix, there will occur no charging of batteries that can power them as learning, thinking beings. If the situations in which they are placed as learners are truly Moebian and interactive, they will become learners and finders no matter whether the curriculum is set up as general, specialized, liberal, or technical education, or whether events are presented in a chronological or topical manner. As human beings, students are both chronological and topical perceivers and thinkers. They are Moebian: they contain in themselves all these ways of perceiving, all these propensities. What they need in school is an arrangement that releases those powers, challenges and extends them.

A few months earlier, the *Times* reported that the Commissioner of Education for New York State was suggesting that maybe kids should start school at age four, thereby eliminating one year of high school and saving money for the taxpayers. He said that there was evidence that young children learned faster than older children. Apparently he didn't realize that this quickness of learning is partly due to the fact that children of four are organizing the bewildering world of new fact and idea outside the crippling forms of the Lecture-Test-Grade System and with the support, encouragement, and high expectations provided by mothers.

Learning by Competing

Several intelligent and competent professionals I've spoken to have insisted they learned to think in conventional school because their teacher took an adversary position and mercilessly grilled them in argument, ridiculing them for false logic and lack of evidence. I'm sure the practice was more valuable for them than the customary impersonal tests administered by conventional teachers. But most students in conventional classes are bored and unconfident. Such treatment demoralizes them. Several of the enablers in this book speak of their aversion to intense competition or ridicule in the classroom. They know that even students who have been relatively little damaged by conventional school remember more and develop more initiative by being challenged by their peers and the enabler doing good works than by being forced into antagonistic postures.

In *Writing without Teachers,* Peter Elbow analyzes the traditional academic "Doubting Game," which consists of countering every statement and opinion made by others seen as adversaries, and the Moebian "Believing Game," which asks a listener to go along with the arguments, experience, and logic of a speaker, as long as possible before looking at them negatively. The tradition of having the last and only word at the lectern is, as I've said before, an ancient one. Many of the worldly wise have resisted it. In his *Autobiography,* Ben Franklin told of taking up the Socratic method (the questioner leads other persons on, step by step, to statements that bring them to the answer the questioner has earlier decided upon):

I found this method safest for myself and very embarrassing to those against whom I used it; therefore I took a delight in it. . . .

Later, Franklin discarded the method because it confused and entangled those he spoke with but failed to help them think better. His friend Tom Jefferson advised people not to argue publicly, saying,

I never saw an instance of one of two disputants convincing the other by argument. I have seen many, on their getting warm, becoming rude & shooting one another. Conviction is the effect of our own dispassionate reasoning, either in solitude, or weighing within ourselves, dispassionately, what we hear from others, standing uncommitted in argument ourselves. (Quoted in Thomas Fleming, *The Man from Monticello.*)

These cautions from two of the most fertile thinkers the world has known. They would be the last to suggest that new ideas shouldn't be examined and tested, but they were among the first to realize the debilitating effect of adversarial response upon thinking, planning, and constructing. In the *New York Times* of April 22, 1983, President Derek C. Bok is quoted as saying in his annual report to the Board of Overseers of Harvard College:

Everyone must agree that law schools train their students more for conflict than for the gentler arts of reconciliation and accommodation. . . . Over the next generation, I predict, society's greatest opportunities will lie in tapping human inclinations toward collaboration and compromise rather than stirring our proclivities for competition and rivalry.

The Power of Professors

In this book I have included more enablers working at the college or university level than at other levels because the professors hold so much power. In "higher" education, as we call it for both valid and invalid reasons, the graduate school wields the most influence and is, customarily, most ignorant of Moebian education.

The split between the researcher and the teacher is an old one. When the scholar, the finder, the translator of the Word of God in ancient tongues, left his study to try to teach the commoners, whose education was slight compared to his, they couldn't understand and didn't learn. And so he was a failure as teacher, and grew wary and weary of that task, and spoke of teaching as something lowly. As he was the teacher of teachers, and the scholar or researcher to whom neophytes in the profession looked up to, his word and attitude carried weight with "educated" people.

In 1964 as editor of *College Composition and Communication,* a journal of the National Council of Teachers of English, I asked ten exceptionally bright persons to write brief case-histories of their experience as graduate students in American universities. All but one reported a bad time: "Literature here is studied as if it were a dead cat . . . The program is a package . . . obstructed the exchange of ideas . . . an interruption rather than a preparation . . . I was thrown a bunch of A's and B's to eat . . . a nagging sense of dislocation . . . I was regarded as an adolescent." Since then, I've asked a large number of people in the Humanities about their graduate experience. About 5 percent reported it was stimulating or valuable.

At the highest reaches of education, when students are often in their late twenties or thirties, they are usually given less responsibility and choice than they were in earlier years. The reasons for this irrational behavior on the part of graduate school professors are many, and not often brought to light. The principal one, I believe, is that professors, like most teachers in conventional educational institutions, seldom find excitement, satisfaction, or fulfillment in their work with students. The conventional system prevents learning more than it enables it. And so teaching is boring. The students appear infantile, stupid, careless. "They just don't seem to know anything any more" is the cry of the professors. They're right to say that, except for the last two words. Most students have never seemed to have known anything. Why should they? People don't remember what they haven't engaged with. So the professors berate the students and "pour it on them" in desperation and bitterness. The professions make qualifying tests for practitioners inhuman ordeals rather than opportunities for showing one's working knowledge. In a year-long study, Dr. Saul Rosenberg of the Stanford University Medical Center found that even "undergraduate students at Stanford are damaged by competition for acceptance at medical school." He said that "the role of being a premedical student is . . . undesirable, stereotyped, frustrating and anxiety-provoking," and he believes that law, business, and engineering students undergo the same debilitating experience (*New York Times,* April 19, 1983). This sort of teaching is a revenge against apparent ignorance and lack of self-discipline.

In contrast, here's a note written to an enabler conducting a seminar in the writings of Thoreau in a large university:

> Before I came into your class, I was afraid of going down the drain with the rest of the sophisticated people and losing any insight I may have gained till then. But I didn't go down. You and the other students wouldn't let me. I was forced to realize that everyone is not a bore, some people care, things count. There was actually room for me. A place where I wouldn't have to "postpone myself," as Thoreau put it.

The Two Virtues of "Higher" Education

In colleges and universities, which so dominate education, scholar-teachers constantly deal with the relationship between fact and theory, and between the views and evidence offered by opposing inquirers or practitioners. They are reluctant to accept an opinion or idea without considering the evidence on, not both, but many sides of a question. This skeptical, and sometimes cynical, habit of mind, often mistakenly called "objectivity," may render its possessors so detached that they become impotent, but ordinarily it has its value. Many of the students these scholar-teachers deal with are accustomed to living and working with people who accept or reject ideas, opinions, theories, or programs without inspecting the evidence and logic for them. They need to be exposed to persons more critical and analytical than themselves.

There are extraordinary institutions and there are extraordinary teachers, or enablers. But the majority operate within the Lecture-Test-Grade System, and the results are disappointing. The preponderant experience for students in this country and elsewhere, while considered "intellectual," is deadening to the mind and initiative. Recently an engineering student at one of the nation's most prestigious universities told me that in the one semester's engineering classes, all of which were conducted by lecture, he never engaged in discussion with fellow students. The professor entered the room and lectured. The students took notes and left. A friend of his told me that he didn't know any students in his engineering classes. He had come to know students in the field only in fraternity and other social settings. The commingling of students outside class and their introduction to analytical minds in the classroom constitute the two virtues of conventional universities. On the campus students from many walks of life and many countries meet and room with each other and thus learn diverse ways of thinking and living. Even in some private schools that enhancement of experience is cultivated through scholarships offered to students from different cultural and economic backgrounds.

I mustn't leave the impression that I believe that every college, university, and high school maintains itself solely by the Lecture-Test-Grade System. The other day an M.D. specializing in eye diseases and care told me that when he attended Yale University Medical School he found classes conducted as small seminars in which students took leading parts. Tests were not given, because they were unnecessary: the professor was observing students perform in ways that revealed both their ability to think and to command facts. This eye doctor received a Moebian, interactive education. A number of other professional graduate schools carry out their mission without giving students grades at the end of their courses because they have come to know their doings, and can describe them for professionals interested in hiring them.

The Power of Groups

Graduate school professors should be the most curious and independent of scholars, and frequently they are. If they want to like and respect their students, they must enable them to become finders, rather than simple keepers of someone else's knowledge. This is what great enablers have done, like Louis Agassiz at Harvard, or Charles Van Riper at Western Michigan University, or Jimmy Britton at the University of London. They have helped their students become finders and thus inescapably become friends and colleagues of theirs.

In my field, called "English," some of the most powerful graduate instruction has occurred in the last forty years, but many teachers know nothing of it. In the 1940s just after the Second World War, Jimmy Britton, his mentor Percy Gurrey, and Nancy Martin, along with others, founded the London Association for the Teaching of English because they felt they didn't know much about how children learn to speak, write, read, and listen. The organization was not a formal part of the Institute of Education at the University of London, but was supported by it in many ways. The leaders brought together English teachers from all levels of school and organized them into interest groups. One task force decided to tape record and study how children talked in and out of school. Another how they wrote, and so on. They engaged in first-hand observation and refined their methods of research and reporting. When a task force had made surprising discoveries out of a substantial body of observation, members presented findings to the whole Association for review. They couldn't resist sharing their news. They were not taking notes on lectures about how to do research but carrying out good works of research themselves, anxious to improve themselves in their profession.

The methods of LATE, as the London Association for the Teaching of English came to be called, were in many ways similar to those of the Bay Area Writing Project, founded by James Gray and associates at the University of California in 1974. The leaders of this movement had grown disillusioned with summer institutes and annual conferences of English teachers which produced participants as apathetic and unaffected by their educational experience as the run of students in conventional schools. So BAWP devised a simple plan. It would invite especially lively English teachers to a summer seminar that met morning and afternoon for five weeks. These writing teachers would be asked to do two things: to write a great deal themselves—of their personal experiences, and of classes they had taught, in both informal and professional style. They would respond to each other's writing helpfully. And each teacher would present to the others the best thing he or she had done with students to help them as writers. The leader of the seminar gave over her or his authority to these teacher/students who were enabling each other.

The result of both these large experiments has been a revolution in the teaching of those English teachers who learned about them. Publications of the findings of these suddenly curious observers appeared by the dozens. BAWP has expanded from one seminar or summer institute in the Bay Area of San Francisco to more than a hundred centers throughout the country and in several foreign countries. It's now called the National Writing Project.

The enthusiasm and drive of teachers who have trained themselves in these two organizations are remarkable. They have been enabled, and they go out to their own learners and to other teachers with knowledge of the best that has been done and thought in their organizations, which are forming ever-expanding networks of enablers and finders who expect other teachers and learners to become finders also.

As collections of enablers, LATE and BAWP inevitably heard about and attracted some of the leading researchers in Great Britain, the United States, Canada, and Australia in the fields of language-learning. And those people, most of whom had been working in isolation, heard about each other, occasionally met, and formed networks casual and unorganized, but influential. At the Bread Loaf Graduate School of English sponsored by Middlebury College, in 1978 Dixie Goswami became coordinator of the Writing Program for Small-Town and Rural Teachers, and began to invite these leaders in to teach and consult. Under her direction, English teachers learn to write and enable, to become themselves researchers of the way their students use language.

These three centers and others, like the one at New York University under the direction of Gordon Pradl, are creating ever expanding networks of enablers. They do not yet dominate the teaching of English in this country or Britain, and may never, but their influence steadily grows. I can see all the disciplines of learning engaging in the same transforming of teachers into enablers. The method is simple: ask bright and eager teachers to write history or philosophy, or do physics or math, or whatever—together, and get responses from their peers. And then ask them to share with the others the most powerful bit of enabling they've ever done in a classroom. The interviews in this book reveal why such a program will work.

Teachers who become students in the summer are usually taught in the conventional way—so that they feel demeaned and powerless. Many English teachers have no confidence in themselves as writers, and that fact embarrasses them in a course in Teaching Writing. But

BAWP, LATE, and Bread Loaf give teachers enrolled in Teaching Writing courses confidence in themselves because they meet each other at their best. The challenge is open-ended: they can improve or reform their profession in cycles that never stop. They can move from success to success, both as learners and enablers. And they can rise on the power of the individual merging with the power of the group.

Organizations in other fields than English, such as the Street Law Foundation, are doing similar things. The recently founded California Math Project is modeled after the National Writing Project.

The need now is for graduate schools to send their professors to such institutes, or to create new ones in their fields, so that so-called "scholar-teachers" can become enablers. Tradition has it that they know how to teach, but their disappointment in their students—in contrast to their enjoyment of research—suggests they need to be introduced to Moebian, or interactive, ways of enabling.

Frequently in my lifetime, professional leaders of the highest stature have called for reform in education in their fields. President Derek Bok of Harvard, cited earlier, has called the American legal system "among the most expensive and least efficient in the world," and laid much of the blame upon law schools. Anyone talking to persons studying for their bar examinations can see that one impetus behind legal education and qualification is to make students do things hard and unpleasant, and sometimes flatly indefensible. The effect of this attitude is to exhaust students, to force them to take on a self-discipline that is masochistic rather than liberating. It should be to arrange their education so they follow something because it pulls them, because they see its place in their world and the larger world beyond that.

Why then, if distinguished leaders continue to point out the failure of education to improve the quality of the professions and of life in general, doesn't school respond with genuine reform? One snag is that reports of failure in this or that community or state or profession appear in the press as isolated cases—and similarly with reform methods and movements—so that no fundamental methodology and philosophy emerge. I know of no person or school in the past that has demonstrated how the practices of individual successful teachers spring from a common base.

The Future of Enabling

Enablers live a blessed life in that they see learning going on all around them. Change. Blossoming. Despair or boredom turned into excitement and that satisfying pleasure which comes from taking initiative and working rigorously. But enabling goes so much against the grain of the Lecture-Test-Grade System that the lives of enablers can be painful and dangerous. Enablers can be harassed by administrators, they can be scoffed at by colleagues, they can be fired.

The careers of most conventional teachers begin with hope and good intentions and turn to desperation and sourness, and sometimes to hatred of students who won't learn and won't try to learn. Drill them harder and they become resentful or bored, and the teachers become policemen of the worst kind. If they give the lectures, administer the tests, and are tough about grades, they won't be harassed or scoffed at or fired. Just bored and sullen, and eventually burned out.

Enablers won't become bored, but they may burn out because they're taking too much of the learners' lives upon themselves. Most adults realize how hard it is to live with other persons in a home. The children and the parents misunderstand each other, irk each other. Two adults living together without the complications of children press each other by the simple fact of their existence. Now consider the days of an enabler at school. Twelve or thirty persons in the class. Three or four classes for the professor, maybe five for the community college instructor, five or six for the high school teacher—perhaps as many as a hundred fifty human beings to keep track of daily. "Don't take their problems home with you" is the advice teachers give each other. But when an enabler invites learners to bring their experience into the classroom so it speaks to the experience of the enabler and the authorities being encountered, the enabler can't blot out those problems and often doesn't want to.

Working in schools is exhausting, and if people are being enabled to learn instead of simply kept in line, the pressure on the enabler is severe and unceasing. I think enablers should work in schools for about seven years and then take a two-year sabbatical, or look for other careers, no matter how good they feel about their jobs. Enabling asks too much of them. It requires them to receive the lives of many learners and to help them fuse those lives with those of others who have gone before, and thus produce something new.

Finally, there is the question whether any society will ever allow its schools to help its young become thinkers. Thorstein Veblen's belief that institutions exist to perpetuate themselves is not to be swept aside easily. Young thinkers are dangerous, or at best annoying. If they seem to be pushing themselves into positions of power, established adults are not likely to sit idly by, watching them.

I've asked the enablers in this book to talk about how they help people learn in their classrooms, not how they feel as agents or pawns in a wrongheaded system. Some of them have left teaching because they were hampered or bullied by that system, or passed over for promotion or tenure by administrators or colleagues who think they are being conscientious. And these teachers are among the best in the world.

Enablers who work for benighted, frightened, defensive principals, department heads, or deans feel oppressed rather than supported in their good work. A school environment that encourages thinking and growth in learners and teachers must be an anomaly in a system so ancient and entrenched. Changing the venerable, coercive ritual of school seems an overwhelming task, as apparently impossible as finding a good alternative to capitalism or communism.

There's no way in any country to institute from above a sweeping successful reform of education. Teachers don't like to be handed a new curriculum and told to put it into practice next semester. They don't want to be advised by the teacher next door or the administrator down the hall that they should change their ways radically. They feel they know their job as well as the next person in the field. But this book presents something new to them: a chance to learn from the ideas and practice of teachers in fields other than their own, and evidence that there may be basic theories and methods that work in all classrooms, described by teachers who have earned their authority as experts. I would like to see administrators, parents, students, and teachers hand this book to teachers they know and say, "Take what appeals to you in it and forget the rest, or the whole thing. You're under no obligation. I just thought you might be interested."

This counter-movement goes on, partly because few people know what teachers do once they close the classroom door and turn to the learners. Most of the enablers presented here—and thousands of others in the English-speaking world and, I'm sure, in other countries whose teachers I know nothing of—continue in the face of incredible obstacles to provide a context for learners to do good works, and to grow out of and beyond themselves.

Indifferently, the sun
Nurtures and kills you.
Its golden words are two, Alpha, Omega.
Write the alphabet in a ring-round
So the two that belong together stand together:
A and Z, beginning and end, side by side.
This is the shape of the world.
God's hoop
To jump through
Once.

(from Winfield Townley Scott's
"—Words to the End of the World")